FROM SLOGANS TO MANTRAS

Religion and Politics

Michael Barkun, *Series Editor*

Hare Krishna members chant on the corner of Broad and Chestnut Streets in Philadelphia on Jan. 6, 1971, as one member holds a placard for the group—an illustration of Krishna. (© Temple University, Paley Library/Urban Archives)

FROM
SLOGANS
TO MANTRAS

SOCIAL PROTEST AND

RELIGIOUS CONVERSION

IN THE LATE VIETNAM WAR ERA

STEPHEN A. KENT

Syracuse University Press

First Edition 2001
12   13   14   15   16   6   5   4   3   2

∞ The paper used in this publication meets the minimum requirements of the American National Standard for Information Sciences—Permanence of Paper for Printed Library Materials, ANSI Z39.48-1992.

For a listing of books published and distributed by Syracuse University Press, visit our Web site at SyracuseUniversityPress.syr.edu.

ISBN: 978-0-8156-2948-1

Library of Congress Cataloging-in-Publication Data

Kent, Stephen A.
    From slogans to mantras : social protest and religious conversion in the late Vietnam War era / Stephen A. Kent.—1st ed.
        p. cm.—(Religion and politics)
    Includes bibliographical references and index.
    ISBN 0-8156-2923-0 (alk.paper)—ISBN 0-8156-2948-6 (pbk. : alk. paper)
    1. Protest movements—United States—History—20th century. 2. Student protesters—Religious life—United States. 3. Counterculture—United States. 4. Cults—United States. 5. Nineteen sixties. 6. Nineteen seventies. I. Title. II. Series
HN59.K44 2001
303.48'4'0973—dc21
                                                                    2001104 2998

I dedicate this book to the memory of
Dr. Robert Blumstock (1934–1995),
scholar, teacher, mentor, friend,
and very humorous man.

Stephen A. Kent is professor in the Department of Sociology, University of Alberta. From 1984 to 1986 he held a Killam Postdoctoral Fellowship in the Department of Sociology. He has published articles in *Philosophy East and West, Journal of Religious History, British Journal of Sociology, Sociological Inquiry, Sociological Analysis, Canadian Journal of Sociology, Quaker History, Comparative Social Research, Journal of Religion and Health, Marburg Journal of Religion* and *Religion*. His current research concentrates on nontraditional and alternative religions.

Contents

Illustrations

Foreword

Within the last decade, books written on the Vietnam War era have sufficient distance from the period that they can put into sociological perspective its various cultural and countercultural transformations. Dr. Stephen Kent's book, with its detailed analysis of the transformation of political radicals into religious revolutionaries, falls into this category. Kent describes and analyzes ideological identity transformations among politically radical youth of the 1970s (including some prominent leaders of student political movements) who ceased, rather abruptly, defining themselves as political revolutionaries and reinvented themselves as spiritual followers of charismatic religious leaders.

This book—which will serve as a useful complement to Steven M. Tipton's excellent study *Getting Saved From the Sixties*—focuses not on the "what" or the "why" but rather on the "how" of this dramatic subcultural change. A commendable feature of all of Kent's scholarship is his concern with the discovery of social and psychological mechanisms. Not content merely to report covariation or to describe cultural patterns, he looks at change in terms of sequences of events and responses to them. By doing so, he seeks to steer us away from an overly exclusive emphasis on inputs and outcomes, instead directing our attention to the in-between steps and stages of the identity-transforming process, steps and stages that many scholars are content to ignore. The larger macrosocial processes that encouraged or impeded the changes being investigated are of secondary interest in this volume. Primarily, this is a microanalysis of the ways in which these identity transformations were accounted for by the people who actually experienced them.

A unique feature of this book is its combination of detailed textual analysis and focused in-depth interviews. Kent's strength as a sociohistorical researcher is his recognition that student movements tend to leave behind abundant written records documenting their ideological struggles and decisions every step of the way. These documents tend to be scattered and hard to come by, but Kent has ferreted out an extraordinary number of them and supplemented them with his own interviews with key players in this drama.

Kent sees this story as a play in three acts: "Drugs," "Revolutionary Politics," and "Transformative Religion." The bulk of the book is concerned with the spiritual stage, but he does lay the groundwork by describing the first two acts. After an introduction to the 1960s generation, in chapter 2 Kent explores the roles of psychedelic drugs and popular culture in creating a self-confident counterculture in the 1950s and 1960s, intersecting with but often opposed to the political culture. Chapter 3 describes the turmoil of student antiwar activism during the late 1960s, the delusions of revolutionary grandeur that ensued, and the subsequent frustration and disillusionment on the part of prominent political activists. Kent argues that there was nothing inevitable about these players turning to religion. He shows how the student antiwar movement adapted to its lost momentum in the early 1970s by transforming the means of bringing about social change (from struggle to control institutions to struggle for psychospiritual transformation), while keeping constant the goals of world peace and universal justice for all.

In chapters 4 and 5, which are the intellectual heart of the book, Kent shows how ten religious groups were able to carve out niches in the tumultuous spiritual market fair that characterized this transformed counterculture. These groups successfully exploited the spiritual seeking of the disillusioned revolutionaries. Kent gives us detailed descriptions of identity conflicts for six Eastern and four Western or syncretic new religious movements: the Divine Light Mission, the Hare Krishnas, the followers of Chögyam Trungpa, the Healthy, Happy, Holy Organization, the Baba followers, Transcendental Meditation, Scientology, the Unification Church, the Christian World Liberation Front, and the Children of God. He argues that the common element in conversions to these ten diverse groups was a persuasive message that the revolutionary goals of the 1960s could still be attained—but only by abandoning direct political efforts and substituting indirect spiritual means.

In chapter 6, Kent concludes with a discussion of the betrayal of his subjects' idealism by what he sees as the fanatical or corrupt (or both) leadership of most of the ten groups investigated. In some ways, this is the most puzzling and disturbing section. The relative ease with which his subjects abandoned their political movements is sharply contrasted with the difficulty some of them experienced in disentangling themselves from these religious movements. Even when tormented by what they saw as obvious hypocrisies and inconsistencies in their newly adopted religions, these people struggled to find ways to justify the practices as embodying some deeper truth, perhaps not yet fully understood. One gets the sense that the members of these groups felt that this was the end of the ideological road for them, where they must dig in their heels if they wished to have any hope of continuing to cling to their battered youthful idealism.

Kent's theoretical focus stays on identity transformation at the individual level. To his credit, he does not obsess over whether the numbers involved were hundreds, thousands, or hundreds of thousands, although he discusses existing controversies on this issue. What is important for Kent are the many variations of the same sociocultural themes. Of particular interest is his treatment of the complex triangular influence of the New Left, feminism, and radical religious cultism. For example, Kent's research helps us understand better by what mental gymnastics some of the most feminist young women of the Vietnam War era justified their inner transformation into passive and subservient vehicles for patriarchal guruism.

Like most truly engaged sociohistorical analyses, Kent's book leaves several important questions unanswered that are crying out for further research. Among these is the question of what happens to these guru-enchanted former Marxists and former anarchists as they grow older. Hopefully, Kent will consider doing a follow-up study. It would be interesting to know how many of his subjects eventually became the "bourgeois bohemians" discussed by David Brooks in his recent book *Bobos in Paradise*. I suspect, based on my own research, that a higher proportion than one might guess continues to cling to these religious commitments, made on the rebound from political disillusionment, well into late adulthood.

Benjamin Zablocki

Rutgers University
August 2000

Preface

One night in 1974, I watched in disbelief as men and women of my generation paid homage to an unimpressive guru who equated levels of spiritual knowledge with increasingly large sizes of airplanes. I was somewhere in Philadelphia, packed so tightly into a church pew that I literally was sitting on top of myself—one leg had to be turned sideways in order to fit between the people on either side of me. As a twenty-two-year-old hippie, I noticed that many others in the audience looked like "freaks" (as we called ourselves) and that there was little discernible difference between the "freak" women and the "earth mother" appearance of the guru's female devotees. In sharp contrast, the male devotees looked like business school aspirants—but I realized that, not long before, they probably had been scruffy and long-haired like me.

One by one, relatives and others in the so-called Perfect Master's inner circle strode to the microphone and proclaimed the spiritual power of their guru's message. Every indication was that, at least in his devotees' eyes, he was no ordinary young man. Indeed, in the middle of the event, one of the organizers asked the audience for use of an available car, because he needed to go somewhere to pick up a pillow for the guru's lotus feet.

Aside from my own excruciating body cramps, I remember little else about the build-up for the guru except for one grand proclamation, from a slightly older member of the guru's entourage. Confidently, clearly, this man announced: "Ladies and gentlemen, I have seen the Lord! He was in New York City last night, and he will be in this church this evening!" Only years later did I realize that this confident speaker had been none other than Rennie

Davis, who had earned the respect and admiration of my generation by his strident opposition to the Vietnam War. In any case, all this hype proved irritating, because I had come not to hear praises from his entourage but rather to experience the Perfect Master himself.

I was profoundly disappointed. Indeed, I found his poorly delivered message to be banal. Drawing an analogy between airplanes and spiritual knowledge, he taught the audience something along the lines that, "If you are a native living in the jungles of Africa and a Piper Cub flies over your head, then you will say 'Oh, what a big airplane.' But ahhh, there are 747s!" I did not appreciate his characterization of African tribespeople, nor was I impressed with his clumsy analogy. Consequently, I could not fathom what so many of my peers found inspiring about this kid, and I was wholly unprepared for what happened after the presentation concluded.

Riding home with a friend that evening in the back seat of a car, I listened incredulously as my companions spoke glowingly about the message that they had just received. In fact, they were so moved by the guru's words that they made tentative plans to return the next day to pay homage to him by kissing his feet. I was flabbergasted, stunned. How could anyone have thought that this guy was a spiritual master? Unable to comprehend why anyone had been impressed by the amateurish performance through which I had suffered, I pondered this mystery for years.

For the past quarter of a century, I have remembered that disorienting night as I have tried to interpret crucial experiences of my generation. My first attempt at doing so (in scholarly form, at least) was an article entitled "Puritan Radicalism and the New Religious Organizations: Seventeenth-Century England and Contemporary America" (Kent 1987). More to the point was an article that appeared the following year, "Slogan Chanters to Mantra Chanters: A Mertonian Deviance Analysis of Conversion to the Religious Organizations of the Early 1970s" (Kent 1988). An edited version of this article was subsequently published in book form as "Slogan Chanters to Mantra Chanters: A Deviance Analysis of Youth Religious Conversion in the Early 1970s" (Kent 1992). Finally, I developed additional ideas in "Radical Rhetoric and Mystical Religion in the Late Vietnam War Era" (Kent 1993), based on a paper presented at the Vietnam Anti-war Movement Conference: The Charles DeBenedetti Memorial Conference at the University of Toledo

(Toledo, Ohio) in May, 1990. I express my gratitude to *Sociological Analysis* (now *Sociology of Religion*), Rutgers University Press, and *Religion* for granting me permission to include sections of these articles in this larger study.

Although my own professional training is in religious studies and now I teach in a sociology department, I realize that this book may have its greatest appeal to students of postwar American (and to some extent Canadian) popular culture. In my previous academic studies I have developed the theoretical frameworks and concepts that lay behind my interpretations, but in this book (for the most part) I have set theory aside and allowed very colorful material to speak for itself. The period upon which I concentrate—the early 1970s— remains relatively unexplored, shadowed as those years are by the intensity of the wild, wonderful, and tragic decade before it. The 1960s, however, were not my time—not really. My friends and I entered young adulthood as one decade slid into another, and we only got to explore ourselves and our world as we watched the 1960s fade. Yet our own era—around the end of the Vietnam War—was filled with excitement and oddities, all of which require their own place as the record of our times.

The era about which I write is sufficiently close to our own that I was able to have access to a wide range of sources upon which to build my argument. Along with several hundred books from or about the 1960s and early 1970s, I consulted extensively both academic and journalistic articles about the late Vietnam War period (although I cannot hope to have gathered and examined everything). Perhaps the most important methodological decision I made was to rely heavily upon commentaries that appeared in the underground and alternative press. I began this aspect of my research by doing systematic searches of youth religious groups through the *Alternative Press Index* at the Library of Congress. After tracking down and photocopying particular items, I browsed thousands of additional alternative press pages that the Library of Congress has on microfilm, in the compilation by University Microfilms International (1985) entitled *Underground Press Collection 1963–1985*. No doubt I missed many articles, but the number of pages that I examined from a wide array of alternative publications convinced me that I identified central arguments and key items.

Beyond these extensive media searches, I collected over twenty-five file cabinet drawers of primary documents, photocopies, and related ephemera from many of the alternative religions that were active in the United States and Canada during the late 1960s and early 1970s. I supplemented my own collection on these new religions by examining files at the Graduate Theological Union at Berkeley, the Bancroft Library at the University of California, Berkeley—especially the Bancroft's excellent Social Protest Collection—and the Institute for the Study of American Religions at the University of California, Santa Barbara.

Finally, I needed to hear accounts from people who actually had passed through the transition about which I was writing. Consequently, I used social networks of both current and former members of these religious groups to locate people whose sectarian involvement came after periods of political activism. I taped twenty interviews with people who followed the politics-to-religion-pattern, and all of these tapes now are transcribed and have been checked for accuracy against the audio recordings. Excerpts from these interviews appear throughout chapters 4 and 5.

Several institutions provided resources that allowed me to conduct research in various locations in the United States and Canada. Two grants from the Social Sciences and Humanities Research Council of Canada (SSHRC) allowed me to gather documents and conduct interviews for research on Canadian "cults" and "new religions," and while doing so I frequently collected research for this project. The University of Alberta provided transcription assistance, release time from classroom responsibilities, teaching assistants, and various forms of support for my document collection efforts. Over the years, many graduate (and occasionally undergraduate) students have aided me by locating countless references in libraries. Among them were Rob Cartwright, Albert Chu, Deana Hall, Theresa Krebs, Jo Lamba, (now Dr.) David Long, (now Dr.) Jane Milliken, Ayse Oncu, and Michael Peckham. Research assistants who provided invaluable service included Lou Bell, Vanessa Cosco, Ken Hutton, Susan Hutton, Jennifer McMullen, Kyla Rae, Elaine Seier, Lori Shortreed, and Kara Thompson. My wife has edited and critiqued various drafts, and has tolerated a writing schedule that usually brought inspirations only after midnight. My long-suffering parents financed various research escapades that contributed to this book, and at times even have driven hundreds of miles to assist me. Their love is never forgotten and always cherished.

Finally, special thanks, and indeed the dedication of this book, goes to a person whose direct influence over me had waned by the time I began serious research on this topic. While I was a graduate student, Dr. Robert Blumstock supported me through very difficult periods, and I often wonder whether I would have made it without his honorable and decent presence. My lifelong gratitude extends to him, and I deeply regret that he did not know about my book dedication plans when he died during the spring of 1995.

FROM SLOGANS TO MANTRAS

I

Introduction
Defining a Generation

As the era of political protests faded in the early 1970s, the United States and other Western countries experienced dramatic numbers of youth converting to new and exotic religions. Where the late 1960s had been characterized by explosions of youthful protest over social issues, in the new decade many of those who had been protesting were turning instead to new religions or undertaking unorthodox spiritual disciplines. Gurus, swamis, teachers, spiritual masters, and "enlightened souls" attracted tens of thousands of baby boomers into what often were unusual and controversial practices.

During this period, American social commentators—including political and social activists observing the actions of their comrades—noticed that a major cultural shift was occurring. Dozens of alternative newspapers carried articles about this emerging cultural pattern, although no uniformity existed either in their portrayal of unfolding events or in their evaluation of them. Some articles spoke highly of the new social values that religion would bring into discussions about political and social change; others reviled former activists who seemingly were turning away from direct social critique and confrontation. Likewise, many social commentators pondered the impact that these unorthodox religious expressions would have on individuals, their generation, and the diminishing political protest movement. In the early 1970s, these topics were among the burning questions of the day.

The focus of this book is the cultural transition of American youth from radical politics to mystical religion in the late 1960s and early 1970s. I con-

1

tend that young adults' attraction to an array of religious figures and practices in the late Vietnam War period was a direct response to their negative experiences with social—especially political—protest. When thousands of youth went from chanting political slogans to chanting meditational mantras or prayers, this transition reflected the social and political frustrations and disappointments of a generation in despair. Certainly, the shift from radical politics to mystical religion was not the only direction that youth took as the 1960s wound down and fragmented. The women's movement, ecology, rural living, communes, gay rights, and other social movements also captured the attention of young adults who had been touched by a shared dream of love and peace (Zablocki 1980, 48–57).[1] The emerging religious phenomenon, however, was the most dramatic and among the most controversial of youth culture options, and it has proven the most difficult for social scientists studying the 1960s generation to understand.

The social and political frustrations that drove many to unorthodox faiths emerged in the context of protests against the Vietnam War—a war that became the defining event for a generation of youth and for the nation as a whole from the mid-1960s to the early 1970s. Television brought graphic images of the war into people's homes, followed quickly by images of chanting protesters at sometimes huge rallies. Even without the grim nightly TV reports, countless direct personal experiences and connections made the war's impact on American life profound and heartrending, as Annie Gottlieb describes:

> Like a massive shock wave, it affected, in widening circles, the 58,022 lost in the war (eight of them women); the 100,000 or more who may have killed themselves since their return; the 153,329 severely wounded, and the 150,375 more lightly wounded; the estimated 250,000 victims of Agent Orange; the half million or more who still suffer from the nightmares and flashbacks of post-traumatic stress; the 3.78 million who saw duty in the war zone; the 11 million who served in the Armed Forces during that time of doubt, drugs, and rebellion; the 27 million men who were threatened by the draft and had to rearrange their lives around it; and all the lovers, wives,

---

1. On the connection between the protests of the New Left and the rise of the women's movement in the 1960s, see Echols 1989, 103–37, 1994; Farber 1994, 240–59. On gay rights, see Teal 1995; Farber 1994, 259–61.

friends, brothers, and sisters, as well as parents, grandparents, and children of those who served, died, vanished, protested, or fled. During the war the generation was divided, but with time its true shape has revealed itself: a set of concentric rings, with the Vietnam Veterans Memorial at dead center. (Gottlieb 1987, 56)

In my own case, the high number that I received in the second military draft lottery is indelibly etched in my mind.[2] On the basis of this and other experiences, I concur with Gottlieb's conclusion that "[t]he Vietnam War was the central event of our generation" (56).[3]

Of course, understanding the 1960s as the Vietnam War era requires placing the closing boundaries for the period beyond the calendrical conclusion of the decade. Tom Shachtman, for example, proposed that the boundaries of the 1960s were the assassination of President John F. Kennedy on November 22, 1963, and the resignation of President Richard M. Nixon on August 8, 1974 (Shachtman 1983, 13). As news items, these events were dramatic, but as cultural influences they were even more powerful because they informed a generation about power, governmental trust, and institutional abuse. As a slight variant to Shachtman's proposal, however, I am inclined to end the 1960s era with Nixon's full and absolute pardon by his successor, President Gerald Ford, on September 8, 1974. The pardon was the final event in a course of political lessons that taught a generation that the good die young and the scoundrels flourish, that being morally right means less than being powerful.[4]

2. The Selective Service System (i.e., the draft board) randomly assigned birthdays to numbers and then called up those young men whose numbers were lowest and who did not have exemptions. For a description of the exact procedure of the random drawing in 1970 for men born in 1951, see Rosenbaum 1970, 12.

3. Another author who concurs with this general analysis is Jerold Starr (1974, 82): "The war in Indochina may have constituted the traumatic sociopolitical event of the sixties, which catalyzed the generation potential of many modern youth, leading to the formation of the peace and love generation unit."

4. Yet another possible cut-off date is proposed by Peter Clecak: "Just what *was* this elusive Movement, which, by most accounts, began fitfully in the middle fifties with scattered cultural and political protests and ended, say, by 1973, when members of the Symbionese Liberation

Lessons such as these—which contrast starkly with deeply held democratic ideals about fairness before the law and a belief in protest as an effective and protected political expression of discontent—have dramatic impact upon a nation's citizenry, especially their idealistic young. Although people of all ages internalize such lessons and (re)interpret them according to their individual life experiences, class, sex, and race, it is for the young that such events can define the consciousness of a generation. Members of a generation are roughly the same age, which means that their social world affects many of them in a somewhat similar manner. Cultural events, including political ones, wash over members of a generation more or less at the same time, dousing people with information that they then must interpret and personalize. In particular, the years from about eighteen to twenty-six are crucial in the development of an individual's political and cultural consciousness. By early adulthood, youth have acquired the cognitive skills necessary for politically moral thinking (Lambert 1972, 24, 36; Rintala 1974, 17) and have had initial contacts with many of society's institutions (such as postsecondary education, government bureaucracies, employment, law enforcement, and, especially for males, the military). Because young adults are "in a formative 'politico-cultural consciousness' stage," dramatic events are "a touchstone, a benchmark to which we compare all our later experiences and sensations" (Shachtman 1983, 15).

Thus, the segment of the population that I am calling the 1960s generation consists of persons who were born anywhere between about 1937 and 1956 (and especially the college-educated among that group). Technically, at least, people in this age cohort would have been between eighteen and twenty-six years of age sometime during the period between Kennedy's assassination (1963) and Nixon's pardon (1974). Moreover, on a practical level, the experiences of political culture were cumulative for this age group, meaning that youth coming into political consciousness at the end of this era had a

---

Army [SLA] murdered Marcus Foster, the first black superintendent of schools in Oakland, California?" (Clecak 1983b, 264). The SLA was a small revolutionary group most known for kidnapping Patricia Hearst (heir to the Hearst family fortune) in Berkeley on Feb. 5, 1974. Regardless of what parameters one places around the era, a useful chronological listing of crucial events from 1947 to 1975 is found in Kleinfelder 1993.

decade of symbolism and events to internalize and to interpret. A remarkable number of political and social events occurred during this period that affected youth, and each event added to the generation's collective experience of the society in which its members lived. Near the end of this period, another new phenomenon appeared: the emergence and popular appeal of new and alternative religious groups as a vital option in youth life and culture. Exploring the genesis of this new cultural current out of the ashes of the old is the central task of this book.

Already a substantial body exists of scholarly description and interpretation of the widespread conversions to mystical religious groups that occurred in the early 1970s. (For a survey and discussion of some of the key works on this literature, see the Appendix.) Many of these scholars understand these conversions essentially as *resolutions to a crisis of meaning*—thus adhering to the widely held but disputable interpretation that religion is necessary to society because it provides a unique sense of meaning and order to social life.[5] This book, however, offers a complementary interpretation of the transition from slogan chanters to mantra chanters. Rather than claiming that a crisis of meaning was what caused activists to convert to religiously ideological groups in the early 1970s, I stress a *crisis of means* within the political counterculture. That is, the combined experience of growing frustration over the perceived failure of political and countercultural protests to end the Vietnam War was the predisposing factor for the massive youth religious conversions that took place in the late 1960s and early 1970s. I propose that the conversions to the new religious groups were responses to activists' appraisal of increasing costs and diminishing returns of political action, with activists-turned-converts believing that through these religious groups they were adopting new means to the same goal.

---

5. For a discussion of religion as providing meaning, see McGuire 1997, 27–37. For the competing position—that many people in modern society no longer need the meaning systems that religion can provide—see Bibby 1979, 9–10.

2

Religion, Drugs, and the Question of Political Engagement

traditionally the American counterculture has included a spiritual element, and the alternative religions to which disillusioned youth flocked in droves in the early 1970s existed within a cultural continuum of religious ideas that stretched back at least to the 1950s (and perhaps even to a period before the abolitionists and other mid-nineteenth-century reformers). The quest for religious vision and insight preoccupied the lives of many prominent cultural figures during the late 1950s and early 1960s, and their spiritual efforts provided a necessary backdrop for the widespread conversions to mystical groups that would occur later. Of particular interest to the midcentury counterculture were Eastern religions. Zen Buddhism, for example, influenced the lives and literature of the Beat generation of alienated writers—and through them, increasingly larger popular audiences—during the late 1950s and early 1960s (Tonkinson 1995). By the late 1960s, several Eastern religious teachers had ventured to the West, and increasing numbers of Westerners had ventured (intellectually, if not also physically) to the East.

At the same time, this "journey to the East" (to use Hermann Hesse's phrase)[1] often coincided with the use of mind-altering drugs. As with the religious quest, cultural elites initiated the use of these drugs and were responsible for disseminating them (both through ideas and by facilitating access)

---

1. Hesse 1970. For an overview and bibliography of Hesse's influence on American youth in the 1960s, see Freedman 1978, 9–11, 397–98nn. 4–8.

throughout the culture. By the mid-to-late 1960s, drug use of various kinds had become so widespread that social commentators spoke of a "drug culture"—really a subculture—that stood in oppositional contrast to the dominant culture. Moreover, this subculture attempted to explain itself and to describe the experiences that people were having on drug trips by drawing heavily on religious language and symbolism.

As expansion of the Vietnam War, however, led to growing opposition against its carnage, critics questioned the value and indeed the appropriateness of these inner-directed experiences (whether achieved through religion or through drugs) in the face of the politically driven human tragedy that was unfolding in Southeast Asia. By the late 1960s, tension existed between the mystically-flavored drug culture and the politically driven antiwar movement.[2] This tension was radically reshaped in the early 1970s, as both sides participated in the rush for salvation. On the one hand, many former drug users came to believe that they could acquire similar insights and visions through the adoption of religious practices that required the renunciation of drugs. On the other hand, many former activists came to believe that the adoption of these same religious practices would lead to the social revolution that they had failed to initiate through political activity. At least in their own minds, religion provided former activists a unique opportunity to resolve otherwise insoluble frustrations that they felt over failing to achieve their revolutionary goals. Not surprisingly, however, what appeared as opportunities to some people looked like cultural capitulation to others, and critics were scathing in their indictments of former activist compatriots who now submitted themselves to authoritarian religious masters. Thus, in order to appreciate the controversial cultural transformations of the early 1970s, we must begin by highlighting the confluence of religion and drugs that began to occur in the 1950s.

2. On the basic distinction between the politically oriented antiwar movement and the lifestyle oriented counterculture, see Westhues 1975; for examples of the tension between them, see Stevens 1987, 291, 296–98, 307–8. As we shall see, however, many young adults moved so fluidly between the two during the 1960s and early 1970s that constructing a rigid boundary to separate them would be artificial. Allen Ginsberg is one obvious example of this fluidity, as was activist Jerry Rubin, who first smoked marijuana and took LSD in the San Francisco hippie haven of Haight-Ashbury (see Rorabaugh 1989, 143–44).

Religion, Drugs, and the Beat Generation

Emerging in the United States amidst the Cold War aftermath of World War II, the Beat generation of writers and other artists felt a profound uneasiness with the confines of traditional society. They lived on society's margins, traveling across the continent and various parts of the world in search of experiences that would revolutionize—and in particular, spiritualize—how they perceived themselves. Pushing outside of conventional sexual boundaries and using a wide variety both of drugs and of religions as twin tools of inner exploration, key Beat figures sought to authenticate and to articulate their alienation. Prose writers such as William Burroughs, Neal Cassady, John Clellon Holmes, and Jack Kerouac along with poets Lawrence Ferlinghetti, Allen Ginsberg, and Gary Snyder saw their art (along with jazz) as expressions of disdain for the collective ennui and psychosis of normal society. "In contrast to the political radicals . . . the Beats proposed a revolt of the soul, a revolution of the spirit" (Stephenson 1990, 6; see also Halberstam 1993, 295–307).[3] As journalist David Halberstam concluded, "Their protest would have significant political implications, but its content was essentially social and cultural" (Halberstam 1993, 296).

For a number of Beats, drugs—especially marijuana and Benzedrine—allowed the writers to explore themselves and their world from different angles, and some drugs (such as speed) allowed them to compose for days on end. Burroughs was addicted to morphine, and in the mid-1940s, Kerouac took so much speed that it caused weight loss and thinned hair (Schumacher 1992, 60). At various times throughout his career (especially before he discovered Buddhist meditation), Ginsberg wrote poems while under the influence of

---

3. Stephenson (1990, 2–3) divides the Beat Generation into two general periods, the first from 1944 to about 1956 and the second from 1956 to 1962 or (at the latest) 1965 and the advent of the Vietnam War: "The first period was characterized by violence, desperation, confusion, and suffering among the early Beat group and their associates," epitomizing one meaning of the term "beat"—beaten, downtrodden, failing to find understanding, entangled with the burdens of sin, crime, and guilt, etc.; "[t]he second, beatific stage of the movement is marked by the attainment of vision and by the communication of that vision to the human community."

marijuana, Benzedrine, methadrine, hashish, morphine, peyote, ayahuasca, laughing gas, and LSD (Portuges 1978, 100–127).

In particular, Ginsberg's mystical quest and (usually) generous temperament seem to have allowed him to benefit most from these experimentations (although some of them proved quite perilous in the images that they produced).[4] During one trip in 1948, for example, Ginsberg believed that his room filled with the booming voice of William Blake reciting poetry (Schumacher 1992, 97–98). The moment transformed him, powerfully focusing his mystical quest, and for the next fifteen years drug-taking was part of his effort to regain the pristine consciousness of eternal connectedness that he felt he had glimpsed in such visionary moments. According to his own report, Ginsberg used drugs "to *catalyze* the world, to catalyze my perceptions." Through them he wanted "a 'break in consciousness,' or a 'break in the natural mode of consciousness, the habitual mode' " (Portuges 1978, 111). He would come to hope that LSD was a tool for entering the mind of God (Schumacher 1992, 313).

Like drugs, Buddhism was a tool that Ginsberg used in his mystical quest, and it proved to be the more durable of the two approaches. He discovered Buddhism in 1953 while reading in the New York Public Library, and he was particularly taken by D. T. Suzuki's description of satori (which Ginsberg related to his earlier vision of Blake). During the same year, Kerouac too stumbled upon Eastern thought while reading in a library (Fields 1992, 210), and in 1954 he intensified his study of Buddhism in an attempt to debate his friends Neal and Carolyn Cassady on their belief in psychic seer Edgar Cayce (Miles 1998, 195–96). In correspondence, Kerouac urged Ginsberg to press ahead with his Buddhist studies, and even prepared for his poet friend a one-hundred-page collection of his notes on the subject (Schumacher 1992, 175). By 1955, Buddhist concepts shaped the nature and content of Kerouac's musings and work.

The most serious (and long-lived) Beat Buddhist was Gary Snyder, who met Ginsberg and Kerouac in 1955 through the San Francisco poetry scene

---

4. For example, see Ginsberg's description of a terrifying peyote trip in Schumacher 1992, 205–6.

(Schumacher 1992, 211). Snyder had formal training in anthropology, linguistics, and literature, and in 1952 he enrolled in the Oriental Languages department at the University of California at Berkeley with the goal (which he achieved) of studying Zen in Japan. He meditated every morning, and the cottage in which he lived was monastic in its sparseness (Fields 1992, 213–15). As with other Beats, Snyder put a personal stamp on religion. His approach to Buddhism was intellectual; Kerouac's, laced with Catholicism, was melancholic, always concentrating on the Buddha's First Noble Truth that "life is suffering"; and Ginsberg's was bound up with Blake. At the same time, the writers had much in common, and later, during the 1960s, both Snyder and Ginsberg would speak on behalf of commingling spirituality with political action (often to the deaf ears both of hippies and of activists).[5] Over their long careers, they brought Beat ideas both into the struggle to end the war and into the struggle to expand the mind.

Psychedelic Sacraments

In and of themselves, mind-altering drugs simply affect brain chemistry. From a scientific perspective, there is nothing inherently religious about the experiences that people have while taking them. A broader perspective on "the effects of drugs on consciousness" includes a complex combination of a particular substance's chemical properties in relation to person-specific long-term, immediate, and situational factors.[6] Taken together, these factors led one researcher to conclude that "the variability of experience with the powerful psychedelics is so great that there seems to be no particular [discrete altered state of consciousness] *necessarily* produced by them" (Tart 1975, 154). In the 1950s, researchers approached mind-altering drugs with widely differ-

5. On Ginsberg's role as "an important link . . . between the vague pacifism and antipolitics expressed in Beat culture and the new, direct-action politics of the 1960s," see Jamison and Eyerman 1994, 159–60.

6. Long-term factors include culture, personality, physiology, and learned drug skills; immediate factors include moods, expectations, and desires; situational factors include physical settings, social settings, and (especially in experiments) explicit instructions and implicit messages (Tart 1975, 147).

ing ideas as to their possible positive uses. The CIA, for example, identified certain drugs as possible truth serums and interrogation tools (Lee and Shlain 1985), while members of the psychological and research communities hoped that psychedelics would lead to insights about psychoses and schizophrenia or even to therapeutic breakthroughs (Stevens 1987, 27–29, 62–63).[7]

Even for scientific observers, however, drugs and religion are not always separate realms, as one early experimenter concluded "that psilocybin (and LSD and mescaline by analogy) are important tools for the study of the mystical state of consciousness" (Pahnke 1966, 308; see also Pahnke and Richards 1972, 415). Indeed, more popular interpretations by prominent cultural figures often identified various drugs as vehicles for religious and mystical insights. Most influential were the writings of the gifted intellectual Aldous Huxley (1894–1963), who ingested mescaline for the first time on May 4, 1953, and the next year published an analysis of his experience in *The Doors of Perception* (1954). This thin but erudite study offered a spiritual interpretation of hallucinogens that served as an inspirational directive to "mind explorers" for well over a decade.

Already well-known for his somber novel *Brave New World,* in which the state keeps its citizens mollified through a drug called *soma,* Huxley was an eclectic spiritual seeker looking for the boundaries of human consciousness. With mescaline, he believed that he had found a way to break through those boundaries. Under its influence, "I was seeing what Adam had seen on the morning of his creation—the miracle, moment by moment, of naked existence" (Huxley 1963, 17). Despite his assertion that "the great change was in the realm of objective fact . . . not the world of visions," he also proclaimed "the Beatific Vision, *Sat Chit Ananda,* Being-Awareness-Bliss—for the first time I understood" (16, 18). He even claimed to understand the Dharma-Body of the Buddha.[8]

7. The term "psychedelics" began to be used in 1957 (Lee and Shlain 1985, 55). See Lee and Shlain 1985, 49–50 for mention of LSD therapy with alcoholics.

8. "The Dharma-Body of the Buddha" is a technical term for Buddhist Scriptures (Conze 1975, 79) along with the Truth allegedly residing in them (Conze 1967, 232–33). For Huxley's Buddhist claims, see Huxley 1963, 18–19, 38, 40. For a general collection of Huxley's writings on psychedelic drugs and the visionary quest, see Huxley 1982.

For Huxley, drugs were a new element in his long-term religious quest, "for until this morning [when I took mescaline] I had known contemplation only in its humbler, its more ordinary forms. . . . But now I knew contemplation at its height. At its height, but not yet in its fullness. . . . It gave access to contemplation—but to a contemplation that is incompatible with action and even with the will to action, the very thought of action" (Huxley 1963, 41). He concluded that mescaline ingestion could be very useful to persons seeking insight into life's meaning, but it could not serve as an end unto itself:

> I am not so foolish as to equate what happens under the influence of mescalin[e] or of any other drug, prepared or in the future preparable, with the realization of the end and ultimate purpose of human life: Enlightenment, the Beatific Vision. All I am suggesting is that the mescalin[e] experience is what Catholic theologians call "a gratuitous grace," not necessary to salvation but potentially helpful and to be accepted thankfully, if made available. To be shaken out of the ruts of ordinary perception, to be shown for a few timeless hours the outer and the inner world . . . as they are apprehended, directly and unconditionally, by Mind at Large—this is an experience of inestimable value to everyone and especially to the intellectual. (73)

Huxley continued his exploration of "the outer and inner world" with additional drug trips, ingesting LSD a few days before Christmas 1955. Soon he and his wealthy friends were holding what retrospectively we would call drug parties (Stevens 1987, 55, 66). The urbane Huxley linked up with a wealthy but rough-edged business executive (and former military operative) named A. M. Hubbard to spread the allure of LSD far and wide. Using his international business connections, Hubbard became the drug's self-appointed distributor.[9] Through him, as well as through CIA research contracts or through direct connections with LSD's manufacturer (Sandoz Pharmaceuticals), growing numbers of psychological researchers and psychiatrists—and through them, artists, writers, and other spiritual explorers—gained access to psychedelics.

Ginsberg, for example, took his first LSD trip at a research institute in

9. For discussions of Hubbard, see Stevens 1987, 53–59; Lee and Shlain 1985, 48–50.

Palo Alto, California, having received entry into the facility through anthropologist and acid-experimenter Gregory Bateson. Ginsberg's expectations
about the experience had been molded by his reading of Huxley's *Doors of
Perception*. As scientists took various psychological measures, he himself "was
waiting for God to show up inside his brain," and he immortalized his experience (which was not entirely positive) in a poem written while still high (see
Lee and Shlain 1985, 58–61). Religious interpreter Alan Watts (1915–1973)
gained LSD initiation through Huxley's social circles, and on his second trip
he had "a full-blown mystical illumination" (Stevens 1987, 68–69). Watts
subsequently wrote about the drug in his books and defended its use as an expert witness in court.[10] Both Ginsberg and Watts would extoll the value of psychedelics to the counterculture in the 1960s (and, in Ginsberg's case,
beyond).

On the East Coast, drugs and religion simmered together in the science-
gone-wild research of Harvard renegade Dr. Timothy Leary. After Leary ingested psychedelic mushrooms during a Mexican vacation in 1960, he
hatched the idea of conducting research on them at his Center for Personality
Research. From Sandoz Pharmaceuticals he acquired pills containing the
mushrooms' psychoactive agent (which the company called psilocybin), and
before the year was out his experiments began. Science rapidly took a back
seat to experience and to cultural vision—too many people took the drug too
often and in too many settings for Leary or anyone else to establish controls or
to conduct measurements.

Having enthusiastically read *The Doors of Perception* and its companion
volume, *Heaven and Hell*, Leary made contact with Huxley during the latter's
autumn 1960 stint in Cambridge as a visiting professor at MIT. They hit it off,
tripped together on psilocybin, and planned the cultural revolution that they
believed psychedelics promised for the future. Huxley urged Leary to: "Work
privately. Initiate artists, writers, poets, jazz musicians, elegant courtesans,
painters, rich bohemians. And they'll initiate the intelligent rich. That's how

10. Stuart 1976, 226. Both Timothy Leary and Ginsberg testified about LSD in 1966 before the Judiciary Subcommittee on Juvenile Delinquency, Ginsberg arguing "that psychedelic
drugs offered the potential for personal discovery that could lead to a better society" (Schumacher 1992, 472; see 471–74).

everything of culture and beauty and philosophic freedom has been passed on" (Leary 1983, 44; see also Stevens 1987, 133–42). After Ginsberg and his lover had a wild (and, for the poet, messianic) psilocybin trip at Leary's rented house,[11] Leary eventually adopted the distribution model that Ginsberg advocated: make the drug available to everyone.

In early 1961, another university psychologist, Dr. Richard Alpert, joined Leary's project, and on his first ingestion of the drug whose effects he was to research, Alpert had a mystical experience. Leary, too, was developing an interest in mysticism and religion (especially from the East), presenting a paper in August 1961 about psilocybin research being "a kind of applied mysticism" (Stevens 1987, 158). Leary and Alpert also wrote the preface to Alan Watts's 1962 inspirational book *The Joyous Cosmology,* in which Watts reversed an earlier position and argued that essentially no difference existed between mysticism and mind-expansion through drugs (Stuart 1976, 216). Even prisoners at a local penitentiary who took psilocybin in a rehabilitation experiment that Leary directed began "talking about love and ecstasy and sharing" (Leary 1983, 83–90; see also Stevens 1987, 157).

Then, Leary's team discovered a different, synthetically-produced drug: LSD. Leary ingested LSD in early December 1962, and later stated that "it was the most shattering experience of my life" (Leary 1983, 118). He saw "an enormous tree" amidst a "teaming and steaming" swamp "on some other planet," and this tree had roots that "were buried miles down and whose branches were foliated out miles high and miles wide." Suddenly, this tree sucked him inside itself:

> Every cell in my body was swept into the root, twigs, branches, and leaves of this tree. Tumbling and spinning, down the soft fibrous avenues to some central point which was just light. Just light, but not just light. It was the center of life. A burning, dazzling, throbbing, radiant core, pure pulsing, exulting light. An endless flame that contained everything—sound, touch, cell, seed,

11. As Leary recalled, Ginsberg and his lover removed their clothes, and the famous poet announced: "I'm the Messiah. I've come down to preach love to the world. We're going to walk through the streets and teach people to stop hating" (quoted in Leary 1983, 48; also summarized in Stevens 1987, 145–46).

sense, soul, sleep, glory, glorifying, God, the hard eye of God. Merged with this pulsing flame it was possible to look out and see and participate in the entire cosmic drama. Past and future. All forms, all structures, all organisms, all events, were illusory, television productions pulsing out from the central eye. (Leary 1968, 246)

A commentator on Leary's trip captured the significance of this new drug experience: "If psilocybin had been about love[,] LSD was all death and rebirth" (Stevens 1987, 165).

As LSD opened new doors, it also closed others, as it doomed Leary's reputed research project and academic career. Even before Leary, his friends, and his research team began using LSD, Harvard colleagues were growing alarmed about ethical and scientific issues related to Leary and Alpert's psilocybin project. Stories about their questionable research hit the newspaper wire services in spring 1961 and quickly spread across the nation (if not around the world). Harvard did a masterful job of damage control (Stevens 1987, 160–63), and the administration looked forward to the expiration of Leary's contract in June 1963. Neither he nor Alpert, however, lasted that long. In late May, the university received information that its psychedelic psychologists still were involving students in their drug activities (thereby breaking an earlier agreement with Harvard officials to stop doing so), and based upon that information, they fired Alpert and relieved Leary of his teaching duties (Stevens 1987, 187, 195).

Not to be suppressed, Leary (through a wealthy patron) set up residence for himself and his fellow mind travelers on a four-thousand-acre estate named Millbrook, two hours' drive outside New York City (Lee and Shlain 1985, 97). Millbrook became the East Coast's psychedelic center, with a steady flow of prominent people and drug experimenters moving through the property. Letters poured in about LSD from around the country, and the media flocked to the grounds (103, 114–15). By the time that local prosecutor (and future Watergate criminal) G. Gordon Liddy squeezed Millbrook out of existence in spring 1967, Leary's gigantic social experiment had interwoven psychedelic drugs and the religious quest into the soul of the counterculture.

Despite his endorsement of George McGovern in the 1972 presidential campaign (see "Instant Karma" 1972), Leary was uncompromising in his hostility to political action. In his near-constant apoliticism, he represented the extreme end of a continuum in 1960s America. On one end were antiwar activists who disdained the counterculture, and on the other end were people (including Leary) who scorned direct political action and insisted instead on the need for a revolution of consciousness. In February 1967, for example, the psychedelic guru pronounced: "The choice is between being rebellious and being religious. . . . Don't vote. Don't politic. Don't petition. You can't do *anything* about America politically." His vision was for bands of "turned-on" (i.e., drug-using) hippies to spread out across the United States and Western Europe, where their eventual effect would be the disintegration of the state. At one point, Leary's apoliticism so enraged the editors of the *Berkeley Barb* that they encouraged political activists to protest against him (Lee and Shlain 1985, 166–67).

Drugs Versus Politics

To be sure, at least some countercultural figures rejected Leary's detached posturing. Ginsberg and Snyder, for example, wanted to bring together people from the two opposing camps, and they saw a festival in San Francisco's Haight-Ashbury district on January 14, 1967, as a means of accomplishing their integrative goal. The festival was the Human Be-In, which attracted some twenty thousand hippies and which helped set the stage for what would come to be called San Francisco's "summer of love." A few days before the event, organizers sent out a press release announcing that "Berkeley political activists and the love generation of the Haight-Ashbury will join together . . . to powwow, celebrate, and prophesy the epoch of liberation, love, peace, compassion, and unity of mankind. . . . Hang your fear at the door and join the future. If you do not believe, please wipe your eyes and see" (Lee and Shlain 1985, 160.)[12]

With the scent of marijuana wafting through the air and LSD being ingested liberally, the crowd undoubtedly saw a great deal—but, as it turned out, little of it had any direct relation to politics. One invited speaker, Jerry

---

12. What appears to be a different press release appears in Perry 1984, 122. For a history of music events that trace their inspiration to the Human Be-In, see Santelli 1980.

Rubin (1938–1994), railed against the Vietnam War, but otherwise only Ginsberg made any mention of the political situation in Southeast Asia (Lee and Shlain 1985, 164). Reflecting upon the day some years later, Rubin concluded that he "got a cool reception from the stoned-out hippies" (Rubin 1976, 80).

While Leary used the event to promote his new group, the League for Spiritual Discovery (abbreviated, of course, to LSD), Richard Alpert at least tried to speak about the vast political force that the counterculture embodied. "In about seven or eight years," Alpert predicted, "the psychedelic population of the United States will be able to vote anybody into office they wanted to. . . . Imagine what it would be like to have anybody in high political office with our understanding of the universe. I mean, let's just imagine if Bobby Kennedy had a fully expanded consciousness. Just imagine him in his position, what he would be able to do" (Wilcock 1967; also quoted in Lee and Shlain 1985, 162). Politically, however, the rhetoric was shallow and simplistic, suggesting how difficult it was to bring together the two sides of the counterculture. Whatever the Be-In accomplished in drawing media attention, few among the masses seem to have been stirred into political revolt.

In other situations, the conflicting worldviews of the hippies and the activists clashed much more dramatically. For example, in fall 1965, organizers for "Vietnam Day" protests in Berkeley made the mistake of inviting author Ken Kesey (b. 1935) to speak against the war. Known to readers as the author of *One Flew Over the Cuckoo's Nest* (1962)—a novel that blurred the distinctions between the insane and their caregivers—Kesey (like so many others) first had taken LSD as a participant in a federally-funded research experiment. It had changed his life, and soon he was helping change the lives of others through LSD. The band of relentless hallucinogen ingesters that formed around Kesey (including former Beat hero Neal Cassady) came to be known as the Merry Pranksters, whose psychedelic bus, blasting music, outlandish clothes, and mass distribution of LSD made them the cosmic explorers of the counterculture. For them, a political rally simply was another opportunity to have fun.[13]

13. On Kesey and the Merry Pranksters, see Lee and Shlain 1985, 119–26; Perry 1984, 13–14; Wolfe 1969. For a "hip" history of the Pranksters, see Perry and Babbs 1990.

Thus, when Kesey addressed the crowd of about fifteen thousand Berkeley antiwar protesters on October 16, 1965, his message was at least as startling as his outfit (see Wolfe 1969, 192–200). In a screaming orange coat (replete with epaulets and service stripes) and Day-Glo World War I helmet, he strode up to the microphone, pulled out his harmonica, and in between bars of "Home On the Range" pronounced: "You know, you're not gonna stop this war with this rally, by marching. . . . That's what *they* do. . . . They hold rallies and they march. . . . They've been having wars for ten thousand years and you're not gonna stop it this way. . . . There's only one thing to do . . . there's only one thing's gonna do any good at all . . . and that's everybody just look at it, look at the war, and turn your backs and say . . . Fuck it." Kesey's antic deflated the rising political emotion of the day, but it captured the attitude of the most extreme hippies and countercultural personalities. Lifestyles devoted to the expansion of consciousness were what mattered, not lives spent ranting against social oppression. Conflicting attitudes such as these plagued various attempts to unite hippies with protesters (Stevens 1987, 290, 304, 307–8).[14] Moreover, they foreshadowed the outright derision that activists would feel towards the religious converts of the early 1970s.

Music, the Counterculture, and Political Protest

Music also reflected the tensions between the inner-directed counterculture and the political culture. As the decade progressed, various artists and their songs took on symbolic importance as representatives of one or the other orientation to the 1960s world. The troubadour of the decade was Bob Dylan, whose complex and sometimes unfathomable lyrics led to endless discussions throughout the decade. Uniting various strands of the folk, blues,

---

14. As another example, a shouting standoff occurred in mid-1967 between hippies and activists at a New York courthouse in which thirty-eight people were being tried for illegally sitting on the grass in a park. The two groups chanted at one another, but the slogans intermingled into a strange mix: "Hare Krishna . . . police brutality . . . Hare Krishna . . . must go . . . Krishna Krishna . . . police state . . . Hare Hare . . . must go." To the reporter covering the event, "they were tearing one another apart in a love-hate dance on the steps of the courthouse" (Nadle 1967).

and protest traditions, Dylan's songs from the early 1960s dealt with a broad range of social and political issues, including "racist murders ('The Lonesome Death of Hattie Carroll'), the compensatory racism of poor whites ('Only a Pawn in Their Game'), [and] Cold War Ideology ('Masters of War' and 'With God on Our Side'). Insiders knew Dylan had written the chilling 'A Hard Rain's Gonna Fall' during the Cuban missile crisis, evoking the end of the world" (Gitlin 1987, 197). Released in January 1964, the title song of the album *The Times They Are A'Changin'* "became a youth anthem" (Shelton 1986, 213). His reputation, however, as the bard of protest outlasted his actual involvement with political statements. Seven months later, *Another Side of Bob Dylan* contained little if any protest sentiment, much to the chagrin of his politically oriented folk music fans (Gitlin 1987, 198). His swing from overt political concern to a more drug-tinged worldview led to one of the classic cultural confrontations of the decade. At the July 1965 Newport Jazz Festival, a mod-clothed Dylan put down his acoustic guitar and picked up an electric one—only to be booed off stage by disappointed fans (see e.g. Rodnitzky 1976, 108–15).

The musical phenomenon of the decade, however, was the Beatles. Dylan's cultural influence peaked in 1964, the same year that the Beatles first landed in the United States. Already with hits on the British pop music charts, the group's February performance on the Ed Sullivan television variety show catapulted them into instant American stardom. Musically and culturally, the Beatles were uniquely innovative; like others during this period, they were looking for answers. In an attempt to find them, they experimented with drugs, but then, in August 1967, they had a private meeting with the founder of Transcendental Meditation, Maharishi Mahesh Yogi. For a while, the meeting profoundly changed the young British rock stars, as the bearded Hindu sage promised them a lasting, drug-free high as the result of practicing his meditation techniques. Captured by this message, the Beatles were excited that his promise might come true.

As the world watched, the Beatles first traveled to one of the Maharishi's ten-day meditation courses in north Wales. While there, they announced their renunciation of drugs (which, not surprisingly, failed to last). Then, in February 1968, they jetted off to the guru's ashram in north India. Ringo Starr and his wife bailed out after only ten days; Paul McCartney and his female com-

The Beatles arrive in Wales on Aug. 27, 1967, to visit the founder of Transcendental Meditation, Maharishi Mahesh Yogi. From left: John Lennon, Paul McCartney (behind the Maharishi), Ringo Starr, and George Harrison. (© T. Stringer, AP/Wide World Photos)

panion hung on for six weeks; but John Lennon and George Harrison remained into May until they discovered that their spiritual (and supposedly vegetarian) guide was serving chicken to select women in his private quarters and often making sexual advances toward them. Although Lennon would express some of his misgivings about the Maharishi in a December 1970 *Rolling Stone* interview, the band's brief involvement with the Indian "holy man" dramatically boosted the public profile of his meditational technique.[15] Certainly few fans would have realized that Lennon's song "Sexy Sadie" (on the

15. On the whole episode, see Brown and Gaines 1983, 264–68, 270–71, 282–91; Goldman 1988, 273–75, 293–97. A very different interpretation of the Beatles's visit to the Maharishi's ashram records that Ringo and Paul appeared to have enjoyed their stay and that George

Beatles's "White Album" of November 1968) was a scornful mockery of his former guru, who had (as the lyrics said) "made a fool of everyone" (Schaffner 1977, 88).

In 1969, despite their disappointment with the Maharishi, the Beatles continued their spiritual explorations through a new channel, the Hare Krishna movement. George Harrison and Paul McCartney (along with Paul's wife, Linda) helped produce a commercially successful record of Hare Krishna chants that "reached number one in West Germany and Czechoslovakia while making the Top Ten in Japan and most of Europe" (Giuliano 1989, 105; see also 97–99; Goswami 1980–83, 4:32–33, 55–57). For seven weeks, Hare Krishna leader Śrīlā Prabhupāda (1896–1977) and various Krishna devotees lived at Lennon's estate (Giuliano 1989, 98, 104; Goswami 1980–83, 4:33, 45–50, 60–67), and in early 1973 Harrison purchased a manor house for the organization (Giuliano 1989, 106). Harrison's spiritual quest also brought him in contact with the work of Paramahansa Yogananda and his Self Realization Fellowship (SRF), the controversial Hindu holy man Sathya Sai Baba,[16] and the young but embattled Guru Maharaj Ji. Ironically, Harrison's chart-topping song in late 1970 and early 1971, "My Sweet Lord"—which contained a Krishna chant—landed the singer in a lawsuit for infringement of copyright in early 1976 that cost him $587,000 (109–12, 155–57).[17]

Although the Beatles were (in varying degrees) spiritual, they were not especially political. The debate about their song "Revolution" illustrates the

---

and John left only after a business deal went sour with the Maharishi (de Herrera 1992, 218–67); however, given that Brown was a close associate of the Beatles, I am most convinced by the first (and more critical) account cited here. Additional glimpses into the Beatles's stay at Rishikesh (along with the simultaneous visits by Mike Love of the Beach Boys and by the popular singer Donovan) appear in Lapham 1968. Mia Farrow (1997, 131–41) gives an account of her time at the ashram with the Beatles and of her departure after the Maharishi tried to put his arms around her after they finished meditating in a cave.

16. Sai Baba (b. 1926) is an Indian holy man living in Andhra Pradesh who claims to be an incarnation of God. He demonstrates his supposed divinity by manifesting ash, crucifixes, gold, and other items. Critics, however, accuse him of being a clever magician.

17. "My Sweet Lord" entered America's Top Twenty song chart on Dec. 5, 1970, and cracked Britain's Top Twenty on Jan. 23, 1971. In both countries, the song reached number one and stayed on the charts for twelve weeks (Nugent and Gillett 1978, 184).

point. In it, lead singer John Lennon intones that while he wants change, he was to be counted "out" when it came to "carrying pictures of Chairman Mao" or even talking about violence. The song was released in August 1968, immediately prior to the riotous Democratic National Convention in Chicago. Chicago's premiere rock music station gave "Revolution" airtime during the period of the riots, even as it refused to broadcast the song that spoke more approvingly to the radicals and their cause, Mick Jagger's "Street Fightin' Man." The underground press criticized Lennon's song, with the *Berkeley Barb* judging that even the name "was worthy of *1984;* the song itself sounded 'like the "hawk plank" adopted last week . . . at . . . the National Demokratik Death Party' " (Peck 1985, 168, quoting the *Barb;* see also Gitlin 1987, 287–88).

A combination of behind-the-scenes tensions and one dramatic stage incident during the Woodstock music extravaganza exemplified the strained relationship between political radicals and the music-oriented counterculture. Upon learning about the plans for the festival and anticipating the size of the event, activist Abbie Hoffman extorted $10,000 from its organizers by threatening to "screw up your show" if the money were not paid to him and his coalition (Makower 1989, 107–12; Spitz 1979, 164–68).[18] Once the festival got under way, activists and radicals established booths and a printing press in an area called "Movement City," but neither these booths nor their antiwar message attracted much attention. By contrast, when Swami Satchidananda unexpectedly showed up at the festival, he quickly was permitted by one of the organizers to address the crowd. His talk about peace " 'was great. It was part of the calming influence. It was like a blessing. It was like an invocation'" (John Morris, quoted in Makower 1989, 193). Significantly, for all its spiritual superlatives, the swami's message was not political.

The apolitical tone of the massive song-fest disturbed Hoffman, and his uneasiness escalated along with his drug use at the event. As he looked across the haze of marijuana smoke rising above a half-million people, he felt compelled to "say something about John Sinclair" (Michael Lang, quoted in

18. Presumably the money went toward legal advice, food, and medical supplies for the extravaganza (Makower 1989, 155, 235; Peck 1985, 178). For an attempt to interpret Hoffman as a religious figure—"a prophetic jester"—see Bianchi 1972, 139–66.

Makower 1989, 236), an Ann Arbor leader of the White Panthers who was serving a ten-year jail sentence for passing a joint to an undercover narcotics agent. In between songs during a musical set by The Who, Hoffman jumped on stage, grabbed the mike, and began his political rap. What followed happened in a flash, and it symbolized the antagonistic tension that existed between the radicals and many music fans. The Who's lead guitarist Peter Townshend (himself a follower of Meher Baba) whacked Hoffman in the head with his guitar while kicking him in the butt, knocking him off stage.[19] Later, Townshend claimed (with satisfaction) that it was the most political thing he ever had done (Makower 1989, 235–37; Peck 1985, 179–80; Spitz 1979, 463). From another perspective, however, Townshend's act certainly constituted "a metaphoric denial of the underground's attempt to fuse politics and music" (Peck 1985, 180).

As the new decade of the 1970s approached, the two strands of (largely white, middle-class) youth culture lived in uneasy relationship. Mystical apoliticism within the counterculture received the scorn of activists, while the often shrill protests of political radicals appeared pointless to persons who believed in the transformative power of (as the Beatles crooned) "love, love, love." Drug use linked the strands at the same time as it accentuated the extreme tendencies in each camp. Put succinctly, "LSD does not make people

19. In a book that came out soon after Woodstock, Hoffman (1969, 143) admitted that "Pete Townshend, lead guitarist, had clonked me over the head with his electric guitar, and I crumpled on the stage." He later minimized the event, however, claiming only that "Townshend, who had been tuning up, turned around and bumped into me. A nonincident really" (Hoffman 1980, 183). Comments by other commentators lead to the conclusion that the earlier account is the more accurate. A biography of The Who, for example, indicates that Townshend both "put one of his Dr. Marten boots squarely into Hoffman's ass [and] swatted him with his Gibson SG [guitar]," after which "the Yippie fell into the photographer's pit" (Marsh 1983, 350). Townshend's own biographer reported that "an enraged Townshend instinctively swung around to ramrod the activist, kicking his little ass in a proud rage" (Giuliano 1996, 94). Later, in a time-line for the musician, the biographer does not mention the kick but does say that Hoffman "was trounced by Townshend's guitar" (287). The incident is captured on the twentieth track on The Who's 1994 retrospective CD. For a discussion of Townshend's devotion to Meher Baba, see Clarke 1979, 106–10, and Giuliano 1996, 111–47; also see the back cover of Townshend's 1972 album *Who Came First?* Thanks go to Michael Peckham for pointing out these Townshend sources to me.

more or less political; rather it reinforces and magnifies what's already in [people's] heads" (Lee and Shlain 1985, 231).

One of the things that was already in many people's heads was the allure of religion, an allure that had appeared in the preceding generation of Beats and that infused Western youth culture with a widely shared but heterodox set of concerns and images. Eastern religions had attained special notoriety, but there were other elements as well—including for example the mystical teachings of Don Juan, who supposedly imparted his wisdom through anthropologist and writer Carlos Castaneda (e.g. Castaneda 1968) but who is now known to be a fictional character (see de Mille 1977; 1980). Only a few cultural personalities of the period, however, (such as Allen Ginsberg and Gary Snyder) made serious attempts to utilize religious self-reflection as a basis upon which to construct political statements. Overall, the religious and the political were held separate. Thus, the wholesale transformation of many radicals and activists to new mystical religions that was about to occur early in the new decade would be startling and unexpected. In understanding this process, we must place the cultural developments of the 1960s in the context of the political history of that decade—a decade that had begun with hopeful expectations but that ended for many in frustration and despair.

3

Political Frustration and Religious Conversions

With hindsight we can see an impressive legacy of social change that originated in the turmoil of the 1960s. That legacy includes civil rights, the "humanization" and reform of education (including student representation), increased public awareness of environmental issues, feminism and the women's movement, community organizing, a lowered American voting age from twenty-one to eighteen, the affective rewards to be found in interpersonal and sexual relationships, the creativity of religious heterodoxies, increased international dialogue between the superpowers, and even some unsurpassed rock music. All of these achievements stemmed from the various efforts, united in the goal of a fundamental redistribution of power, that together came to be known simply as "the Movement." In countless instances, youthful challenges to authority had paid off. By demanding accountability from people in politics, business, and education, students and other young people had altered important aspects of the existing power structure. Even family dynamics changed as many youths took home with them—and acted upon—the popular slogan "Question authority!"[1]

The often verbalized goal or aspiration of the Movement was "the Revo-

1. For the basis of this interpretation, see Levitt 1984, 101—2; Kendrick 1974, 265, 267; Oberschall 1978, 281–83; Albert and Albert 1984, 28–29, 38–39. Garfinkle 1995 gives an extensive discussion of the impact of the antiwar movement on American society. For a sustained discussion of religious activity, see Ellwood 1994.

lution"—a term often used but rarely defined, except perhaps in the popular phrase "power to the people." (Indeed, in many cases the terms "the Movement" and "the Revolution" were used interchangeably.) An article written in the latter part of the Vietnam War era (November 1970) attempted to define what the Revolution envisioned for society:

> Just what are the goals of the Revolution? Since "the Revolution" is not one coherent party, movement, or force but a kind of loose psychic alliance of many groups, ideologies, life-styles, and constituencies bound together primarily by a general realization that the present American political, economic, and social structure stinks, the overall goals of the Revolution are little more than a set of general criticisms couched primarily in negative terms.
>
> Domestically, the Revolution wants an end to racism, an end to all artistic censorship, an end to the economic exploitation of the many by the few, [and] an end to all puritanical laws against drugs and human sexuality. In foreign policy, the Revolution wants an immediate end to the Viet Nam war, an end to the interventionist policies which caused the war in the first place, an end to American economic control of other countries, and in general, an America that minds its own business. (Spinrad 1970, 3)

Broadly speaking, the Movement wanted to achieve a fundamental restructuring of social and political power in society.[2]

Although an outright revolution never came to pass, protests directed specifically against the war did bear fruit. The Movement's continuous antiwar activities contributed to the U.S. government's decision to withdraw its ground troops from Vietnam in late March 1973, two months after the government had ended the controversial military draft. Earlier, in 1969, unbeknownst to protesters at the time, opposition to the war had prevented President Richard Nixon and his National Security Adviser, Henry Kissinger, from escalating the conflict—an escalation that, had it occurred, might have included the use of nuclear weapons (Zaroulis and Sullivan 1984, 296).

Those of us in subsequent decades view all of these achievements with the

---

2. The theoretical framework that lies behind my interpretation of the 1960s power redistribution movement is found in McCarthy and Zald 1977, 1218–21, passim.

grace of retrospection. For many activists and radicals during the late 1960s and early 1970s, however, these significant changes were not enough. Even taken collectively, they fell short of the radical activists' dreams and rhetoric. Most concretely, the antiwar movement had experienced a number of demoralizing setbacks and defeats to its cause, as the war continued despite the strident efforts of (at times) hundreds of thousands of protesters and (at least in the early 1968 Tet Offensive) stunning displays of military prowess by the North Vietnamese. As one social movement theorist commented some years later, "the U.S. involvement in the war did not end as rapidly and as completely as the Movement sought," nor did the efforts of the broader social movement in the era "result in a major redistribution of power in the U.S. as was hoped by some activists" (Oberschall 1978, 281; see also Levitt 1984, 101). Indeed, Movement literature from the early 1970s indicates how disillusioned, if not despairing, many activists were with regard to the efficacy of their political efforts. Thus, in order to understand why so many young adults abandoned political protest and confrontation for mystical means of societal transformation, we must appreciate the frustrations that Movement participants felt about their efforts during the final years of the Vietnam War.

In 1968, when so much happened that entire volumes are devoted to it (e.g. Ali and Watkins 1998, Caute 1988, Fraser [et al.] 1988), the power redistribution Movement—and especially the antiwar efforts—suffered major setbacks. The two most violent episodes tore away the embodiment of the civil rights movement, Martin Luther King Jr. (by then a critic of the war), and presidential aspirant and Democratic peace candidate Senator Robert Kennedy. Both fell victim to assassins' bullets—Kennedy's death coming minutes after he had won the California Democratic presidential primary. With their deaths, "the possibility for nonviolent change—for the country under either man's leadership to turn itself around from its self-destructive course of war and racial conflict—seemed lost" (Zaroulis and Sullivan 1984, 159). With Kennedy absent, the hopes of many turned to Senator Eugene McCarthy, who had made a strong showing as the peace candidate in the New Hampshire Democratic primary.[3] In August 1968, however, supporters saw Mc-

3. Realistically, McCarthy's strong showing was more the result of anti-Johnson feelings than of his peace platform. See Zaroulis and Sullivan 1984, 157–58.

Allen Ginsberg (seated, on far left) leads a prayer meeting in Grant Park during protests surrounding the Democratic National Convention in Chicago, Aug. 28, 1968. (© Archive Photos, File)

Carthy skipped over at Chicago's Democratic National Convention, as thousands of disillusioned youth fought rioting police.

For militants, the Chicago street-battles were a resounding success. In front of the nation's cameras, "they were able to feel themselves in active confrontation" (Farber 1988, 244). The riotous events led some commentators to suggest that "the war in Southeast Asia . . . was causing a kind of civil war in the United States" (Zaroulis and Sullivan 1984, 200). Moreover, "[b]y raising the specter of civil war, the protesters in Chicago had also dramatically raised the costs of prolonging that [Vietnam] war" (J. Miller 1987, 305). To others, however, the Chicago demonstrations made clear the potentially high costs of defiant protest. For example, reflecting on the conflicting effects that these violent demonstrations had on the public and on sympathizers themselves, activist Sidney Peck admitted that "the anti-war movement won a great deal of sympathy although at the same time the nature and character of the action at Chicago stimulated a great many fears in people about participating in demonstrations." That fear, he added, "was going to be a huge political problem that we had to overcome" (Zaroulis and Sullivan 1984, 200; see also Gitlin 1987, 420).

The protests in autumn 1969 "were a high point for the anti-war movement, the time of its greatest success" (Zaroulis and Sullivan 1984, 299), but both the moderates and the radicals suffered seriously from terminal weaknesses and external assaults. Internally, within the antiwar movement, the fragmentation of Students for a Democratic Society (SDS) eliminated effective contacts on college campuses.[4] Moreover, the movement's leadership, uncertain about how to follow up its recent efforts, became divided over future tactics—and these divisions were helped along by government agents provocateurs who continued their meddling subversion among the ranks (see Davis 1997). Externally, the government pursued its damaging strategy of entangling the Movements' leaders in court (Zaroulis and Sullivan 1984, 299–300).

Commentaries from the period reveal a sobering climate during the opening months of the new decade. In February 1970, for example, one writer identified her fear about the state of the nation and her sense of helplessness to do anything about it. Composing her thoughts four days after the jury began its deliberations in the Chicago conspiracy trial,[5] and two days after

---

4. The radical group Students for a Democratic Society emerged out of the Civil Rights movement in May 1960, but its most coherent critique of American society appeared in its 1962 policy formulation, commonly referred to as the Port Huron Statement (written by Tom Hayden). As the 1960s progressed, SDS became more aggressive in its resistance to social inequality and (increasingly) to the Vietnam War, and by the end of the decade had become a revolutionary and often violent organization (Franks 1981; Sale 1974).

5. The Chicago conspiracy trial involved federal charges against activists who had been involved with the protests (that led to riots) at the 1968 Democratic national convention in Chicago. The trial began in September 1969, and the jury delivered its verdict on February 18, 1970 with sentencing two days later. Initially eight activists went on trial together, all on charges that they had crossed state lines with the intent to riot, and that they had conspired to do so—in violation of the 1968 Federal Anti-Riot Act. Two defendants—John Froines and Lee Weiner—were accused specifically of teaching and demonstrating the use of incendiary devises. The other six were charged with various actions allegedly related to crimes involving conspiracy and intent to riot. Three of the defendants—Rennie Davis, David Dellinger, and Tom Hayden—were mem-

someone bombed a local police station, Anna Darden revealed: "I think I'm scared because I do see what's happening—and not only do I dislike it, I don't think there's a damn thing I or anyone else can do to change it" (Darden 1970, 5). While others in her era saw revolution about to break out at any moment, Darden was more somber. Believing that the militant Black Panther Party was "the strongest, most hopeful group of radicals in the country today," she nonetheless admitted that they also "are a tragedy of our time": " 'All power to the people, and Panther party to the vanguard,' is a beautiful slogan, but I say it with sorrow, perhaps not only because they are going to die [presumably in police battles] but because I see no guarantees, no signs that the vanguard is even beginning to make a successful revolution, or provide a force for social change of any kind." [6] With equal pessimism, Darden added: "I am beginning to think of political activism as the noblest and most quixotic

---

bers of National Mobilization Committee to End the War in Vietnam; Abbie Hoffman and Jerry Rubin were Yippees; and Bobby Seale was chairman of the militant Black Panther Party. As the trial began, these defendants became known as the "Chicago 8." Amidst the trial, however, Judge Julius Hoffman had the disruptive and verbally-challenging Seale gagged and bound to his chair, after Seale repeatedly demanded the right to act as his own attorney and called Judge Hoffman a racist and fascist for his refusal. Judge Hoffman finally removed Seale from the court on November 5, and declared a mistrial in his case. He was never retried. The remaining defendants became known as the "Chicago 7." Froines and Weiner were acquitted of all charges, and the remaining five were acquitted of the conspiracy charges but convicted on lesser charges of crossing state lines as individuals with the intent to riot. In addition, Judge Hoffman sent to jail all seven defendants and their two attorneys, on a total of 175 contempt of court citations. The Chicago 7 defendants had their convictions overturned on appeal in late 1972, and all but two contempt charges (both against Dellinger) were overturned in December 1973. On the trial see Schultz 1993; for a summary see Zaroulis and Sullivan 1984, 302–8; and for an edited trial transcript see Levine, McNamee, and Greenberg, editors, 1970.

6. The Black Panther Party was founded by black revolutionary nationalists Bobby Seale and Huey P. Newton in Oakland, Calif., in October 1966. It called for independent, self-governing black communities, an end to police brutality against blacks, full employment, decent education, and opposition to capitalism, which they saw as an oppressive system. The group developed free food programs and legal and medical services for the poor, but it also ran afoul of the law. Moreover, internal disputes, shoot-outs with the police, problems with the FBI and with the IRS, and dirty tricks by various law enforcement agencies and their agents provocateurs took their toll, and by early 1971 the party fragmented and fell apart. Summaries of the Black Panther Party appear in Butwin and Pirmantgen 1972, 74–78; Heath 1976, 2–214.

failure of our time. 'I have seen the best minds of my generation destroyed by madness,' wrote Allen Ginsberg. Or by gunfire, drugs, apathy, anger, jail, starvation and frustration" (8).

Within a few months, Darden and the rest of the nation would see a few more lives destroyed, this time by National Guardsmen. After Nixon's admission on Thursday, April 30, 1970, that the American military had been making ground and air incursions into neutral Cambodia,[7] campuses around the country spontaneously erupted. Over the weekend, several campuses became battlegrounds. These battles only intensified after Ohio National Guardsmen at Kent State University killed four students and wounded nine others on May 4. Horrified and angered, students at over half the nation's college campuses protested. Fifty-one colleges closed for the remainder of the semester, and over five hundred schools canceled classes (Scranton 1971, 17–20; Zaroulis and Sullivan 1984, 320). One radical at the time summed up student sentiment by saying that "the War is coming home."[8] Tragically, ten days after the killings at Kent State, the statement was proved true when Mississippi National Guardsmen opened fire on students at Jackson State College, killing two and wounding ten (Spofford 1988, 71–75). Student protest had reached a sobering turning point.

An alternative press article at the time snarled that "Amerika was shocked but not surprised at the news that broke Monday, May 4, that the white, working-class-student segment of the Movement had suffered its first multiple slaughter" (Marshall 1970, 8).[9] Another person, writing to the *Los Angeles Free Press,* interpreted the events as signs of the Movement's failure:

> We can misspell America all we want, we can slander this country as pignation until time ends, [but] we'll get nowhere. The more windows we break, the more the establishment makes replacing them, and the more the police have against us for persecution and the more the politicians have to rave about come next election. We've been fighting for ten years and what really do we

7. Nixon's speech is reproduced in Pratt 1984, 434–36.

8. Excerpt from Michael Rossman, "The Day We Named Our Child We Had Fish for Dinner," reprinted in Pratt 1984, 440.

9. Spelling "America" with a "k" was popular among radicals of the period. It played off the word "swastika" and indicated their feelings that the country was a fascist state.

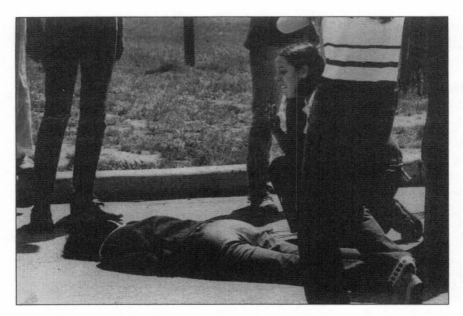

At Kent State University on May 4, 1970, Mary Ann Vecchio realizes that the man on the ground (Jeffrey Glenn Miller) has been killed by National Guard fire. This photograph, by Howard Ruffner, first appeared in Life magazine on May 15, 1970. (© Time Inc.)

have to show? Which direction are we headed now? All our leaders from Medgar Evers to Timothy Leary are either jailed, dead, or in exile. They sure the hell aren't doing this revolution any good at all in these circumstances!! We've burned, become violent animals, protested, chanted, marched, and signed petitions until we are blue. It simply isn't enough. (Klein 1970, 5)[10]

From this perspective, a generation of activists had tried almost everything to bring about massive social change, and nothing had worked. Meanwhile, Nixon and his vice-president, Spiro Agnew, had inflamed the activists with

---

10. "Pignation" alluded to the practice of calling police by the pejorative term "pigs." The allusion to pigs as oppressors may harken back to Orwell's *Animal Farm* (1946). Black civil rights activist Medgar Evers was the NAACP's field secretary in Mississippi and was fatally ambushed near Jackson, Miss., on June 11, 1963, during a period of heightened integration efforts in the area. Timothy Leary served time in prison for drug convictions.

derogatory rhetoric at the same time as they instituted policies of government surveillance, harassment, and persecution against a wide range of power-restructuring organizations (Albert and Albert 1984 36–37; Oberschall 1978, 275–80; see also Kent 1987, 20).

However much the shootings at Jackson State and (especially) Kent State inflamed antiwar protesters, it also tempered them (Ellwood 1973, 16; Richardson 1973, 461). An astute participant in and commentator on the period, Michael Rossman, reflected on the demise of a theater troupe he had helped to form: "[A]fter this venture's failure I entered a paralyzing depression which lasted two years. Many people were going through similar depressions around that time, perhaps as much from having tried to do too much too soon as in response to the grim theater of Kent State" (Rossman 1979, 94). In essence, Kent State was a watershed event for radical protesters and activists, and "in the months following the 1970 strike [over the Cambodian invasion], the campus Left collapsed" (Heineman 1993, 257; see also Ellwood 1994, 295).

The collapse, of course, was neither instantaneous nor uniform across campuses, and many students still made their voices heard. Memories of the spring 1970 campus protests, for example, probably contributed to the New Mobilization Committee's ability to draw upon students to participate in its governmental lobby efforts in spring 1971 and in its massive road blockade of Washington, D.C., on May 1 (May Day).[11] Despite attempts by the Trotskyites and their Socialist Workers Party to subvert the blockade (Lerner 1971, 20), about thirty-five thousand people attempted to shut down Washington through civil disobedience against commuters. After using their bodies

11. The New Mobilization Committee to End the War in Vietnam was formed in summer 1969 by the Cleveland Area Peace Council. Working through contacts that key organizers had on college campuses, New Mobe (as it often was called) initially directed its energies toward organizing a national demonstration in Washington, D.C., to demand the immediate withdrawal of Americans from Vietnam. That march drew more than 500,000 people to Washington on Nov. 15, 1969; the size of the crowd reflected New Mobe's effectiveness in working with over 100 moderate and radical New Left organizations (Davis 1997, 138, 152, 155). A hastily organized and smaller (perhaps 130,000 people) protest on May 9, 1970, against the American incursions into Cambodia was less successful (Zaroulis and Sullivan 1984, 320, 322–29). New Mobe broke up in summer 1971 (DeBenedetti 1990, 295).

to block major traffic arteries, more than twelve thousand people were arrested and detained. By the third day, however, the demonstration was crushed, and despite its hopes, New Mobilization's lack of a national support network prevented its actions from having any direct repercussions in local communities across the country (Lerner 1971, 41; Zaroulis and Sullivan 1984, 355–64). Somberly reflecting on the event, Norman Spinrad (1971) concluded that Nixon "has indeed made it perfectly clear that any future mass demonstrations of civil disobedience (presumably as defined by Nixon and Reichfuerher [Attorney General John] Mitchell) will be broken by similar mass arrest tactics."

Focusing upon the absence of a national network within the New Mobilization Committee and the internecine factionalism that this absence fostered, Michael Lerner (a prominent organizer of the committee's efforts in 1971) warned his fellow activists about the bleak future that lay ahead. Several months after the May Day efforts to shut down Washington, Lerner correctly predicted that "without the development of this kind of [broad, democratic, national] organizational structure, the next year will see the forces of the New Left splitting in equally useless directions" (Lerner 1971, 42). The editors of the leftist magazine in which his comments appeared, *Ramparts,* echoed Lerner's concerns. After first asserting that, metaphorically, the May Day protest "sent shivers" down Washington's spine, they then admitted that "if it was a success, it was a greatly qualified one" because it "pointed up crucial weaknesses in the Left which must be overcome" ("[Editorial Introduction]" 1971, 20; see also Oberschall 1978, 280; Bellah 1976, 83).

Other activists and radicals in the period were expressing similar concerns and frustrations. Writing in January 1971, for example, the Chicago Seven defendant David Dellinger bespoke the toll that seemingly ineffective protests were having on his fellow Movement adherents:

> [T]he anti-war movement is paying a price for a period of ideological confusion and tactical mistakes. Even more serious, it has been struggling to overcome the feelings of frustration and despair that have gripped people after they discovered that neither a million people in the streets (November 1969) nor several hundred schools and colleges on strike (May 1970) altered Wash-

ington's determination to escalate its war of aggression in Indochina. (Zaroulis and Sullivan 1984, 343)

These feelings of frustration and despair continued to grow as the early 1970s unfolded.

Already demoralized by the political process and by their apparently unsuccessful efforts to transform it, activists and radicals had their worst fears reinforced by the results of the 1972 presidential election. Even though prominent radicals and countercultural figures issued a combined plea (which they cleverly called "Instant Karma" [1972]) for the youth counterculture to work on behalf of Democratic candidate George McGovern,[12] Nixon won by a landslide. Subsequently, the *New York Times* reported that "the election of 1972, which swept hundreds of thousands of young people into politics, only to crush their hopes with the stunning victory by Mr. Nixon, apparently did almost as much to sour young people about working to elect national leaders" ("Student Volunteers" 1976). Radical organizer Rennie Davis captured the mood of youth in early 1973 when he reported that "students say 'we tried this tactic, we tried that tactic. We petitioned, we voted, nothing works' " (T. Wood 1973a, 3; see similar sentiments reported in Szatmary 1991, 198–99).

The January 28, 1973, treaty that extricated the United States from direct military involvement in Vietnam knocked the wind out of the peace movement (Kent 1987, 20; Oberschall 1978, 281). By the time of South Vietnam's collapse on April 30, 1975, peace demonstrations (on campuses and in the streets) had all but disappeared from the American landscape. Certainly some truth exists in the observation that "the sixties were over because, compared with 1960, there was much less to protest against" (Anderson 1995, 409).[13] At the same time, American foreign policy remained basically

12. Signatories included Leary, Ginsberg, poet Lawrence Ferlinghetti, Abbie Hoffman, singer Phil Ochs (1940–1976), Jerry Rubin, Ed Sanders, and John and Leni Sinclair.

13. As is Anderson, I certainly am aware of the economic nosedive that the American economy took in the mid-1970s (partly as a result of the military demobilization and certainly a result of the oil crisis), which forced recent college graduate baby boomers to spend more time and effort working and job hunting. However, I attribute relatively little importance to these economic

unchanged in its support of various dictatorships around the world, and corporate influence on all levels of government remained. Much *had* changed, but much also remained the same (Zinn 1995, 534–36).

Within the frustration, fear, and despair about the perceived failure of the Revolution lies the key to the rapid transformation of the slogan chanters of the late 1960s into the mantra chanters of the early 1970s. Whether the power redistribution Movement actually *had* failed was not the point; radicals and activists *perceived* that it had, and they were at a loss about how to proceed. Viewing the political climate of protest in the early 1970s, many activists were concluding that continued confrontations with political power were not worth the risks to their own safety and well-being. Although they still desperately wanted the Revolution to occur, activists and radicals did not see evidence that their strident efforts were bringing down "the system" and the capitalist engine that reputedly drove it. If they continued their legal or illegal protests, they risked their freedom and their safety for a goal that still remained elusive.

In the very period when radicals and activists were expressing profound doubts about the efficacy of their protest actions, academics and cultural commentators began observing a new trend among young adults: a shift from radical politics to mystical religion (see, e.g., Bellah 1976, 87; Cooper 1972, 59, 95; Judah 1974, 115; Richardson 1973, 461; Wallis 1981, 98). Religion was becoming central to the lives of thousands of people who, just a few years earlier, had been protesters in the streets. Always a strong current within the counterculture (see Ellwood 1994), never before the 1970s had religion been central to the lives of so many people of that generation (Anderson 1995, 381–83, 408–10). Moreover, for the rising generation as well, religion seemed to be replacing political protest and drugs as the vehicle for channeling post-adolescents' societal disdain. Although cultural commentator Tom Wolfe (1976) would immortalize the 1970s as "The 'Me' Decade," *Harper's* magazine more accurately captured the tenor of the early part of the decade with its 1971 article on "The Rush for Instant Salvation" (Davidson 1971).[14]

---

conditions in understanding the shift toward mystical religion in the early 1970s because the alternative religious groups flourished (at least for a time) in this same economic environment.

14. A similar pattern involving a youth-oriented shift toward mystical religions seems to have taken place in the United Kingdom. In 1973, Frank Musgrove supervised research in En-

Alternative religions in the early 1970s provided hope for social revolution in a manner analogous to the hope for social revolution provided by political protest a few years earlier. Some social commentators at the time picked up on this new cultural trend,[15] and often were angered by it. For example, the incursion into the New Left of so many new religions spurred an alternative paper in New Jersey, *The Free Aquarian*, to complain about "Pacified Hippies":

> If the loss of former radicals to straight society didn't deal a death blow to the movement, then the pacification diversions did. The people who refused to join the mainstream have too often been caught up lately in more inwardly-directed activities that have little or nothing to do with changing the social order and are basically counter-constructive, counter-revolutionary, selfish diversions of the white middle class.
>
> The rise in popularity of the Jesus Movement and other assorted religions and quasi-religious groups are a prime example. The move to find one's self through Jesus and other self-proclaimed gods like Maharaji [*sic*] Mahesh Yogi—or through meditation, the occult or soul travel or whatever—has become insincere, a hip plaything of poor little rich kids who became burned out, bored, scared or disinterested in working for change and improving the situation of the oppressed.
>
> Many of the hipper religions are insidious, embracing cop out philosophies of follow-Jesus-and-things-will-be-all-right or discover-yourself . . .
>
> "Love Jesus and be saved." A great line, unless you happen to be starving in a ghetto, pushed onto a reservation or rotting in prison. The rise in

---

gland's urban northwest (involving interviews with over 100 members of the counterculture) and discovered that members of the youth community "were involved in three main areas of activity—social and political action (including writing 'alternative' publications); mysticism; and community music and drama" (Musgrove 1974, 126). Similar to countercultural conditions in the U.S., Musgrove found that "anarchists and political activists showed considerable interest in Eastern matters, including Eastern philosophy and religion; but they were not, as a rule, 'into mysticism,' and were deeply contemptuous of the Divine Light Mission, Jesus Freaks, the Festival of Light and the Children of God" (139). On the "shift from political activism to religious alternatives" in Australia, see Blaikie and Kelsen 1979, 136.

15. See, e.g., Rossman 1979, 20; "On Being an Atheist" 1975, 28; "From Politics to Yoga" 1975; Marin 1975.

popularity for another self-proclaimed god, the [Guru] Maharaj-ji, the teen-age idol from India whose followers are massing a gigantic public relations campaign in this country, is another ripoff religion that thrives on the unhap-piness and searching of the younger generation, offering "the answer" to people willing to shell out the dough for the master's playthings. (Edwards 1973, 10)

To be sure, the article continued with a somewhat more sympathetic—but still challenging—comment: "Of course, there's the argument that to im-prove society, one must get his or her self together first. But isn't it possible to try to do both at the same time?" (Edwards 1973, 10).

Two months later, from Michigan, the September 1973 *Workers' Power* complained that

notably absent from the press is the New Left. "Mystic chic" is the new style of the campuses and the streets. Who would have thought it was such a short step from the streets to the ashram?

The defection of New Left stars Rennie Davis, Jerry Rubin, Sally Kemp-ton [16] and hundreds of lesser lights seemed almost to flow from their political activity. One day Rennie Davis was flying to Paris to meet with Madame Binh [from North Vietnam], the next day he is in India, receiving knowledge from Maharaj Ji. . . .

They wanted to change it all and make a revolution. After a while, it be-came clear that there had been no revolution—they hadn't smashed racism, smashed imperialism, won the "war on poverty" or even made education relevant.

Many learned the wrong lesson and decided that politics doesn't work. So, if you can't change the world, change yourself.

The author scorned this new effort to change oneself through various mysti-cal religions and therefore entitled the article "New Mystics: The Great Guru Rip-Off" (Russell 1973).

16. Sally Kempton had written a widely circulated feminist article in 1970 (Kempton 1970), but by 1973 she had become a follower of Swami Muktananda (Kempton 1976).

On the West Coast, Art Kunkin of the *Los Angeles Free Press* expressed his ambivalent emotions in a front-page article about "The Great Guru Hunt:"

There is very definitely something in the air, and it is not, as I originally thought last year, just the cycle of individualism and personal mystical search which could have been expected to fill the vacuum left by the failures of mass political activism in the 1960's.

A certain cat is being let out of the bag, accidently or by design, which will either result in the creation of many socially motivated individuals of great personal energy who can stop mankind from destroying itself, or the widespread dispersal of these same energies utilized by egoistic persons will accelerate the crisis. (Kunkin 1973, S-1)

The recent turn toward mystical religion, according to Kunkin, could lead either to a goal shared by spiritual seekers and radical activists alike (that of "stop[ping] mankind from destroying itself") or to self-absorbed egoistic quests.

Perhaps the most thoughtful and academically informed explanation of the conversions came from former SDSer Andrew Kopkind (1935–1994). In 1973, he used cognitive dissonance theory to explain the politics-to-religion transformation that he was witnessing at the time:

The "failure" of revolution, according to the hyberboles employed by the political movements of the late '60s, freaked out the people who had set their life-clocks according to the apocalyptic timetable. What happens "when prophecy fails?" . . . the moment of disconfirmation—the day the world does *not* end—creates extreme dissonance in the minds of those whose belief systems are based on the fulfillment of the prophecy. . . . The un-success of rapid, radical political change in America; the reelection of Nixon; the "winding down" of the war in Indochina without the unconditional surrender of the Pentagon—all that created an amount of dissonance (not to mention despair) among those who had invested the most in the expectation of a quick victory. Everyone has a way of blunting that dissonance: and one of them is the acceptance of a new belief system that either *confirms* the success of the Left in new terms, or *invents* drastically new terms. (Kopkind 1973, 49)[17]

Although scholars may debate the social-scientific rigor of cognitive dissonance theory (especially when applied to a broad social movement), Kopkind nevertheless clearly understood what he was observing around him.

Moving from the historical to the analytical, we can further interpret the shift toward mystical religion in the early 1970s through a sociological theory known as resource mobilization, originally put forward by Mayer Zald and Roberta Ash (1966). Resource mobilization theory examines how social movement organizations acquire and utilize such necessary resources as wealth, talent, power, etc., insisting that an organization "must have a payoff to its supporters"—a claim that seems equally true for an entire social movement, such as the power redistribution effort of the late 1960s. "Aside from the joys of participation," the theory adds, a social movement organization's "major payoff is in the nature of its promise; its goals or at least some of them must appear to have a reasonable chance of attainment." Moreover—and again in language easily applicable to an entire social movement—resource mobilization theory proposes that a "failing [social movement organization] loses members because they no longer believe their goals can be achieved with that instrument" (333, 334). In sum, a social movement will lose support when its adherents lose confidence in the feasibility of achieving its goals through its established patterns of social behaviors. This insight, however, leaves open the possibility that members of an apparently failing social movement may attempt to reinvigorate it by adopting a new "instrument" in their effort to achieve the social movement's goals.

One way in which the instrument or means of a social movement loses its attractiveness to adherents is when major societal or political events render those means ineffective. Politicians, for example, may satisfy one social movement demand among many, but in doing so eliminate a major rallying point

17. The essay is also reprinted in Kopkind 1995, 236. For another example of cognitive dissonance theory being utilized to explain "the movement of the new culture from the quietism of Zen to the religious proselytizing of psychedelia and new cults, and from the politics of the civil rights movement to the Jesus movement," see Ellwood 1973, 21–22.

used against them by their opponents. Politically disarming events of this nature happened to the floundering power redistribution Movement during early 1973. On January 27, the United States signed a cease-fire with North Vietnam and ended the draft, then on March 29, it withdrew its remaining troops from South Vietnam (Karnow 1983, 684). Through these three acts, the U.S. government removed the most contentious issues that power redistribution organizations had used to gain support from adherents. Perhaps paradoxically, the power redistribution Movement (already slowed by activist disillusionment and fear) suffered a further blow from the occurrence of the very events it had been clamoring to bring about. Thus, the Movement's partial success was also its most dramatic failure, as America's disentanglement from South Vietnam took place *without* the longed-for revolution in social and political power.

Writing about the consequences of a social movement organization's failure, sociologists Zald and Ash reflect that one consequence of such failure is "the search for new instruments" among disaffected adherents: "Either they search for a more radical means to achieve their goals within the movement, decrease the importance of their goals, or change the focus of discontent" (1966, 335). The theory thus suggests a new interpretation of the shift from politics to religion in the early 1970s: converts believed that they had adopted a more radical means to reach the same political end or goal of revolution (see McCarthy and Zald 1977, 1235). On this view, conversions to the religious groups of the 1970s were, *for the converts,* behaviorally innovative responses to the perceived failure of the power redistribution social movement of the 1960s—innovative responses that, paradoxically, renounced most of the symbols and social activities of the 1960s counterculture protesters while still maintaining (in some form) "the Revolution" as their goal.

Adapting Zald and Ash's terms, the new religious organizations to which former leftists converted *changed the primary focus of discontent* from society to the individual, and this change indicated their *adoption of new means to achieve the same goal.* Moreover, these converts felt that their new means were more revolutionary than ones previously used by 1960s organizations—a feeling that many activists and radicals firmly rejected. In the early 1970s, having failed to bring about the Revolution by direct action against political and economic structures, many participants in the Movement adopted what they believed to be new means to their goal by taking personalized religious or psychotherapeutic action against themselves. For participants in these new religious movements, the Revolution still would come, but its arrival would be heralded by a personal transformation of purified individuals, and its appearance would (have to) be a divinely orchestrated event (since bitter experience had taught them that it could not be a *socially* orchestrated occurrence). Transform the "self" of each adherent, the new logic went, and the heavenly sanctified revolution would immediately follow, if not coincide (Foss and Larkin 1979, 271). Radical-turned-mediator Jerry Rubin epitomized this new logic when he stated that "soon the spiritual and political revolutions will be joined: the inner and the outer" (Rubin 1973, 71). As the power redistribution Movement searched to find a successful method for achieving an ever-elusive revolution, the techniques and the promises of the new religious groups became beacons of hope.

The flexibility with which people can interpret religious ideologies and texts makes religion a particularly useful device for adherents of a failed social movement who are attempting to redefine the means by which they hope to achieve an elusive social goal. Religious ideologies are so flexible that members of an unfulfilled social movement can take solace in ideas that allow them to project the achievement of their defeated goals in the apocalyptic future, blame the failure of their "righteous" cause on the enemies of God, or even declare that God has in some way actually met their expectations (Zygmunt 1972). Each of these possibilities has profound effects on the valuation placed upon social action, including social protest.

The following two chapters will argue that new religious groups and their ideologies provided the cognitive and social structures by which many former activists reduced the tensions caused by their commitment to an apparently failed social movement. From the perspectives of the new religions, the ultimate rewards for participation would be reaped in the imminent millennium (see Stark and Bainbridge 1980, 121–22). In complementary fashion, religious organization provided the social-structural means by which former activists established alternative sources of immediate rewards (such as status and community) in contrast to those offered by the dominant society. If we view the new religions of the early 1970s as constituting another segment of a broad, social movement industry whose members saw themselves as striving to achieve a humanistic society, then apparent defections or religious conversions of former activists simply were shifts of allegiance from one failing movement to another, rising one, both of which claimed to share the same basic goal.

4

Radical Rhetoric and
Eastern Religions

during the late Vietnam War era, radical political rhetoric and pervasive countercultural symbols took on new meaning as religious groups either adapted or rejected them according to their own doctrinal positions. Hundreds of long-haired men sheared their locks down to their scalps—except for the topknots or short pigtails by which they expected their Lord Krishna to pull them up into heaven. Others of that generation (including the renowned radical Rennie Davis) fell at the feet of a teenaged Indian guru who had a penchant for fast cars, jewels, and ice cream but who also promised to bring about world peace. Persons whose lives a few years earlier had been committed to resisting authority now literally kissed the feet of their "perfect master." Other former radicals—now members of the Healthy, Happy, Holy Organization (3HO)—stuffed their long hair under white turbans and forswore drugs and premarital sex as they attempted to transform power that operated, not in social institutions, but instead in the base of their spines. Despite the variations, however, the words and symbols expropriated by religions of the early 1970s had the threefold effect of further diminishing direct social and political confrontation, sanctifying patriarchy, and further fragmenting an already divided New Left movement. Gods came alive as the 1960s Movement withered.

I base my analysis of rhetoric and symbolism on primary documents from numerous 1970s religions in conjunction with alternative press articles and

Guru Maharaj Ji (sitting on chair) lectures at the Divine Light Mission in Hollywood, Calif., on Sept. 2, 1971. The orderly worship-room is typical for ashrams in the period, with the guru's picture in the center, surrounded by additional photos of the leader and other "holy" figures. This picture first appeared in the Sept. 15, 1971, issue of Newsweek. (© Lester Sloan)

my own interviews with political-to-religious converts.[1] The groups examined include the Children of God, the Christian World Liberation Front, Divine Light Mission, Hare Krishna, Meher Baba, Naropa Institute, Scientology, 3HO, Transcendental Meditation, and the Unification Church. Most of the examples taken from and about these groups demonstrate the introspective, patriarchal, and divisive consequences of radical rhetoric and borrowed symbolism in the popular but unorthodox religions that flourished during the final years of the Vietnam War.

Religious imagery permeated much of the 1960s debates, even if political

---

1. As far as I can tell, the alternative press's coverage of various youth-oriented religions in the late 1960s and early 1970s has never been examined. Peck's (1985) study of the underground press, for example, barely mentions the religious groups that concern me in this study.

concepts took center stage. To be sure, in the popular mind religion and protest often were opposing paths. Marx's adage about religion being "the opium of the people" expressed the Movement's disdain for organized religion;[2] and when mainstream religious groups and individuals—including the Catholic Church, Reverend Billy Graham, and the "positive thinker," Dr. Norman Vincent Peale—did make their voices heard in political debate, they often actively supported America's efforts in the Vietnam War (see Connelly 1972).[3] Nevertheless, an amalgam of clergy and laypersons from many denominations resisted the general pattern, including the Catholic fathers Daniel and Philip Berrigan (Polner and O'Grady 1997), liberals in the Clergy and Laymen Concerned About Vietnam (CALCAV) (Hall 1990), Martin Luther King Jr., and various peace churches such as the Quakers, Amish, and Mennonites (Connelly 1972, 22–23; Kent and Spickard 1994). Thus, the political impact of religious groups in the 1960s was split between those who upheld the status quo and those who produced a rhetoric of governmental opposition and resistance that enhanced direct social action.

In the early 1970s, the politically-inspired rhetoric generated by the heterodox religions contained the express hope that a major political restructuring would occur, and on this point it was little different from typical New Left and Movement slogans from the period. The new religious rhetoric differed dramatically, however, when discussing how that restructuring would come about. In 1970, the director of the Ananda Center in Long Beach, California, succinctly summed up the new view by asserting that "the only revolution which will change the world is a revolution of consciousness in the individual through self-awareness" ("What is Ananda?" 1970, 8). The idea of "working

2. See, e.g., "On being an Atheist" 1975, 27; "Jesus Communes" 1973, 16. For Marx's original formulation, see Marx 1964, 42.

3. Billy Graham (b. 1918) was the most popular and presidentially connected Christian evangelist throughout the 1960s and 1970s; for his (often inconsistent) positions on the Vietnam War, see Martin 1991, 343–48. Norman Vincent Peale (1898–1993) was a highly popular American religious minister whose theology was "based on the belief that through the mind and subconscious, utilizing techniques of positive thinking and affirmative prayer, one can achieve spiritual harmony and personal power" (George 1993, 6); on his friendship with Richard Nixon, see 198–200, 210–11, 214–15.

on the self" as the vehicle for political change captured the imagination of heterodox religious persons in the early 1970s, who fundamentally believed that a religious foundation of pure individuals would provide the basis for a perfected and just government. Members of widely diverse nontraditional religions believed in the foundational necessity of individual purity underpinning the social state, even though they differed hotly and bitterly over what set of doctrines provided the best (if not the only) way to holiness. Thus, despite dramatic doctrinal differences, any number of religious leaders would have agreed with Ananda Marga's North American head in 1974 when he stated that "social institutions must be founded on spiritualism. With a lack of spiritualism, things fall apart. That is what is happening around the world today" (Acarya Yatishvarananda [Dada], quoted in "Ananda Marga" 1974, 18).[4]

Some form of "spiritualism"—or, more accurately, spirituality—had played a role in the New Left almost from its inception. In July 1969, an article in the leftist New York City publication *Liberation* indicated one of the ways that the New Left "shows its differences from all the old ones is by the re-

4. To be sure, it would be inaccurate to portray Ananda Marga in the early 1970s as having been completely uninterested in social issues. For example, because both the Black Panther Party and Ananda Marga experienced what were to their members forms of oppression, the two groups were able to carry off at least one cooperative undertaking involving a free clothing program for Washington D.C.'s poor. Furthermore, on its own, Ananda Marga apparently sponsored "a benefit for a Halfway House for women ex-convicts" in 1975 ("Ananda Marga" 1975, 13), and the group ran medical clinics, food projects, and nursery schools in various American cities in the 1970s and 1980s. Note, however, that the actions that most of its members took were charitable, not structurally challenging. Although space prevents me from examining the charitable programs of the various groups that I discuss, suffice it to say that almost all of them (on social issues) were structurally nonconfrontational like most of Ananda Marga's. For an example of someone (Steve Ross) who "burned out" after having been "intensely involved in the whole Berkeley scene—demonstrations, drugs, sex" and joined Ananda Marga in 1971, see Silverman 1985. (On a different level, a small faction within Ananda Marga utilized bombings, attempted assassinations, etc. to attack perceived opponents—often people attached to the Indian government, which in 1971 imprisoned the group's leader, Prabhat Ranjan Sarkar [b. 1921], who had political aspirations and a political party in India that rejected both communism and capitalism as it aspired to lead a world revolution under the group's own principles. Critics accused Sarkar of megalomania and fanaticism; see Bauer 1982; Melton 1991, 3:190.)

markable interest in religion, magic, astrology, and the other 'opiates' of traditional Left ideology" (Waskow 1969, 36). Even yoga played a role in some revolutionary ideology, with Berkeley's Red Yogi Collective arguing that "by the practice of hatha yoga (exercises), pranayama (breathing exercises) and meditative techniques we can greatly increase and intensify our ability to function creatively in a hostile environment. . . . Our approach to yoga is based on attuning, cleansing, and harmonizing ourselves to better struggle against the death-machine" ("People's Yoga" 1970, 5).[5]

In most cases, however, proponents of action were little concerned with religion. Political efforts dominated much of youth protest culture, and religious or spiritual undertakings either were valorized when they contributed directly to politics (Lee and Shlain 1985, 126–38) or were thought to be "Another Road" altogether (Monk 1972; see also Everyman 1969, 3). In the 1970s, political and religious priorities reversed, as participants in spiritual or mystical groups believed that their new roads were leading to the same goals that previously they had sought through direct political action.

Divine Light Mission

Nowhere was the new prioritizing of religion or spirituality over politics more dramatic than among followers (called "premies") of the adolescent Guru Maharaj Ji, who was born December 10, 1957 (for a brief "official" biography, see "Who Is Guru Maharaj Ji?" 1973). Rennie Davis's conversion to the "Perfect Master" (as the guru's followers called him) sparked bewilderment and anger within the New Left, and during Davis's speaking tours on behalf of the Divine Light Mission (DLM), activists and radicals alternatively ridiculed him and sat in dazed wonderment as he propounded his message about the new path to peace ("Rennie Davis on Tour" 1973, 2; Rossman 1979, 17). Davis told a Berkeley crowd comprised of many former and current activists that "the Perfect Master teaches perfection, and will bring perfection on Earth—not after the Millennium, but right now, in three years. A

---

5. See also "Revolutionary Yoga" 1970, 17. Despite the attempt to unite yoga with revolutionary action, the Red Yogi Collective's representation of a yogi using an *asana* as a means of balancing a firing rifle seems a bit far-fetched ("People's Yoga" 1970–71, 17).

revolutionary perfection, realizing all our ideals of peace and justice, brought about not by struggle and conflict but by the perfect working of a perfect organization" (Rossman 1979, 16). In essence, Davis offered his former comrades a career move into the ideal organization, from which they finally would achieve the heretofore elusive goals of the 1960s. After people received "the knowledge" that Maharaj Ji imparted to his followers, Davis insisted, "then we can do what the street people sought in the sixties—abolish capitalism and other systems that oppress" (Davis, quoted in Lewis and Thomas 1973).

The primary political word that Maharaj Ji and his organization used to attract disaffected activists and radicals was "peace." As it stated in various ways, the DLM offered converts the road to achieving peace in a manner as universal and grand as they ever had dreamt of accomplishing in the 1960s. In typical fashion, the guru's posters advertising his September 9, 1972, appearance at the Oakland City Auditorium boldly proclaimed "IMAGINE WHAT IS PEACE / COME AND REALIZE THE PRACTICAL EXPERIENCE." On the application form for Millennium '73, the DLM's major media event of the early 1970s, the teenaged guru said, "I declare I will establish peace in this world."[6] During the event itself, held at the Houston Astrodome, a giant video screen behind the main stage showed a barrage of shots from the tumultuous 1960s—assassinations, riots, peace protests, and Vietnam War footage (Levine 1974, 48; Gray 1973, 39; see also Kent 1987, 22–23). When the DLM's newspaper reflected upon the Houston event a few months after it was over, it again contrasted the contentious political events of the preceding decade—the civil rights movement, VISTA (Volunteers in Service to America), the October 1969 Vietnam Moratorium, draft-dodging, and the Vietnam War itself—with the guru's message of peace: "Give me your love, I will give you peace. Come to me, I will relieve you of your suffering. I am the source of peace in this world" ("Story" 1973, 9).

Various accounts from the period suggest that many former protesters accepted the guru's promise for peace.[7] Prior to his own conversion, Rennie

6. For another statement of this claim, see the interviewer's question to Maharaj Ji in J. Wood 1973, 48.

7. See e.g. Downton 1979, 31–32; Kent 1988, 104, 104n. 2; Rossman 1979, 22; Snell 1974, 21. It seems likely that most of the conversions of former activists and radicals took place

Followers of Guru Maharaj Ji march in downtown Houston in early November 1973, in anticipation of Millennium '73. (© Houston Chronicle)

Davis met numerous leftist veterans in the DLM, and their presence helped him to decide to explore further the guru's message. While visiting the group's ashram in India,

> I kept getting more and more freaked—the whole thing stank of fraud. But there were about 60 western young people at Prem Nagar [near the Himalayan Mountains], and I kept having these great raps with them. People

---

before 1975, at which time a major upheaval occurred in the DLM that led to the recruitment of a new type of convert. After 1975, "one had to accept Guru Maharaj Ji as a personal savior in order to become a member," and the people who were able to do so tended to have "been very religious in their pre-adolescent years" (Derks and van der Lans 1983, 305).

would come up to me and say "Far out—I was with you in the streets of Chicago," or "Good to see you again, last time I saw you was at May Day." Slowly my resistance began to break down as I saw that these great people were really into this kid. So I decided I would at least try and receive knowledge. (Davis, quoted in Kelley 1973b, 35)[8]

In turn, Davis's conversion influenced other activists to explore Maharaj Ji's teachings (Kelley 1973a, 9). Former activist Sophia Collier read about Davis's new direction in a copy of the DLM's newspaper, *Divine Times*. From the article, she learned that Davis

> now felt that the work of the peace movement, in which he had labored so long, would not bring about society-wide changes. Instead, he "envisioned a spiritual movement with the aim of raising the collective consciousness of the nation as the first step toward any other meaningful change."
>
> Although this idea was not really new to me, when I read it in [*Divine Times*] it seemed to click. Maybe Divine Light Mission could help me with both my personal spiritual aspirations and my hopes for the world. (Collier 1978, 111)

Other prominent activists and radicals who converted to Maharaj Ji included Michael Donner, whose term as vice president of the DLM was interrupted in 1975 by a twelve-month imprisonment (as a "Beaver 55" member) for destroying draft board files and erasing Dow Chemical's computer tapes.[9] Sandy

8. For Davis's mention of meeting another former activist-turned-DLM convert prior to his own conversion, see also "Serendipity of Peace" 1973, 3. Elsewhere Davis said about his Indian ashram trip that "I was expecting a secluded mon[a]stery. When I got there, to my shock, there were 50 or 60 westerners there. I found people who had been arrested at May Day, Chicago, one woman from a Women's collective in New York, another guy from a Marxist Leninist study group in Buffalo. I never felt so comfortable with a group of people in my life. I thought it was like an early SDS convention in the Himalayas" (T. Wood 1973b). According to Allen Ginsberg, Davis had been doing zazen meditation (learned from friends of Gary Snyder) for several months prior to his conversion ("Rennie Davis" 1973).

9. On Donner's activities with the Beaver 55, see Cameron 1973, 146–53; Kelley 1973b, 54; Collier 1978, 179; "Michael Donner" 1976, 1. His first prison term of fourteen months for a related conviction appears to have taken place mostly during 1969, prior to his conversion. On

Rennie Davis, former antiwar protester turned Divine Light Mission premie, speaks at the Millennium '73 extravaganza in Houston (which he helped to coordinate) on Nov. 11, 1973. During the event, Davis told the crowd of about 22,000 attenders: "All I can say is, honestly, very soon now, every single human being will know the one who was waited for by every religion of all times has actually come." (© Gerald Israel, Archive Photos)

the Beaver 55 in general, see Zaroulis and Sullivan 1984, 288. An undated, unattributed statement about the Beaver 55's actions against draft board records in St. Paul, Minneapolis, and Indianapolis and against Dow Chemical Company (because of its manufacture of the chemical agent napalm, a jelly that burned off skin) appears in Bloom and Breines 1995, 252.

Meadows, managing editor of the DLM's publication *And It is Divine,* had been a member of the Denver Weathermen Collective (Haines 1973–74, 8). Steve O'Neill, who in 1973 was a twenty-five-year-old DLM organizer in Boston, was an ex-GI and "a revolutionary of sorts" before his conversion (Kelley 1973b, 54). Finally, the DLM's director of public relations in 1973, Richard Profumo, had served a seven-month prison sentence for draft evasion (Levine 1974, 42).

Michael Rossman captured the logic of the attraction that Maharaj Ji held for former activists when he observed:

> If Rennie was a heretic, his heresy was not one of ends, but of means; and it struck us where our faith is weakest. We have all been struggling for personal fulfillment and the social good in the same brutal climate. Few now can escape the inadequacy of the political metaphor to inspire and guide even our political actions, let alone to fulfill them. It is not just a matter of the correct line; the problem is with process. All is accomplished by organizing. But was there an activist present [in Davis's Berkeley audience] who had not felt despair, simple and terrifying, at the frustrations and impossibilities of working in the organizations we form: their outer impotence, their inner conflicts and ego games and wasted energy, the impoverishments of spirit which lead us to drop out of them again and again? Here Rennie was, proclaiming the perfect means to our various ends, the ideal, impossible Organization, working in perfect inner harmony, and outer accomplishment. *Lay down your arms, your suffering, and the Master will give you bliss.* And yet to work in the Left, to be of the Left, has meant to bear these arms, this suffering; we have known no other way. (Rossman 1979, 22)

For Davis and many other political activists and radicals, the rhetoric of the DLM provided hope that an ungraspable and ill-defined "peace" still could be achieved, even as the organization's staunchest workers submitted themselves to the absolutist authority of a guru who retreated from confronting institutions that fostered war. As one of many DLM ironies, the tents and water tanks for its 1974 New England rummage sale and festival were provided by the National Guard (Boulanger 1974).

"Blissed out premies" attend Guru Maharaj Ji's Millennium '73 in the Houston Astrodome, Nov. 8–10, 1973. This photo is a still-shot from a one-hour national broadcast by the Public Broadcasting Service entitled "The Lord of the Universe," Feb. 24, 1974. (Photo courtesy of Urban Archives, Temple Univ., Philadelphia)

The Hare Krishnas

Of all the Eastern-based religions that flourished in the early 1970s, the DLM was the most Westernized, with the guru rarely pictured in traditional Indian garb but rather in a business suit, which was also the accepted clothing of his male devotees (Morgan 1973, 94). The opposite was true, however, of another prominent Hindu-based group that attracted former activists, the International Society for Krishna Consciousness (ISKCON)—more popularly known as the Hare Krishnas. Their leader, A. C. Bhaktivedanta Prabhupāda, always dressed in a *dhotī*, the long, wrapped loincloth that is the traditional garb of Indian men, and the Western converts to his group followed his lead. For both potential converts and members themselves, this attire was part of the group's otherworldly image—an image that embodied a rejection of the

Western world. As one former-activist-turned-Krishna-devotee, Subhananda, explained in an interview in New York in 1986:

> A strong part of the attraction of devotees for me was their sheer defiant otherworldliness. Because . . . my ideology basically was just [that] the world as it is is just in such bad shape it's not worth saving. . . . Destroy it and start over again; things are really hopeless. And here are these people who clearly were making a statement that they had really . . . entered another realm of consciousness and being. And even though I knew very little about it ideologically, philosophically, just *that* itself was enough to cause me to have great interest.

Subhananda illustrates J. Stillson Judah's observation that "in their extreme dissent, [converts] exchanged our Western culture and its value system for an Eastern civilization and one of its popular religions" (Judah 1982, 14).

In a survey of residents of Hare Krishna temples along the Pacific Coast conducted in 1969 and 1970, Judah discovered that "before becoming members a large number had been involved in protests against the Vietnam War, the government, the educational system, the growing secularism, and even the American way of life because of its alleged involvement in materiality" (Judah 1982, 13; see also Judah 1974, 115–16).[10] Similarly, from a sample of devotees, E. Burke Rochford, Jr. found that "over half of the early converts to Krishna [between 1967 and 1971] had taken part in the anti-war movement" (Rochford 1998, 64).[11] Subhananda exemplifies Judah's and Rochford's characterization. His account of encountering Krishna devotees at a major antiwar march in Washington, D.C., in late 1969 or early 1970 is especially revealing:

> And there was a stage set up, and all the big . . . Movement people were speaking. And at one point Allen Ginsberg was on stage, chanting mantras

---

10. Presumably the survey results discussed in Judah 1982 extend beyond the sixty-three questionnaires (from Berkeley and Los Angeles disciples) to which he refers in Judah 1974, 1.

11. The chart in which this figure appears, however, does not tell us how many people Rochford sampled, so this percentage is difficult to interpret. For an account of a female convert who had been active in anti-Vietnam War groups, see Shinn 1987, 98.

Upon Swami Prabhupāda's arrival at Heathrow Airport in London on July 7, 1972, devotees set up a carpet and a throne in the VIP lounge, and one adherent kneels before the guru on a flower strewn floor to pay homage to him. (© Popper-foto/Archive Photos)

for peace. And Allen Ginsberg at that time was my role model/hero. I was very into Allen Ginsberg, mainly because he symbolized for me utter rebellion against society . . .

But at the same time as I was moving towards the stage to get closer to hear him, I hear on the left side the Hare Krishnas, who were—there were about thirty of them, under a tree, chanting. Chanting up a storm. And they had a big crowd around them. And I remember being almost physically pulled between the two. On the one hand, Ginsberg was like . . . God to me. On the other hand, I had heard of the Hare Krishnas . . . but knew virtually nothing about them, and was very intrigued to get a little up-close look at the Hare Krishnas doing their thing.

And I remember thinking, "Well . . . should I go see Ginsberg or them?" And I really was torn, and I sort of pulled myself off to see the devotees. . . . And so I watched for a little while, and then I joined the chanting line . . . with my gas mask and helmet hanging from my belt, my . . . leather jacket, which I had bought used at a thrift store. . . . I just got swept up in it. I just really thought the chanting was great and joined in the line.[12]

Ironically, Ginsberg himself usually led Krishna chanting at political events (Rubin 1970, 43), including when he was on the witness stand during the Chicago conspiracy trial (Levine, McNamee, and Greenberg 1970, 115). It appears, moreover, that Subhananda was not the only leftist for whom the rhythmic sounds struck a chord. As early as October 1967, a large body of demonstrators chanted away as they marched toward the Pentagon, in what became an unsuccessful attempt to levitate and exorcize the building (Mailer 1968, 142; see also 136–38; Rubin 1970, [70]; Zaroulis and Sullivan 1984, 136, 138).

Several years after Subhananda joined the Krishnas in summer 1970, he became a campaign manager for Balavanta, a devotee who ran for mayor of Atlanta, Georgia, in 1973 as a candidate from the Krishnas' religiously-based political party. The party, which eventually (and briefly) worked on the national level as the In God We Trust Party, played a small but neglected part in the Krishna's story in the United States. The content of its political message embodied the pattern of self-transformation-before-world-transformation that characterized the goals of numerous religious groups in the early 1970s. Surprisingly, only one academic seems to have paid attention to the party. Writing in 1974, Francine Daner argued insightfully:

> The swami began by promoting his movement as a political alternative to the doctrines of contemporary leaders such as [Black Panther Party leader Eldridge] Cleaver, Mao, [SDS's Tom] Hayden, [Republican Nelson] Rockefeller, [right-wing Democrat George] Wallace and Nixon by claiming

12. I am unable to ascertain the demonstration to which Subhananda was referring. After 1968, Ginsberg "was a featured speaker at a number of anti-war rallies and demonstrations" (Schumacher 1992, 567), and in 1972 he spoke at "a huge demonstration outside the White House" (Miles 1989, 448), but these observations are not enough to allow me to identify the particular demonstration discussed here. For an allusion to Krishna converts reacting against the politics of the 1960s, see Johnson 1976, 34, 40.

that "they can't help you," and offering chanting of the Hare Krishna
mantra as the "highest form of social work" . . . With the "In God We Trust"
party ISKCON points a finger at the current moral state of American
government and presents ISKCON's philosophy, while realistically understanding that the election of its candidates is improbable. (Daner 1974,
11–12)[13]

Indeed, party candidates propounded that philosophy in several city and state
elections.

The conversion accounts of two Krishna candidates shed light on how
some people (perhaps especially men) evolved from political activists to devotees in the early 1970s. The first devotee to declare himself a political candidate was Amarendra, who ran for city commissioner of Gainesville, Florida, in
1972. He and I discussed his conversion and subsequent political activities
when I interviewed him at his law office in Culver City, California, in summer
1988. Prior to his life as a Krishna devotee, Amarendra (then known as David
Leiberman) had a colorful activist history. Having enrolled in the University
of Florida at Gainesville in 1966, he was inspired by the political protest activities that he witnessed during a visit to Boston on the eve of the 1968 Democratic convention.[14] He returned to Gainesville and over the succeeding
months became a prominent and effective campus organizer and speechmaker
at rallies and demonstrations. At a 1969 or 1970 riot in St. Petersburg,
Florida, Leiberman felled a police officer whom he said was about to billy-club
a person from behind, but for his valor he himself was beaten and arrested. Reflecting on his actions and feelings at the time of his arrest, Leiberman remembered: "I know when they threw me in the paddy wagon, I was furious. I
was swearing at them, threatening them. And at that point . . . that was an important—[a] critical point in my life . . . because I was thinking . . . either—

13. As one example of the Krishnas' approach to politics, I found in the Social Protest Collection of the Bancroft Library (Univ. of California, Berkeley) as undated handout from the San
Francisco Hare Krishna center entitled "The Sanctification of the Peace Movement," in which
"Swami Bhaktivedanta Gives You The Peace Formula." The formula turns out to be "the simple
process of chanting the holy names of God," which are, "Hare Krishna, Hare Krishna, Krishna
Krishna, Hare Hare. Hare Rama, Hare Rama, Rama Rama, Hare Hare."
14. For a brief biography of his life as David Leiberman, see Sachs 1979.

the next step was violence . . . in terms of real revolution. You know, getting guns and . . . taking the next step. Or just looking for an alternative." While in jail, Leiberman tried meditation, an activity he had heard about from one of his professors. After being released,

> the meditation while I was in jail had left an impression on me. So then I started looking in Eastern philosophy. . . . I did start to do some hatha yoga, a little meditation, and start to look into things a bit more. And essentially, just—in a very short period of time, [I] just got beyond the political thing, seeing that it was only one small part of an overall problem. And it was just like if you—if you have a bubble in your carpet and you put it down over here, it's just going to come up somewhere else. And you really had to trans- form everything in order to solve the fundamental problems—that was just a manifestation of a deeper problem regarding the purpose of life. And I wasn't prepared to go the next step and start killing people and blowing up things and . . . so forth, and didn't feel that that would be effective anyway, cause who's going to beat the United States government in terms of a showdown, a military showdown?—it was stupid! And I just couldn't see giving up my life for a political cause. It just wasn't worth it to me.

Still believing that a fundamental cultural revolution would transform the country, Leiberman had reached a point where he felt that his former political activities were ineffective but that heightened violence was both unsavory and (in the face of American military might) pointless. In Eastern religion, how- ever, he began to see the possibility for orchestrating the desired revolution through religious channels: "By 1970, [I] met Hare Krishna devotees in Gainesville who came to campus, and from the first day I met a devotee it was like, that was it. I mean, I heard what he had to say, and I said, 'This—this def- initely sounds exactly what I'm looking for.' "

The other major Krishna political candidate, Balavanta—also known as William Ogle—also had an activist past before joining the Krishnas. Now (like Leiberman) a lawyer, Ogle spoke with me at the end of 1987 in his office in Knoxville, Tennessee. Entering Atlanta's Emory University in 1966, Ogle gradually became politically active in subsequent semesters. After spending the first semester of his junior year in Europe, his growing political consciousness led him to civil rights protests in Sylvester, Georgia, and to frequent discussions about the thought of Herbert Marcuse.[15] By his senior year, however, his campus was dividing between "the peace and love crowd" and the "SD-Sers [who advocated that we] 'kill the pigs, and . . . take over the administration building.' " Already experimenting with drugs and dabbling in Eastern philosophy, Ogle sided with the "peace and love crowd" but maintained his antiwar sentiments. He visited the Krishna community in New Vrindaban, West Virginia, and upon his return to campus shaved his head except for the topknot *(śikhā)*. In his words, "politics had evolved into . . . an Eastern view of things."

With politically active backgrounds in protest activities, both Amarendra and Balavanta ascended to leadership positions in the growing Krishna devotional movement in the southern United States, Amarendra assuming the presidency of the Gainesville temple. Their tensions, however, with mainstream society did not end. Balavanta frequently ended up in jail because of charges stemming from regular Krishna activities—chanting, distributing literature on the street, visiting and preaching on college campuses, and so on.[16] Then, as both Amarendra and Balavanta recall, in the final months of 1971 a devotee named Shyamsundar who was traveling with Prabhupāda[17] wrote a letter to all of the temples in which he quoted the guru as saying something to the effect that "devotees can do anything for Krishna, [including] enter politics and preach Krishna Consciousness." Commenting on this letter, Ogle re-

---

15. Herbert Marcuse (1898–1979) was a founding figure in the Frankfurt School of sociological theory who attempted "to amalgamate elements from Freud and Marx in a new utopian synthesis" (Manuel and Manuel 1979, 794). A useful outline of his life as an "author, University professor, and political activist" is Kellner n.d.

16. The only two charges about which I am specifically aware involved trespassing (on the campus of the University of Tennessee, Chattanooga) and playing drums on the street (in New Orleans during Mardi Gras!). Given that Ogle said that he had been arrested many times, it seems likely that he and other Krishnas were picked up for such alleged offences as creating a public nuisance and soliciting without a licence. Perceived harassment from the police was one line of continuity between a former life of countercultural push toward social change and postconversion involvement with the Krishnas.

17. Prabhupāda's letters indicate that he was in Africa on Sept. 8 or 9, 1971 and departed on Oct. 19, 1971 (see Prabhupāda 1987, 3:1759–85).

lated, "Well, that's all a couple of us needed . . . that little bit of encourage-ment." Leiberman recalled that "when I saw that [letter], something clicked, I guess."

On January 22, 1972, Amarendra wrote Prabhupāda concerning his plans to run for election as city commissioner. Prabhupāda responded in his somewhat choppy English on March 4, 1972, indicating that "especially I am glad that you are entering politics. . . . This will be a good opportunity to preach widely and sell our literatures, so take advantage." He was very critical of politicians, calling them "pick-pocket[s]" and "rascal leaders." Conse-quently, Prabhupāda told his disciple that "I am very serious that you all boys and girls should expose these Nixons and remove them, there is ample scope for protest in this Sankirtan [devotional] Movement, and you yourselves be president, that is my hope for saving the misled mankind from total chaos." Despite, however, his harsh words against current politicians and his hope for the political success of idealistic devotees, the guru's political platform was a far cry from the confrontational and structurally challenging efforts of the 1960s. In instructions that would remain consistent throughout the Krishnas' various attempts to gain political office, he informed Amarendra

> our platform must be very simple, that there is no other sacrifices necessary for the well-being of the citizens save and except this Sankirtan *yagna* [cere-monial sacrifice by chanting Krishna's names]. Regularly the town citizens can everyone congregate and chant Hare Krishna and hold festivals of cele-brations continually, with wide distribution of tasty foodstuffs—who will not be attracted by such programme? This is our simple method, nothing more. (Prabhupāda 1987, 3:1935 [letter no. 72–3–1])

In essence, Prabhupāda's entire political platform revolved around the at-tempt to convince people to orient their lives and lifestyles around devotion to Krishna. As a result of that devotion, in his view, national and international problems would diminish and then disappear.[18]

18. The lifestyle changes involved the avoidance of gambling, intoxicants, meat-eating, and what the Krishnas called "illicit sex." Prabhupāda's emphasis on distributing "tasty foodstuffs" al-lowed Balavanta to distribute food in some of Atlanta's poorer black communities during his 1973 mayoral campaign.

Prabhupāda avidly supported his disciples' political efforts in their early days. In an encouraging letter to Amarendra on June 12, 1972, the swami stated that "Krishna desires to have His own men in the top posts. . . . So gradually we shall also try to influence the leaders of this country and other countries to base their political activities upon a God-conscious platform." At the end of the letter he added that "you are the pioneer in this matter amongst the devotees in your country, so whatever experience you have gained you may pass on to others who may also attempt to engage in political activities. I am very thankful to you for your bold attempts, may Krishna give you His all blessings" (Prabhupāda 1987, 3:2028 [letter no. 72–6–8]). Endorsing for a second time Balavanta's campaign for mayor of Atlanta,[19] Prabhupāda reiterated the simplicity of the political platform on which the candidate was to run: "You may present the simple programme to the citizens for becoming purified and regaining their lost happiness by meeting together frequently to chant Hare Krishna, that's all. We have no complicated political platform" (Prabhupāda 1987, 3:1913 [letter no. 72–2–23]). Neither candidate was elected, but in January 1973, Amarendra got on the ballot in the mayoral race in Dallas, Texas, and received about a thousand votes in the actual election (in addition to my interview with Amarendra, see "Hare Krishna Devotee" 1973, 1B). Also during 1973, Balavanta tried to be elected to the twenty-seventh district of the Georgia Legislature.[20]

In 1974, Balavanta was back in another mayoral campaign, and apparently these and other devotees' political efforts had greatly impressed Prabhupāda (largely because of the opportunities that campaigners had to spread Krishna consciousness through public speaking events). So favorable, in fact, was the impression on Prabhupāda that he told Balavanta that all temple presidents were to run for public office, in part because the experience was such

19. Prabhupāda's first endorsement in a letter to Balavanta dated Dec. 22, 1971 (1987, 3:1835 [letter no. 71–12–26]). In this letter Prabhupāda acknowledges receipt of two letters from Balavanta, one dated Sept. 24 and the other dated Nov. 22. Presumably Balavanta expressed his political intentions in one of these.

20. Balavanta's candidacy for the legislature is described in a pamphlet entitled "Who Shall Lead Us?" A copy of this pamphlet, along with copies of items from Balavanta's 1973 mayoral campaign, are in the author's personal possession.

Krishna temple president and occasional political candidate Balavanta/William Ogle lecturing in Atlanta on Feb. 3, 1975, as he sits amidst Krishna Consciousness books and a picture of his leader, Swami Prabhupāda. (© Billy Downs, The Atlanta Journal-Constitution)

"good training [in] how to preach [and] how to deal with the public" (Balavanta 1987). Following their guru's instructions, ISKCON launched the national In God We Trust Party, which had devotees ready to run in Atlanta, Dallas, the District of Columbia, Gainesville, Los Angeles, New York, and Philadelphia.[21] In an April 28, 1974, letter to Balavanta, Prabhupāda told the political aspirant: "Your work in America with the God We Trust Party [*sic*] is

21. The July 4, 1974, issue of the DLM's *Divine Times* refers to the party as the "In God We Trust Party of Purified Leaders" and mentions that a *Divine Times* staff member had received a copy of the party's newspaper, *The New World Harmonist.* "The party is anti-communist, prescribes a strict moral code for all politicians, advocates the caste system for American schools and recommends chanting the non-sectarian names of God" ("Quick Cuts" 1974, n.p.). On the party's political campaigns, see Cook 1974; "Krishna Movement" 1974, 14; Wright 1977b, A3. An undated (1974?) letter from Balavanta on "In God We Trust Party for Purified Leaders" sta-

very inspiring to me. If anywhere they will take seriously the principles of *Bhagavad Gita As It Is*, that will be America." In this letter and elsewhere, he also insisted that one goal of the party was to establish the traditional Indian caste system in the United States (Prabhupāda 1987 4:2475–2476 [letter no. 74–4–51]; see also 2477 [letter no. 74–4–52]).

Less than two months later, however, Prabhupāda killed the political party that he had fostered. On June 8, 1974, the guru informed one of his disciples that "I have stopped the political movement because it will not help us. It is a very filthy atmosphere. Better you do not indulge in those things with expenditure of money and spiritual energy" (Prabhupāda 1987, 4:2516 [letter no. 74–6–12]). Two days later he wrote separate letters to Amarendra in Gainesville, Balavanta in Atlanta, and Rabindra Swarupa in Philadelphia, elaborating upon his objections to the organization's burgeoning political efforts (see 4:2520 [letter no. 74–6–22], 4:2520–2521 [letter no. 74–6–23], and 4:2521 [letter no. 74–6–24]). To Balavanta, he stated:

> My point is that I cannot employ the society's money in political campaigning. Moreover it is illegal for the society which is a religious society to pay for political campaigns and would cause us to lose our tax exempt status. The alternative, to make a separate brain [*sic*], separate funds, and separate manpower is a diversion from our spiritual goal. The other political parties are spending lavishly so how can we compete with them. We do not have enough money nor do I wish to spend our money in this way. Therefore I say it is better to stop. You say you plan to run for U.S. Congress. But for this, you can draw no money from the society. So your plan is Eutopian [*sic*]. Better concentrate on developing the brahminical qualities in the devotees there; that is more important than running for political office.

ISKCON's political party quietly disbanded, but with seemingly long-lasting effects on both Amarendra and Balavanta: both became lawyers, and, on his own, Amarendra ran (again unsuccessfully) for the Florida State Legislature in

---

tionery (photocopy in the author's possession) mentions a concluding campaign in Gainesville and pending campaigns in Georgia, Washington, D.C., Philadelphia, and New York.

1978, receiving 20 percent of the vote (Amarendra 1988; see also Sachs 1979, 4).

In 1975, however, disenchanted ISKCON members in Hawaii maintained devotion to Krishna (under the direction of His Grace Siddha Swarup Ananda Goswami/Chris Butler) even as they formed their own political party, entitled Independents for a Godly Government (IGG). They ran candidates for local, state, and federal offices both in 1976 and in 1977. The party's 1976 congressional candidate, Kathy Hoshijo, received 17 percent of the vote in a three-person contest, and local candidate Wayne Nishiki took 20 percent of the vote in Maui's three-way mayoral race (Wright 1977d, A3). The IGG's political platform for candidates—which prohibited meat eating, nonmedical drug use, sex outside of procreative efforts with spouses, and gambling—resembled positions taken a few years earlier by the In God We Trust Party. The similarities may have come through mutual devotion to Krishna, as mediated by Prabhupāda (Wright 1977c; see also "Hoshijo Calls" 1977, "Link Acknowledged—Finally" 1977, and Wright 1977a).

Other Krishna leaders had activist or radical backgrounds, even if their careers inside the religion were not as political as were those of Amarendra and Balavanta. For example, in a 1987 interview, the prominent Krishna leader Jagadisha Goswami (b. 1948) recalled his days as a "pacifist-anarchist" student at a university in Buffalo, New York. In 1966, he protested against "the illegitimate activities of the government" regarding the Vietnam War. After only a year, however, he "came to the conclusion that the real problem was spiritual, not political. And if the spiritual problem could be solved, then the political problem could be solved." In February 1968, Jagadisha had his first contact with the Krishna Consciousness movement when he (along with other members of the audience) performed Hare Krishna chants that Allen Ginsberg led before a poetry reading. Also around that period, he chanted with friends while they vacationed at a cottage. Direct contact with ISKCON occurred when he visited a friend who had moved into the Buffalo temple around April 1968. He obtained some Krishna literature and began chanting:

> And right away I could see that the explanations given by Prabhupāda were clearing up . . . the relationships between all the other things that I'd been

studying. Things fell into place. I could understand in perspective how all the different philosophies and spiritual teachings that I'd been studying were linked together. That was the first experience I had. And the next experience I had, through chanting, was that . . . [the] feeling of existential fear of existence—of the world around me—evaporated, and I felt a sense of having come home, of having found the security that I was looking for through my spiritual search. And from then I've been maintaining my discipline in Krishna Consciousness.

When he and I spoke in Toronto's Hare Krishna temple in October 1987, Jagadisha was serving on ISKCON's Governing Body Commission, responsible for major policy and administrative decisions for the organization.[22]

More dramatic was the background of Bhakti-Tirtha Swami, who—as John Favors and then as Toshombe Abdul—had been a member of the Student Nonviolent Coordinating Committee (SNCC),[23] the Black Panther Party, and (as a Princeton University student in 1970) president of the Association of Black Collegians (ABC). In line with the policies of violent confrontation of some of these groups, Favors "was committed to thinking that violence was necessary to make people live better." Eventually, however, he "became disenchanted with political activism, feeling that it was bringing little or no progress." After traveling overseas, Favors "saw racism and class struggles and started to realize that it's not just one political paradigm versus another that's going to bring man equanimity, peace of mind, and a more just order. . . . What we really need is for man to have a change of consciousness." His conversion to Krishna Consciousness (apparently in 1973) was gradual,

22. For a discussion about the Governing Body Commission, see Shinn 1987, 48–60.

23. SNCC began in Raleigh, N.C., in 1960 as a civil rights movement comprised of black and white college students. Early in the decade it led a number of peaceful protests against segregation and sponsored a successful voter registration drive for previously disenfranchised African Americans. In 1966, under the leadership of Stokely Carmichael, the organization became more radical and racially exclusive, with the infusion of ideas and rhetoric of the Black Power movement against (what it identified as) white oppression. By the end of the decade, the organization was no longer operational.

occurring after he spent time studying with "Sri Chinmoy,[24] Swami Satchidananda, and other Indian gurus who related Hindu philosophy to the Western world." As he studied with these teachers, he continued his political
activities; and later recalled, "I would leave a Black Panther rally or an ABC
meeting and go to New York and study meditation for a couple of days with
some swamis." In 1979, he became an ISKCON renunciant monk[25] and directed ISKCON's Urban Spiritual Development Committee, which provided
"humanitarian, social welfare, and spiritual programs in the U.S. and Africa"
(McCray 1983, 35–36).

My final example of a political radical who converted to ISKCON is a
Canadian whose activist career and Krishna conversion followed patterns that
we already have seen in his American counterparts. Peter Chatterton (whom I
interviewed in 1989) was born in 1948 and entered McGill University in
Montreal in 1967, transferring after one year to the University of Victoria in
British Columbia. He and another person formed a branch of Students for a
Democratic University,[26] and he was a successful candidate for Victoria's stu-
dent council, having run on a radical platform. While at the University of Vic-

24. Sri Chinmoy (b. 1931) came to the United States from East Pakistan (now Bangladesh)
in 1964 and has lived in Queens, New York, for a number of years. He stresses the importance of
following a Master, who assists students in their meditations on the heart with the goal of God-
realization. In recent years, he and his students have set a number of records in various sports-
endurance areas, and he remains a prolific writer, artist, and musical instrument player. For years,
he has held meditations at the United Nations, and in 1976 he proclaimed: "Constant meditation
will help us solve all of our problems and all the world problems. We will immerse in a sea of wis-
dom-life instead of sinking in the sea of ignorance-life" ("Transcendental Meditation" 1976).

25. A monastic renunciant is required "to observe strictly the 'four regulative principles' of
abstinence from: the eating of meat, fish and eggs; all forms of intoxication; illicit (nonmarital and
nonprocreative) sex; and gambling and 'frivolous sports' (which refer to indulgence in nondevo-
tional, mundane entertainments including television and movies)" (Gelberg 1989, 143).

26. I am not aware of any systematic studies of Students for a Democratic University (SDU),
but Kostash (1980, 82–83) offers some impressionistic conclusions about it: "SDU was influenced by certain Americanisms of the international student power movement, notably
'yippie!ism' (Youth International Party) with its emphasis on the politics of outrageous life-style
and extravagant gesture. . . . It included in its ranks advocates of women's liberation, of Third
World struggles, of 'touchy-feelyism,' of revolutionary culture; published manifestos rather than

toria, Chatterton's radicalism grew as he felt increasingly alienated from mainstream society:

> We started getting into this whole we-them type of attitude, where we were the radicals, [and] everyone else was the straights. They were all out of it. They were establishment. We did things like organize a tent protest at U. of Vic[toria]. I can't remember what it was about but I took part in an occupation of Simon Fraser [University]'s administration building. It must have been '68 where [sic] we took, you know, a bunch of us occupied the administration building for at least 24 hours and, you know, that was a pretty intense event. We were, you know, not sure if the cops were going to come and get us and so on.[27]

Apparently Chatterton was not there for the entire event, given that police did arrest 114 students on the protest's fourth day (Kostash 1980, 94).

In retrospect, this event soured Chatterton's attitudes about radical political action. Reflecting upon it in our 1989 interview, he surmised: "Actually, I think it was the occupation of the administration building that disillusioned me about the radical movement because I saw [that] the leaders of the radical movement in the building were very—[they] seemed to be power hungry and just jockeying for position. . . . I think that helped push me more towards the hippie movement, you know, more towards that." While an undergraduate, Chatterton began exploring Eastern spirituality. As a psychology student, he wrote a major paper that discussed Eastern philoso-

---

programs; and adopted a strategy of confrontation through mass meetings, rallies and marches rather than of party politics."

27. The administration building takeover in which Chatterton participated almost certainly occurred in November 1968. Student research had determined that "17 per cent of SFU's student population comes from the working class" while prominent and wealthy businessmen sat on the University Senate; students who did not gain admittance to SFU went to community colleges, but SFU would "disqualify" many of their earned credits if and when they applied to transfer. Consequently, when the University Senate turned down a motion for "an 'open admissions' policy to SFU from the colleges," more than 100 students occupied the administration building (Kostash 1980, 93–94).

phy and Western psychology, and he began dipping into the works of Alan Watts, Gurdjieff, and Ouspensky.[28]

Upon graduating in 1970, Chatterton was uncertain as to whether he wanted to go on for more education "or really cop out of the whole system, and I decided to move up to a commune in Bella Coola . . . and we spent about six months up there with . . . no electricity, no contact with the outside world. Our goal was to, our idea was actually to go off in the woods and create our own separate ideal community and it was up there that we first started, I first started chanting Hare Krishna." When Chatterton returned to Vancouver in fall 1970, he accompanied some friends to the local Krishna temple. His impressions of it was that "it was just so exotic and so unworldly." It had a powerful impact on him, as it often did for "people who were already totally disillusioned and [who had] written off our whole western culture." The singing *(kirtan)*[29] gave him "a real feeling of exuberance and euphoria which at that time I felt was a very powerful experience." He joined the Krishnas in early 1971 (along with two friends who also had been student activists), later recalling that one strong motivation for doing so was his dream of "creating an ideal, alternative community, an ideal community that would be perfect." Once in ISKCON, Chatterton became one of its leading Canadian figures, especially in the western part of the country.

Chögyam Trungpa, Rinpoche

Although Allen Ginsberg was sufficiently sympathetic to Krishna Consciousness that frequently he intoned the Hare Krishna chant at public events, he ultimately became a devotee of a Tibetan Buddhist teacher, Chögyam

28. Georges Ivanovitch Gurdjieff (1872–1949) taught that people were to break out of their self-limiting, sleeplike habits through (often harsh) regimes of difficult physical undertakings, frenzied dance, "rhythmic exercises to music, breathing exercises, fasting, sleep deprivation, and mental training" (Barrett 1996, 178). He began his teaching in Russia but in 1922 moved to France, where he established an institute. His talented student P. D. Ouspensky (1878–1947) collected, systematized, and clarified his teachings.

29. Brooks (1989, 250) offers a more technical definition of the term: "Glorification of a deity, usually by congregational responsive singing."

Trungpa, Rinpoche (1939–1987).[30] The poet's third meeting with the sage took place in Berkeley during May 1971, at which time Trungpa's "drunken influence" (as Ginsberg himself called it) convinced the poet to shave off his beard. Ginsberg was quite aware, however, of the monk's deteriorated state: "I came up to see him in the motel where he was staying. And he was not there, but sort of tipsy in the bar across the street. He came up accompanied by two disciples, and fell down off the balcony; they had to help him up. It reminded me of Kerouac's genius for being drunk and inspired." Trungpa asked Ginsberg why he did not cut off his beard, and shortly thereafter Ginsberg excused himself, obtained a pair of scissors, and cut off two inches. Ginsberg had to insist that the two of them leave for Trungpa's scheduled lecture, since the lama preferred to stay in the bar. Trungpa dismissed the fact that disciples were waiting to see him with the offhand comment, "They know me. I can be late" (Harris 1971, 14; see also Miles 1989, 440–44; Schumacher 1992, 549–51). The last thing that the inebriated Trungpa (the name is Tibetan for "the precious one") said to Ginsberg that evening was, "Fuck off," a phrase that the chuckling bard himself used to a reporter to whom he related the story (Marin 1979, 45n.; Harris 1971, 15).

Despite Trungpa's obvious problems, Ginsberg took formal Buddhist vows (committing himself to the Buddha, to Buddhist teachings, and to the Buddhist community) under Trungpa's instruction on May 6, 1972. He also took Bodhisattva vows, promising (among other things) to postpone his own enlightenment in order to facilitate the enlightenment of all sentient beings. In 1973, he accepted Trungpa's invitation to teach poetry at one of the latter's retreats, which in turn led to Ginsberg's establishment of a poetry school at Trungpa's newly formed Naropa Institute in 1974 (Miles 1989, 446, 454–55). All the while, in his lectures and teachings, Trungpa gave little if any attention to antiwar or Movement teachings.

The Healthy, Happy, Holy Organization

Just as Krishna devotees were distinctive in their orange robes and (for men) shaved heads, so too were the followers of the immigrant guru Yogi

30. For a sympathetic discussion of Trungpa, see Layman 1976, 82–110.

Allen Ginsberg listens to his spiritual teacher, Chögyam Trungpa, Rinpoche, on the day that the poet took formal Buddhist vows in Boulder, Colo., on May 6, 1972. (© Ginsberg Trust Collection)

Bhajan in the Healthy, Happy, Holy Organization (3HO) known for their modified version of Sikh garb. Both men and women adopted an all-white outfit, complete with turban (which most traditional Sikh women do not wear).[31] As with their contemporaries in both the DLM and the Krishnas, some members of 3HO had histories of political activism prior to their conversions, and these former radicals saw their new religious involvement as a means of keeping alive their 1960s dreams of sociopolitical reform and cul-

31. I shall not enter into the debate about whether 3HO should be included in the Sikh community, but I note McLeod's conclusion on the issue: "Sikhs who come into contact with [3HO] Sikh Dharma are frequently perplexed by it, not knowing whether to embrace its followers as unusually devout or to avoid them as perversely unorthodox. . . . The answer appears to be to let them live their life of obedience, and Punjabis will live another, seldom the twain meeting in any meaningful way. They are accepted as Sikhs provided they maintain a separate existence" (McLeod 1989, 118–19).

tural revolution. The programs in which they participated as religious figures, however, eschewed challenges to political or structural systems and instead involved techniques ostensibly designed to purify the bodies, minds, and (as 3HO members would say) the spirits of practitioners. By attempting to make themselves models of virtue that others in society would want to emulate, 3HO members replicated the pattern found in other heterodox religions of the period by focusing on self-perfection as the means of transforming political and social inequality and injustice.[32]

A summer 1976 editorial in 3HO's magazine, *Sikh Dharma Brotherhood,* indicated that the organization saw itself within the context of disillusioned 1960s American youth:

> In the 1960s, America's young let out a cry of disillusionment heard round the world: America had failed to live up to the ideals it had so proudly touted. Now it faces a hungry and materially lopsided world, an exploited and depleted mother earth, and a confused and demoralized populace. It must make good on its promise or suffer the karma of its actions.
>
> It is no accident that Sikh Dharma took its new roots here: that the first in America to wrap the white turban and to don the Master's kirpan [ceremonial knife] were also the first to experience the new technology: the first to speak out against the hypocrisy of the old order; the first to rediscover what it means to be simple, joyful creatures of this creation; and the first to attempt to forge a new way of life based on the long-cherished ideals of truth, love and brotherhood. It is no accident that the pioneers of Sikh Dharma in America were the pioneers as well of the American youth movement, for Sikh Dharma in America is part of the new wave. (Khalsa 1976, [1]; see also Tobey 1976, 21–22)

In essence, 3HO members saw themselves as pure examples of the healthy alternative to a decaying American culture.

Among North America's leading 3HO members was Gurutej Singh

32. In addition to the 3HO interviews that I conducted, I heard several more stories of former activists among 3HO members. I was, however, either unable to reach these people (such as the high-ranking official who allegedly had been part of a Marxist collective in Buffalo) or I could not link up with people who agreed to speak with me (such as a woman who had been active in the tenant-rights movement).

Yogi Bhajan teaches his turban-wearing followers at the 3HO summer solstice celebration in Pecos, N.M., circa late June 1971. (© Lisa Law)

Khalsa, who was instrumental in establishing the religion in Canada. In February 1987, I recorded his conversion account as we sat in an ashram office in Toronto. Gurutej, in his earlier life as Ted Steiner, had been prominent as a campus organizer at the University of Kansas at Lawrence, activities that got him suspended from the school and, consequently, in line for the draft in 1969. He had led demonstrations both in Lawrence and in Kansas City against the Presidio Stockade shooting and the subsequent mutiny trial of military personnel who protested against it.[33] Soon afterward he organized a reenactment of the shooting on the university campus. Probably because of the success of the reenactment, SDS members contacted him about helping to organize a protest against an upcoming parade of the Reserve Officers' Train-

33. On October 11, 1968 a guard at the Presidio military stockade in San Francisco shot and killed Private R. Bunch as he tried to escape. Subsequently twenty-seven prisoners protested his shooting (along with general conditions in the stockade, racism, and the Vietnam War), which led to their convictions on charges of mutiny or related offenses (see Gardner 1970).

ing Corps (ROTC).[34] Steiner agreed, and he mobilized a wide array of students (including fraternity brothers and cheerleaders) to participate in the demonstration. On the day of the parade, as Steiner recalled, about a thousand protesters entered the university stadium, and two or three hundred of them got onto the field where the ROTC cadets were to march. Once on the field,

> We basically just danced in a big circle. Over the hill comes these ROTC candidates in full regalia and [they] marched down the hill and they actually came onto the field, and we just ran, skipped, and jumped in around them. . . . And so what happened is, the Chancellor actually canceled the ROTC review and we then went to the nearest pub and celebrated. And then about a week later I got a notice in the mail saying that I was to appear before a judiciary committee, and I was being expelled from school and the army had taken photographs at that point. So we had a trial and they were not willing to listen to why we were there but they wanted to know if we were there.

Soon after his expulsion, in July 1969, Steiner was drafted, and, after considering imprisonment, he fled to Canada.

On September 3, 1969, the day that Steiner departed Kansas and headed north, he asked himself (in his diary) the following question:

> If I would do better to stay and try to change the society after my two year stint with Uncle [Sam], could I still be effective or would I be *near* as effective in this kind of role after joining the army and submitting for two years to a power which I don't recognize? I am going to Canada primarily on the assumption that I could not—That if I were forced to swallow the affirmative

---

34. The ROTC was an American college-based program (compulsory for men in many schools until 1969) that provided scholarships and some spending money in return for military-type training that often funneled graduates into the armed services. The program itself, along with its facilities and activities, was a frequent target of antiwar campus protesters. SDS was the first organization to protest against the ROTC, and by 1970 anti-ROTC protests "had eliminated thirty units, made eighty-three voluntary, and reduced enrollment by 56 percent from 1966" (Sale 1974, 9).

"ME" for that period of time and was subjected to the waste of the military in human initiative and energy, it would stifle growth[—]constructive, humanitarian, simplistic growth of character. (Steiner 1969–72, 4–5)

With considerable doubts about what lay ahead, Steiner hitchhiked north to Winnipeg, then east to Toronto.

After several months in Toronto, Steiner (along with science fiction writer Judith Merril) founded an organization for draft dodgers and resisters called Red, White, and Black.[35] The group provided music; a twenty-four-hour-a-day switchboard; assistance in locating housing, legal aid, and medical services; and immigration assistance to displaced Americans. The organization (and its two leaders) received international attention, with articles appearing in the *New York Times* and *Newsweek* (Cowan 1970; Alsop 1970a). Columnist Stewart Alsop assessed that Steiner "in another time . . . would have had a brilliantly productive career in America." In *that* time, however, Steiner was angry, if not bitter: " 'You're raised to believe in the American dream and then the time comes when you see through the lies and deceptions. You see that we have a very rotten and very imperialist society, that war and racism are just an expression of the American culture, and there's nothing you can do to stop it. Then comes the rage when you discover the terrible hypocrisy' " (Steiner, quoted in Alsop 1970b, 80).

Steiner's diary contains gaps for the final months of 1969 and throughout 1970, but it suggests that he slowly integrated religious issues into his political concerns. Comments on American and world political issues filled parts of his 1969 and early 1970 entries, and by late June he had become convinced "that the U.S. is in for civil war." He even considered writing his parents about the imminent danger (Steiner 1969–72, 213, 215). By August 4, however, aspects of spirituality begin to appear in his writing: "I continually pick

35. I cannot date exactly when the group started, but the first reference to it in Steiner's diary appears to be from around mid-February 1970 (see Steiner 1969–1972, 197). Certainly he was worried about the group's success in an entry that appears to be dated Mar. 19, 1970 (201). By June 19, Red, White and Black had appeared in the *New York Times,* on CBS news, and in the Canadian media (209).

up [from things around me] and feel myself that something extremely 'big' is happening in terms of this social & political revolution in the world today. [It] involves reaching another level of mind development. . . . When Eastern thought tries to communicate a state of Nirvana-like oneness that is possible for the mind to achieve, the Western man has no idea of what that experience actually *is*" (223). He also observed that he was "getting more and more people saying there [*sic*] moving away from drugs—Don't need them anymore— can get high off life" (225). By November 5, he was meditating "each morning and when it is necessary during the day" (228–29). By November 17, 1970, he was speaking strictly in religious terms:

> I know the answer to the riddle—It's to stop the inner mind[']s constant chatter—to be—I have experienced the Light—I have seen & experienced liberation—total liberation. It's simply no doubt that I am liberated . . .
>
> Now, these liberated moments come in spurts—In between the moments—I busily try to find ways to stay liberated—Yoga, meditation, Christianity—praying, drawing . . . But all of this is still up & down. Why can't I stay "up" forever henceforth since I know that the answer is just thinking I'm up. (229)

Apparently, something profound had occurred in Steiner's life, but his diary does not tell us what it was.

In his interview, however, Steiner, recalled vividly what happened. He did not give a date for this momentous event, but diary evidence suggests that it was in October 1970 (see Steiner 1969–72, 228–29).

> Well, what happened with me was one night late I was just staying up with a friend and I had a rebirth or a spiritual experience, where I was God, God was me. It wasn't a drug experience; it was something fundamentally profound. It didn't come with being saved by Jesus Christ, thank God. In other words, it didn't come through any particular vehicle except the news itself that the "struggle was over"—was the term that caught my mind. Someone told me, "Hey, did you realize the struggle was over?" And the combination of the lateness of it being at night and the magic of the times and the opening of the heavens (in quotes) for me was I heard this message that whatever internal

struggle was involved in my own psyche was mended enough to awaken into a different consciousness. I did not know what it was but I felt a massive amount of healing energy and I felt as though I was capable of great things . . .

I made three statements as soon as I experienced this: that I would never kill a person; I want to tell people about it [presumably the healing energy]; and I'll never eat meat again. It just came out spontaneously.

Interpreting such a profound event in another's life always is risky, since outsiders may read meaning into it that would not ring true to the person who was involved. Steiner's account, however, provides some interpretive leads. American politics, especially the draft, provided much of the backdrop to his "struggle." With considerable anxiety he had fled his country, settled in Canada, and then started over in his struggle against American militarism and values. Slightly over a year after his Canadian move, and several months after cofounding Red, White, and Black, he told himself that his "own psyche was mended enough to awaken into a different consciousness." Seemingly part of the awakening involved the realization that he had struggled in the political realm long enough. He had (so to speak) paid his dues—his political "struggle was over." As a summation of what he had learned from his years of protest, he embodied his opposition to war and his commitment to peace by extending his refusal to kill people into the world of higher animals. For Steiner as for many others in his generation, vegetarianism was the logical consequence of his desire to stop the killing in Vietnam, his opposition to the war leading him to ponder what he called "the unity of all of life." [36]

The overwhelming release from the emotional burden of direct political struggle, in the context of the mystical material that he had been reading and the meditative practices that he had been performing, provided Steiner with a powerful, emotional experience that he attributed to a religious realm. He did not know, however, how to repeat the intense experience, nor even what to call it. He began looking everywhere for a precise interpretable framework in

36. For a differing interpretation from a psychological perspective, see Sarwer-Foner 1972, SS54.

which he could replicate what had occurred. He even obtained fake identification and drove back to Kansas, hoping that a friend of his who had joined Transcendental Meditation would be able to help him. When his friend was unable to do so, he drove back to Toronto, arriving just at the time when a follower of Yogi Bhajan was about to start yoga classes. As Steiner recalled in his interview, when he attended the class on November 3, 1970, he was overwhelmed to hear that the 3HO yoga teacher

> was talking about all the experience I had and he was talking about it as if he was living in that [consciousness]. And he said that in order to maintain it you have to get your nerves and your glands together and you have to learn how to live group consciously, and you can't use drugs and . . . the do's and the don'ts of all religion. Then we had this experience in doing yoga where by increasing the breathing and doing the postures I understood the relationship between the experience I had and yogic experience. And I then at the same time said, "I have to master or learn whatever this person has to teach."

Believing that he had found an explanation for his own intense experience, and expecting to be able to reproduce it after rigorous study, Steiner converted to 3HO.

Through a complex series of events that unfolded over an extended period, Steiner again illegally reentered the U.S., this time to study for three months at a California 3HO center. In early 1971, under Yogi Bhajan's direction, he returned to Toronto to start an ashram, which initially consisted of eighteen people crowded together in one room in Toronto's notorious counterculture haven, Rochdale College (Khalsa 1983, 302; for more on the college, see Sharpe 1987). The first yoga class that he conducted in Rochdale took place on the roof of the building, with many of the participants practicing their postures and techniques in the nude. Of the initial ashram members, Steiner remembers that about four or five of them were deserters or American draft dodgers like himself.[37] Regarding his previous political activities, Steiner

---

37. Another account of an American draft dodger joining 3HO in Canada (apparently in Vancouver) appears in Levine 1984. This person, Dennis Ericson, had espoused politically conservative views prior to getting his draft notice and fleeing the U.S.

(who changed his name to Gurutej in late 1971) essentially had lost interest in them. Red, White, and Black, the widely-publicized organization that he had cofounded, dissolved, but he never looked back. Part of his new message was saying to people, " 'O.K., the time for drugs is over, folks. You can get high without drugs.' But we weren't born again people, we were not fanatic. We could still speak the [counterculture] language, [and] we kept our hair. We had a Sikh teacher who never cut his hair. So we were very able to translate the street values into a yogic value without missing a beat, not one beat." [38] Gurutej—and many others who made the transition from radical politics to mystical religion—kept much of the counterculture parlance in their speech. From their perspective, they simply had moved on to the next or "higher" stage of the sociocultural revolution. They strove to become both spiritual counselors for a deeply troubled society and cultural models of inspiration, who would mold the future in large part by their wise advice and solid example of devotion, purity, and hard work. Direct political effort became far less important than purifying one's own consciousness, because, as Yogi Bhajan exclaimed, "The politicians will soon be coming to us for advice." Still believing that they were a part of the movement for fundamental societal change, former radicals who joined 3HO became part of an "apolitical" organization (Bailey 1973, 220; see also 193).[39]

Part of the group's apoliticism took the form of heightened concerns about diet and health. To the extent that one's food choices affected one's consciousness, eating became a new form of political statement—albeit one that was largely concerned with issues that did not involve challenges to structural issues. Diet and health concerns, for example, helped Gurutej to receive a $10,646.00 grant from the Canadian federal government in March 1972 to "establish a centre to teach 'Kundalini yoga, naturopathic massage, pre-and-

38. In early 1977, Steiner (Gurutej) offered other views in a Kansas City, Kansas, newspaper article written in response to president-elect Jimmy Carter's announcement of a proposed pardon for Vietnam War draft dodgers. The reporter highlighted Gurutej's life after fleeing to Canada and then interviewed him about his current life and retrospective views (Tammeus 1977a, 1977b).

39. Interestingly enough, however, Dusenbery (1975, 17n.) expressed surprise at "the number of 3HO members who in 1972 were supporting Richard Nixon in an election where the youth vote was supposed to go [to] George McGovern."

post-natal child care, nutrition and drug abuse counselling and rehabilitation.' " Although he had no formal training in any of these areas, Gurutej pronounced that " '[o]ur diplomas are registered on our faces, our bodies and our minds' " (quoted in MacDonald 1972, 1).

Health food sales helped to establish strong connections between 3HO and another former activist, whose business relationship (as a supplier) with a 3HO health food store paved the way for his conversion. Harinam Singh Khalsa, whom I interviewed in 1987, was born in 1952 and grew up in Toronto.[40] Before the end of the 1960s, he was involved in the hippie communities of Yorkville and Rochdale, where he did some drugs and read Beat poets Ginsberg and Ferlinghetti in the *East Village Other* and the *Village Voice*.[41] For a brief time (around 1966 or 1967), he practiced Transcendental Meditation, later claiming to have been one of the first practitioners in Toronto. While working at a summer camp in 1970 or 1971, Harinam befriended a couple from the Boston area who were interested in many of the spiritual explorations of the time. At nineteen, he moved in with them for a year, living in New Bedford, Massachusetts. During that time, he also discovered the free school movement, absorbing the progressive ideas of Vermont's Goddard College, which he hung around for a while but which he did not formally attend.

Upon returning to Toronto in 1972, he became involved in some of the city's communist political collectives, joining a small Maoist organization called Newsreel, which had chapters in various American cities and distributed political films. His involvement in Newsreel marked two or three years "of very deep involvement politically; that began my deep political involvement in the subculture, political movement of Toronto, which included . . . the Marxist-Leninist Party of Canada." He and his associates analyzed the ostensibly negative consequences of capitalism in continental terms: "We believed

40. I do not know Harinam Singh Khalsa's preconversion (birth) name, and I decided not to look for it because I see no need to identify his prominent Toronto family, which apparently is well known in the business world.

41. For a glimpse into the activities going on in and around Yorkville in the late 1960s, see Kostash 1980, 124–26.

in [the existence of] North American imperial-capitalism—we were North Americanists. . . . We believed that there was no difference in the political structure of Canada and the U.S. They were both imperialist-capitalist nations, and they were basically all one."

Continuing his work with grass-roots community organizing, Harinam became involved in an intense fight to stop development of an area called Bleecker Street, in which (among other things) protesters chained themselves to porches by the street in an effort to stop the plans of local developers. These community activities were only a part of his intense political involvement, which he divided into "overt work" and "covert work." Overtly, Harinam and his group organized sports teams for local children, and they were successful in attracting corporate sponsors for them. Covertly, "we were involved in a prison program where we were sending literature into prisons around North America. . . . We considered [inmates] prisoners of war, you see. . . . And then we developed links with the Black Panthers, at that time, out of New York. . . . One of our people actually went down and met frequently with the Black Panthers out in New York." The literature that they sent primarily consisted of "position papers on the North American imperialist-capitalist society and how prisoners were part—how prisoners were prisoners of war, political prisoners who were in jail for political crimes."

In preparation for a possible armed struggle, Harinam began studying martial arts: "We didn't carry weapons. But we were definitely in favor of armed struggle. I mean, that was, I think, more rhetoric than reality. But it was—it was something where we said that if [it] needed to be that—that armed revolution, as what was stated by Mao Tse Tung, that armed revolution would be the only way that the proletariat could win. And we were prepared to do that if we had to, so, you know, we began getting our bodies in shape in kung fu." Eventually, in 1973 or 1974, "political differences" and romantic jealousies arose within the Newsreel group, but by then he and his friends had "moved into health foods." Before long Harinam had become a distributor of honey throughout the city, and he soon introduced Toronto to various nut mixes.

Through a close friend who happened to be meditating and reading widely in spiritual issues during the time "when things sort of broke down politically," Harinam had his earlier interest in religion rekindled: "For those years when I was political, I really denied in myself my spiritual beliefs. I said . . . 'God is an opiate of the masses.' You know, dialectical materialism is the way to deal with things—you know, look at it that way. So I denied in m[e] that—that spiritual aspect." Going into the 3HO health food store for the first time around 1975, Harinam recalled that, "I'd say at that time, the first time I saw them, I said, 'This is what I want.' " Over the next few years he kept in touch with the community, took a few courses with the group's leader, Yogi Bhajan, and began meditating: "And then all of a sudden when—the summer of '78, I just woke up one morning and this voice came into my head that said, 'Go to the ashram.' And I said, 'What?' And the voice—'No, not what; just go.' " It took a few months for him to get his affairs in order, but by December 1978 he had moved into the ashram and, he added, "never looked back." When we spoke at his office in September 1987, Harinam owned an impressive and successful printing business in Toronto.

Harinam's conversion to 3HO is unique only with respect to how late in the decade he converted. As early as January 1970, for example, a 3HO member indicated: "Now that we are through dropping out, rebelling, finding ourselves, getting it together, etc., we can look for ways to reintegrate our new selves into society. One splendid way is to teach the old dog new tricks. Everyone likes to be healthy, happy and holy and now by the Grace of the Guru we have the technical know-how to turn them on" (Singh 1970). 3HO sees itself as providing a Sikh model of integrity to society—a model that includes "running our businesses with integrity, and with consciousness, and with an eye to the bottom line, 'cause we're not in business to go broke" (Khalsa 1987).

Transcendental Meditation

No guru from the East had a higher public profile in the late 1960s and early 1970s than Maharishi Mahesh Yogi of Transcendental Meditation (TM). His fame in the West had been a long time coming. Arriving in the United States for the first time in early 1959 (Olson 1979, 22; Rose 1976, 50), the Maharishi's mission to convert Westerners to his form of Vedantic

Hinduism grew slowly.[42] Only after one of his followers established the Students International Meditation Society in 1965 to target the college crowd did the Maharishi's message attract substantial interest (Rose 1976, 92, 100). Then, in 1967, when the Beatles and Mia Farrow traveled to the Maharishi's retreat in northern India to receive private instruction, the world took note (Brown and Gaines 1983, 282–91; Ebon 1968).

The Maharishi's message was simple: receive a secret mantra from his organization and meditate on it for twenty minutes twice a day. Around this technique, the Maharishi made grand claims. In late January 1968, he packed a 3,600 seat forum in Madison Square Garden (at ticket prices ranging from $3 to $10), calling on Americans to practice TM "every day to bring about world peace":

The lights were dimmed, and the Indian told his listeners: "My heart is bouncing with bliss." The reason for his happiness, he explained, was his conviction that permanent world peace could be achieved if global, national and regional problems could be reduced to the quest of individual peace.

Softly gesturing with his right hand while the left gently defoliated a hyacinth, the guru talked about a happy world "where frowning will be missing, [and] tensions will be absent." He spoke in English without notes.

"Wars, epidemics, famines, earthquakes are all symptoms of tensions," the guru declared. "Tension is as contagious as any other disease."

If only 1 per cent of the world's population followed his easy-to-learn method of half an hour's meditation every morning and night, the Indian

---

42. Several schools of Vedantic Hinduism exist, all adherents agreeing "that the world is the manifestation of Brahman [Absolute reality], that knowledge of Brahman is the *marga* [path] which leads to liberation, and that Brahman can be known only through the *shruti* [revealed or heard] teachings of the *Upanishads* [a collection of Indian teachings from antiquity that most Hindus believe are holy]" (Organ 1974, 242). Vedanta's greatest proponent was Śaṅ (ca.788–820), whose *advaita* (monistic) philosophy asserted that "on the highest level of truth the whole phenomenal universe, including the gods themselves, was unreal—the world was *Māyā*, illusion, a dream, a mirage, a figment of the imagination. Ultimately the only reality was *Brahman,* the impersonal World Soul of the *Upanishads,* with which the individual soul was identical" (Basham 1959, 328).

said, "it will be enough to dispel the clouds of war for thousands of years."
(Hofmann 1968, 24)

For the Maharishi, the quest for peace was to take place within each person's consciousness. In 1967, he had expressed his antipoliticism by indicating that "he was 'no more interested in Vietnam than anywhere else in the world' " and that President "Lyndon Johnson [was] a peacemaker" (Goldstein 1989, 88). Not surprisingly, Allen Ginsberg judged that "[h]is political statements are definitely dim-witted and a bit out of place" (Ginsberg 1968; see also Miles 1989, 408–10; Schumacher 1992, 499).

Despite Ginsberg's harsh evaluation, the Maharishi's basic claims had widespread appeal in the late 1960s and early 1970s, even to those of a more political or activist bent than the guru himself. For example, in a 1968 cover story in *Look* magazine, a Los Angeles-based civil rights worker named Tim Crawford stated his belief that "Transcendental Meditation can cool the riot-prone racial scene. I am slowly working on getting leaders in the ghetto to start meditating. I don't see how it can help but do good." After a Berkeley presentation by TM practitioner Jerry Jarvis at which seven hundred people signed up to attend a second lecture, *Look* author William Hedgepath concluded that "now, at this juncture in the history of the world—and to the applause of student revolutionaries, ex-hippies, and 'straight' kids as well—here has come Maharishi Mahesh Yogi with a safe, natural and inexpensive vehicle for the continued exploration of inner space" (Hedgepath 1968, 75, 71). By the end of 1975, approximately 729,000 Americans had received TM initiation (Bainbridge and Jackson 1981, 144).

The political dimensions and implications of the Maharishi's teachings also appealed to Canadian Keith Plummer (not his real name), who joined the TM organization in Kingston, Ontario, several years after having been radicalized in the U.S. In early November 1987, he recounted his conversion story to me as we sat in his living room in a central Canadian city. Born in 1955, he spent the years 1966 to 1969 attending school in the Washington, D.C., area. Living in the vicinity of that politically charged city, he and his fellow classmates were acutely aware of the social turmoil swirling around them: "People in my grade nine class had tear-gassed themselves at recess so they'd be ready to graduate to university and get into the demonstration thing." By the time he returned to Canada and was finishing high school, however, he sensed that an important shift was occurring in youth culture: "I had the sensation . . . that the political movements on campus lost some of their force. And they didn't interest me. . . . The climate was such that you didn't feel that the political movement was going to change the world. And that may be where all of us kind of imploded and started looking inside."

Plummer's implosion included reading a popular religious book of the period, Paramahansa Yogananda's *Autobiography of a Yogi,* which "tremendously impressed" him.[43] He saw Yogananda as one of the first Hindu swamis "who tried to maintain some kind of integrity to Eastern knowledge, but still present it to the West and make it palatable to the West." This book launched him on a quest for a "yogic master," and at some point he happened to walk past a poster of the Maharishi that announced an introductory lecture on TM. Plummer thought, "He's a monk; [he's got] long hair and a beard; he's Indian. I'll go." That lecture included a movie about the Maharishi's visit to beautiful Lake Louise, Alberta, and "I thought it was great." In a subsequent meeting he received his mantra, and upon his first effort at meditating, "I felt a terrific, immediate, very profound change. It was terrific; it was a real experience, and it worked." He was hooked—so much so, in fact, that he became an active TM practitioner for six years and even did important missionary work for the organization in the Middle East.

Meher Baba

Meher Baba was born of Persian parents in Poona, India, in 1894. As the self-proclaimed Perfect Master or avatar (God incarnate) of the age, Baba's love, joy, and playfulness bespoke Sufi and Indian *bhakti* (devotional) influences, as well as possibly Christian strains. From 1925 until his death in 1969,

43. Paramahansa Yogananda (1893–1952) arrived in the United States in 1920, and subsequently established the headquarters for the Self Realization Fellowship in Los Angeles, which continues to teach various meditational and yoga techniques designed to lead people to self-realization or God-realization (Melton 1991, 3:217). The first U.S. edition of his autobiography was published in 1946, the first British edition appeared in 1969, and the book first appeared in paperback in 1972.

he refrained from speaking and communicated only with either an alphabet board or hand signals. Because he claimed to be the embodiment of grace and love, his teachings emphasized the importance of serving and emulating him, despite his apparently erratic personality. Given the focus on loving Baba, the movement that grew up around him deliberately lacked any central organization (Ellwood and Partin 1988, 216–17, 283; Robbins and Anthony 1981, 197).

Followers of Meher Baba have not attracted scholarly attention for their political backgrounds; rather, scholars have concentrated on the "disillusioned drug enthusiasts" who went "straight" as "Baba lovers" in the early 1970s (Robbins 1973, 20; see also Robbins and Anthony 1981). In fact, at least some converts had been politically active before participation in the group led them to forsake political concerns. Perhaps representative was one woman who "came to California and I thought it was important to get involved politically. For a long time I thought the antidraft work was compatible with Baba! Then L. talked to me—he'd been with Baba for fourteen years. He told me how Baba wanted his lovers to stay out of politics." Soon she devoted her energy to accepting Baba's love (Needleman 1984, 93–94).[44]

The movement's emphasis, however, on living God's love had a profound impact on at least one political activist, Thomas Ross (Tom) Wolfe (b. 1952) (not to be confused with Tom Wolfe the author). Wolfe felt repelled by the violence and destruction that he witnessed during his protests against the Vietnam War, protests that held particular salience for him because his father had been the head polygraph operator for the Berlin sector of the U.S. Army's Counterintelligence Corps—in essence, a spy. I spoke with Wolfe about his journey from activism to Babaism in his business office outside Washington, D.C., in December 1994.

In high school, Wolfe combined student leadership with both athletic and scholastic achievement. Already, however, he was opposed to the Vietnam War, having concluded that it "was immoral." Wolfe's first "political state-

---

44. Another person with an activist background who became a Baba lover is Danny Einbender, but it is not clear from his biography how politically involved he was prior to his conversion (see Kessler 1990, 187–90).

ment" against it involved leaving the Episcopal Church (where he was an acolyte), because many army officers were members of the congregation. Then, in spring 1970, the shootings at Kent State "really affected me." First and foremost, "I saw that you could die. It was not a joke, which made me even more committed to it. I was not afraid." Having been recruited by the University of Pennsylvania to play freshman basketball, Wolfe arrived on campus a week early. The head coach told him:

"I bet the [other] coach that you would have your hair cut when you came here, and you didn't, and it cost me five bucks, and I'm pissed, and you're going to cut your hair."

And I said, "No sir."

Anyway, then he gave us the God and Country and School speech, which was that the three priorities in a college education were first God . . . then your family, then your school, then your basketball. And, before you leave the University of Pennsylvania, some hippies will offer you marijuana and don't take it. And I just realized that, at that point . . . my values were too different, and that I really was charting a different course, and that I was no longer a basketball player. I called my father that evening, and he cried. He just couldn't believe it.

This decision was only the first in what would prove to be a tumultuous year of major decisions.

In January 1971, Wolfe "decided that the Vietnam War was the highest priority in my life," so he decided to work with organizers of the upcoming May Day demonstrations that were being scheduled for Washington, D.C. He traveled to the nation's capital and lived with a collective of homosexual men who were helping to organize the protest. Even though he had to fend off their frequent sexual advances (having no personal interest in their lifestyle), he found them to be "intelligent, politically astute people." He worked with them for "a couple of weeks"; they gave him a stack of literature that advertized the event; and Wolfe hit the road to distribute the information. He hitchhiked to five campuses along the southeast coast, passing out posters featuring a picture of Gandhi with a raised fist, the simple slogan "Strike," and the date of the upcoming protest in Washington.[45]

When May Day came to pass, Wolfe and others from his university decided:

> We would not sit in the streets, that our role would be just to keep everyone's temper, and keep them in good humor. We would hand out doughnuts. Hence, the infamous Doughnut Brigade from the University of Pennsylvania. So, we bought a lot of coffee and doughnuts and tried to give them out to everyone—spectators, policemen, demonstrators, army men, anybody. Just try to make everybody realize that it was not the end of the world, there was not a war. That was the idea.

The street action involved protesters attempting to snarl traffic by sitting in the roads, and Wolfe was startled at some of what took place.

> First of all, I just saw a number of people get beat up . . . and gassed, and that was violent enough. But the biggest thing that had an effect on me was I saw two young gentlemen with long hair smash up a car, which—everyone [had] agreed, we were not going to destroy property. That was not what our intent was. So, myself and someone else—I don't really remember who, at this point—followed these gentlemen to try and talk reason with them, and they got in a police car and drove away. . . . That really was an eye-opener for me.

Soon after observing this provocative violence, Wolfe was arrested.

> We were walking down Pennsylvania Avenue, the Capitol in view, and, we were suddenly—we were handing out doughnuts, doing nothing illicit, [but] *looking illicit,* and we were suddenly surrounded by ten to twelve police cars, and they said, "Up against the tree." And then, in counterculture, "up against the wall" [was a] real slogan about what the police say—"Up against the wall." And so I . . . just cracked up laughing, and [said], "I can't

45. On this trip, Wolfe visited the campuses of the University of Maryland (College Park), Randolph Macon (Ashland, Virginia), Duke (Durham, North Carolina), University of North Carolina (Chapel Hill), and University of Florida (Gainesville).

believe he said, 'Up against the tree.' I mean, there's no dignity in this"
[laughing]. So, we put our hands up against the tree.

As were the thousands of others arrested that day, Wolfe was cuffed with "little plastic handcuffs," put on a D.C. transit bus, and taken to the stadium. Wolfe was impressed by his fellow prisoners, including Abbie Hoffman (who apparently had a broken nose), Jerry Rubin, and pediatrician and pacifist Dr. Benjamin Spock (1903–1998), with whom Wolfe spoke for a while.

On the same day that Wolfe observed the agents provocateurs smash a car, he also witnessed another scene that chilled him:

> I just remember marines dropping out of helicopters with the Washington Monument in the background . . . [with] M-15, or whatever, attack rifles across their chest[s]. There was a full military maneuver. I mean, they didn't fool around. They arrested eight thousand people very fast,[46] but they had, you know, National Guard out there on maneuvers in Washington, D.C. But I just—I remember that scene particularly vividly because it was war, and I really realized that this was not the arena I chose to express myself in because it was so out of control, particularly the incident with the provocateurs, and then the—I mean, full battle. I mean, this is helmets and attack fatigues and, I mean, it was war. It didn't matter what we felt about it. . . . Their perception of it was that the nation's capital was under siege.

Too much of the day's protest scene was violent and ugly, and it drove Wolfe and his doughnut brigade to renounce any further direct political action. Wolfe remembered the renunciation, which took place while they were imprisoned in the stadium: "We sat down and we swore off politics. Yeah. I remember that. The delegation from University of Pennsylvania—we sat down. What to make of this? It happened so fast, and we decided that this was it. This was our last political demonstration . . . [because] to really change society for a lasting peace, people's hearts had to change, and you

---

46. Wolfe's figure of 8,000 people being arrested may be slightly high; Zaroulis and Sullivan (1984, 361) indicate that about 7,000 people were arrested on the first day of the May Day protests.

Tom R. Wolfe (third from right, tall, with long, wavy hair) stands with other arrested protesters near the bend in a fence at the Washington Coliseum on Monday, May 3, 1971. (© Bettmann/CORBIS)

have to have communication." Thousands of his peers were arriving at similar conclusions.

While at Penn, Wolfe was involved in one other noteworthy incident that both epitomized the issues of the period and highlighted student discontent with persons in power. In autumn 1972, the university held a forum on the future of education at the institution, which perhaps eight hundred people attended. Organizers, however, had failed to invite any students to sit on the panel, and Wolfe and a friend were so irritated by this omission that they took over the microphone. Wolfe's friend spoke first, and his nervous comments about the ridiculousness of the panel drew mild applause. Next, Wolfe went to the podium and spoke extemporaneously for twenty minutes. He raised issues about the costs and quality of education, and he spoke about the "gross arrogance and impoliteness of the university" in its failure to have student representation on the panel: "The students in the audience were just [whooping, clapping, and cheering], and I was having a good time, and [the panel members] didn't know what to do. So, they waited for me to stop."

He ended his talk on a respectful note by thanking the officials "very much for your time." As he was returning to his seat, however, "the president of the University yells into the microphone, 'You have no business being in this school.' And I turned around and he really showed where he was at. And I said, 'I only want my money's worth.' And he said, 'Well, just quit the school then.' And, he was just so angry, he couldn't think." The next day, the forum had another seminar, still without student representation. Once again, Wolfe challenged university officials, this time asking them to set up a forum in which select faculty and students could debate key issues. After the organizers refused to do so, Wolfe felt so disgusted with the educational environment that he dropped out: "I was out of school. It was not the arena. They were not ready for me. I was not patient with them. Change was not forthcoming. They wouldn't allow change. They wouldn't allow change." For the next two years, Wolfe dedicated himself to working at a collective cafeteria called the Eatery on the university campus.

After the cafeteria work, Wolfe experimented with various life options as he tried to find direction. For a brief period he was a hospital orderly in Nantucket, after which he lived alone in a relative's house near Myrtle Beach, South Carolina. While there he met a group of people who were going to the international Meher Baba center located in Myrtle Beach, and out of curiosity Wolfe decided to accompany them. Although he already had some knowledge about Meher Baba from previous reading and discussions, while at the center "I felt a deep stirring within my own soul, if you will, to follow his teachings." For a while afterward, Wolfe remained spiritually eclectic, "but as things winnowed out, I really realized that . . . it was really the one path [that] I was on, and that I was going to follow that until I felt like I outgrew it, which never happened."

As his commitment to Baba was growing, Wolfe returned to his former campus for a visit. By chance, he happened upon a demonstration at which an activist faculty member was attempting to rouse the students. The professor spotted Wolfe, and to the crowd of several hundred people he proclaimed:

"And here's one of the few students who ever had the guts to do anything at the University of Pennsylvania. And he stood up in front of the . . . University forum, and Tom, do you have anything to say?"

And I got up there and said, "I'm really not very political anymore. I really believe that God is the answer, and if you're interested in God, what you need to do is go down to Myrtle Beach, South Carolina." And I walked away. Mild applause, and everybody just sort of went, "Oh." And they went back to their rabble-rousing.

Wolfe, like so many others of his generation, left confrontational politics and embarked on a quest for God. Indeed, that quest continues three decades later, and Wolfe's commitment to Baba remained steadfast into the 1990s, at which time he became involved with the Religious Society of Friends (Quakers). Partly because his faith lacks intrusive demands upon believers, Wolfe has managed to avoid most of the coercive restraints that followers endure in other new faiths. His place of business, Smile Herb Shop (near College Park, Maryland), served as a form of Baba-inspired service. Filled with a pleasing potpourri of smells, colors, music, foods, and textures, the shop enriched and delighted its customers as it turned a profit. As Wolfe himself indicated, his business "gave me an arena in which to put Baba's motto of mastery and service into practicality." In various places in the store (at least through the early 1990s), photos of Baba bespoke Wolfe's continued devotion to a man he considered to have been the avatar of the age.

Beyond the intrinsic complexity of its philosophical ideas, Eastern thought held special attraction for youth culture in the early 1970s. This attraction existed in large measure because the material came from outside Western culture—a culture from which large segments of North American youth felt alienated and estranged. The traditional Christian religions of their parents failed to express outrage at the Vietnam War, and many even supported it. Politicians, for the most part, insulted youth and ignored their protests, and law enforcement harassed if not hurt them. Western culture seemed moribund, and youth felt that their political and countercultural efforts to rejuvenate it had failed.

Commitment to Eastern religions, by contrast, provided new hope for

Tom R. Wolfe outside the herb shop that he and his wife own in College Park, Md. (© Tom Wolfe)

initiating a much-desired social revolution. Although direct confrontation with authorities seemingly had failed, direct confrontation with the self (at the feet of one's enlightened master or guru) promised to be the first step in changing the world. Spiritual energy and effort, not political energy and confrontation, would bring about the changes that radicals and activists intensely desired in the late 1960s. To the new religious converts, it seemed strangely fitting that a corrupt America was bombing the very part of the world from which true wisdom came.

5

Conversions to Syncretic and Western Religions

In the early 1970s, former radicals converted not only to Eastern-based groups but also to various syncretic organizations that claimed to integrate Eastern and Western religious ideas, in their view synthesizing the best from both worlds. This synthesis could occur in a great variety of ways: the Scientologists, for example, understood themselves as extracting Eastern mysticism and spirituality and combining it with Western technology and science. The Unification Church members believed that their founder invigorated Western religious ideas with Eastern wisdom. Despite, however, the markedly different ideological beliefs of the groups, the fact that a similar conversion pattern occurred supports an interpretation that understands the behavior in terms of structural conditions within American social and political life. Political frustration, despair, fear, and growing hopelessness propelled people into searches for alternative means to accomplish the Revolution, and a wide range of groups offered spiritually or mystically justified solutions that attracted many former activists and radicals. Eastern-based and Western-based groups—not to mention those somewhere in between—utilized the radical rhetoric of the Movement to their own ends, both attracting leftist converts and allowing existing members to feel a sense of continuity with their previous political lives.

Scientology

Evolving out of a form of lay psychotherapy named Dianetics, Scientology claimed to address the issues in people's current lives in part by referring to events in their previous ones. Both Dianetics and Scientology were created at midcentury by pulp fiction writer L. Ron Hubbard (1911–1986).[1] Considerable controversy rages around Scientology's later assertion that it is a religion: critics point out that Hubbard's initial claims in 1954 that Scientology contained religious elements were poorly received by his followers, who insisted that they were conducting scientifically verifiable mental and physical health procedures. These same critics emphasize that Hubbard's ever-increasing insistence on the religious nature of Scientology merely was an attempt to secure the privileges and protections that most governments grant religions.[2]

From its beginning in 1952, Scientology has marketed itself as a powerful and effective "technology" for personal advancement. An important aspect of applying this technology involves a staff member (called an auditor) recording another person's reactions to hundreds of standardized questions while connected to a device called an E-meter. This simple instrument registers (on a monitoring gauge) fluctuations of the skin's resistance to an electrical current flowing to tin cans that the person holds. Rounding out the technology are thousands of policy bulletins, talks, lectures, articles, and books that Hubbard produced on a wide range of subjects and that his followers carefully read, study, and implement. Scientology has placed many of these materials into courses that intend either to advance people's own auditing or train them to deliver the auditing, in either case facilitating their advancement up the "Bridge" to the organization's highest levels of commitment and "spiritual" insight.

Having developed a "religious" system, Hubbard insisted as early as 1954

1. The December 1949 issue of *Astounding Science Fiction* contained an announcement that Hubbard was preparing an article on a new science of the mind (Campbell 1949); Hubbard's article "DIANETICS: The Evolution of a Science" appeared in the May 1950 issue; and his pivotal book *Dianetics: The Modern Science of Mental Health* was published that same month. In 1952, Hubbard's philosophy (and organization) took on the name Scientology. The history of the belief in past lives in Dianetics and in Scientology is complicated, with discussion about past life events causing considerable division within the Dianetics community. See Atack 1990, 115; Hubbard 1951, 1:61n.; R. Miller 1987, 197; Whitehead 1974, 579; Winter 1987, 188–91.

2. I discuss a variety of issues related to Scientology and religion in Kent 1996, 1999a, and 1999b. See also Evans 1973, 81; Atack 1990, 193.

Scientologist Robert H. Thomas demonstrates the E-meter to Arthur J. Maren in Washington, D.C., June 8, 1971. Both men had ministerial status in the organization. (© New York Times Pictures)

that his technology had much in common with the major religions of the East (see e.g. Hubbard 1976c, 2:72–73). In a series of lectures delivered in July 1954, he asserted several key connections between his system and various Eastern faiths. He would publish these lectures in book form in 1968, at a time when Eastern religions were influencing Western culture dramatically (Hubbard 1968, 10). He and his followers even came to claim that Scientology's "earliest known ancestor" was the Vedas (Church of Scientology World Wide 1970, 8–10).[3] A late 1973 article in a Scientology magazine attempted to make the link unequivocally, and in the attempt alluded to the antimaterialism that colored the youth rhetoric of the day: "The wheel of history has

3. The *Vedas* are ancient hymns (probably composed between 1500 and 900 B.C.E.) that originally were recited at Aryan sacrifices and became the foundation for much of what we commonly call Hinduism (Basham 1954, 232).

turned and from materialism we are about to enter a new Vedic age, a new spring-time of life at a higher level. The modern word for Veda is Scientology. . . . the great Rishis of the Vedic age would join us in inventing a thousand ways to thank him for his gift to Man's future: L. Ron Hubbard, the Founder of Scientology" (Advanced Organization 1973b, 26).

Apparently, however, it was not sufficient for Scientology to be a modern manifestation of the ancient Vedas, for the group also claimed to provide the "inner meaning" to key concepts of a central Taoist text. A 1973 Scientology publication claimed that "Lao Tzu's greatest successor is L. Ron Hubbard. And from the pinnacle of Scientology we can suddenly look down the ages and see the inner meaning of the *Tao Te Ching*" (Advanced Organization 1973a, 8). As early as the late 1950s, Hubbard argued that one of Scientology's spiritual and social concepts (known as "Clear") "was envisioned 2,500 years ago by Gautama Sidhartha and was attained by a very few and then was seen no more" until the advent of Hubbard's system (Hubbard 1958, 6). Indeed, the achievements afforded by Hubbard's technology propelled people into a spiritual state beyond the levels of either the Buddha or Jesus (Hubbard 1963, 3). "From the ashes of a dying world," a Scientology article told its readers in 1974, "from a world sinking into the death trap of materialism, L. Ron Hubbard has arisen to again confirm the goals of Buddha and develop as well a technology to lead Man toward even higher states" (Advanced Organization 1974a, 21).

Discussions of Buddhism always contained the implication that Scientology completed ancient Buddhist teachings. In the mid-1950s, Hubbard went so far as to hint that he was the Maitreya Buddha (which he and his followers spelled "Metteya"), and his organization published these suggestions in 1974 (Hubbard 1974). A 1974 article entitled "A 2,500 Year Old Prophecy" claimed:

In 1955 Buddhists worldwide celebrated the 2,500 year anniversary of the Buddhist era. These celebrations coincided with the earliest date predicted for the arrival of Metteya which works out, more or less, to 1950.

Dare we hope that Metteya is real and that he has answered the call? *He has arrived.* . . .

Metteya has arrived, on schedule. Through him Man now has a complete technology through which the ancient goals of philosophy and religion can be achieved and new vistas even beyond these lofty goals can be reached. (Advanced Organization 1974f, 5)[4]

Scholars may wonder exactly which Buddhist scriptures predict the return of Metteya two and one-half millennia after the Buddha's life, but apparently the prediction came from Hubbard himself, in a 1966 taped lecture excerpted in a box alongside the article. It almost goes without saying that the predicted date of Metteya's return, 1950 "more or less," coincided with the publication of the book that catapulted Hubbard into the limelight, *Dianetics: The Modern Science of Mental Health* (Hubbard 1950a). Despite the implausibility of these reputed links to various Eastern traditions (see Kent 1996), they nonetheless allowed some youth in the late 1960s and early 1970s to believe that Scientology combined the best of the East with a technology from the West.

As a social and political influence, Scientology (according to Hubbard) had the capacity to make the world free of insanity, war, and crime. Hubbard had written about the insanity of war in his pre-Scientology *Dianetics:* "No self-interest can be so great as to demand the slaughter of Mankind. He who would demand it, he who would not by every rational means avert it, is insane. There is *no* justification for war." Several sentences later, Hubbard announced that "Dianetics addresses war because there is in fact a race between the science of mind and the atom bomb. There may be no future generation to know which won" (Hubbard 1950a, 406).[5] Scientology—which kept *Dianet-*

4. In another issue of *Advance!*, Scientology claimed that the Jataka (a collection of legends, tales, and stories about the Buddha's alleged past lives) was unexceeded in its "concept of past lives . . . until the appearance—2,500 years later—of L. Ron Hubbard's trilogy of books, *Mission Into Time, Have You Lived Before This Life?* and *History of Man,* which give the first full and accurate account of the whole track as well as the verification of past life recall" (Advanced Organization 1974b, 5). "Whole track" is a Scientology term referring to "the moment to moment record of a person's existence in this universe in picture and impression form" (Hubbard 1975, 468, quoting a Hubbard Communications Office Bulletin of Feb. 9, 1966).

5. A 1976 Scientology pamphlet entitled "The Cessation of War" (Hubbard 1976a; copy in author's possession) contains this passage and several related ones. From comments of former members who had been in the group during the late 1960s and the early 1970s, I suspect that Scientology had used some of these quotes in pamphlets during the late Vietnam War era.

ics as required reading for its adherents—claimed that its techniques eliminated the insanity that caused war, and in the early 1970s members used this
claim in their defence of the organization and in pamphlets and flyers that
local missions produced.[6] For example, a flyer that a franchise distributed in
San Francisco's November 15, 1969, Moratorium March contained a lofty
statement of the goals that Hubbard espoused for his technology: "A civilization without insanity, without criminals and without war, where the able can
prosper and honest beings can have rights, and where Man is free to rise to
greater heights, are the aims of Scientology. . . . Scientology is the most vital
movement on Earth today" (Hubbard 1969).[7] In an atmosphere of Vietnam
War protests and general societal hostility, the claim that Scientology was a scientific technology that would end war throughout the world spoke to many
disillusioned youth.

On January 1, 1969, Scientology propounded similar claims in *Astral
Projection,* an alternative newspaper in Albuquerque, New Mexico. In a short
column "generally reserved for the publication of articles dealing with groups
or religions which do not ordinarily meet the public eye," a write-up on Scientology proclaimed:

Around the world is a growing movement of truth which brings order where
there was confusion, sanity where there was insanity, health and purpose

6. In 1959, Hubbard established a franchise system that allowed a person to offer various
Scientology services and material in return for payment to the Hubbard Communications Office
"of ten percent of his/her gross weekly income" (Hubbard 1972, 6:246). In April 1971, Scientology ceased using the word "franchise," claiming that it "has become associated in common
usage with mere commercial or business activity. Since the Church is not, and never has been concerned with that type of activity, this word will no longer be used to describe its religious field activity. From this date, any legally chartered Scientology field activity will be properly designated
only as MISSION OF THE CHURCH OF SCIENTOLOGY" (Hubbard 1972, 6:293). In my interviews,
former members from the early 1970s were not always historically accurate in distinguishing between "franchises" and "missions."

7. Hubbard's original statement was written in September 1965, and is also reproduced in
Hubbard 1976c, 6:88. The earliest form of this statement appeared in Hubbard 1951, which said
that "a world without insanity, without criminals and without war—this is the goal of Dianetics"
(xxxv). On the 1969 San Francisco Moratorium March, see Zaroulis and Sullivan 1984, 295.

where there was only sickness and despair, and rapid advance for the able to states of Beingness hitherto only dreamed of by Man.

Scientology is the science of how to change conditions through knowing how to know. This knowledge and the phenomenal states of being, known in Scientology as "Release," are achieved through a combination of auditing and training.

The article concluded with the warning that Scientology "is literally the only hope man has of halting his rapid plunge toward global disaster" ("Challenge of Scientology" 1969, 2).

Because of their conviction that their technology was an effective antidote to society's ills, Scientologists attempted to recruit youth who were concerned about pressing social issues. An example of this recruitment strategy was a flyer (probably from 1969) that Scientology Berkeley distributed about People's Park.[8] The top half of this flyer contained a circular picture of a tree from the perspective of looking up its trunk from the ground. Around the top of the tree was the foliage of several others. Beneath the photo was the sentence (in quotation marks): "No one bothered to ask us trees about People's Park!" Continuing the text as if the trees themselves were speaking, the flyer stated:

Here's what we would have said if you had asked:
Parks are groovy because the [*sic*] they provide a safe environment for us to grow in.
They also can provide a safe environment for people to grow in—if the people are helping to make a safe environment themselves.

8. Advocated by the *Berkeley Barb* as a citizen project, People's Park emerged when hundreds of people began developing a vacant lot owned by the University of California, Berkeley, on Apr. 20, 1969. University and city officials grew increasingly concerned as the park project continued, and on May 15, police took over the lot and oversaw the construction of a fence to keep people out of the space. The rallies of People's Park supporters led to riots in which police shot 110 people, killing one and blinding another. The National Guard had to be called in, and the antagonism that local residents developed toward local authorities over their handling of the park issue had significant political implications (including the propulsion of California governor Ronald Reagan toward the antiliberal stance that eventually helped him win the American presidency). For a summary of events, see Rorabaugh 1989, 155–66.

> Scientology is a world-wide self betterment and human rights organiza-
> tion. The Humanitarian Objective of Scientology is the creation of a safe en-
> vironment in which you people and us trees can grow.
>
> If you are willing to *demand* improvement in our society . . .
>
> If you have *hope* that you *can* bring about change . . .
>
> If you are able to seek and accept *help* . . .
>
> Scientology has tools *you* can use! Come in & discover how! (Scientol-
> ogy Berkeley [1969?])

As we soon shall see, thousands of young people visited the Berkeley Scientology headquarters during the late 1960s.

Several of Scientology's programs received favorable alternative press
coverage in the Los Angeles area, where the organization had many of its national offices. During the first few years of the 1970s, at least three articles
about artists or artistic programs inspired by Hubbard's techniques ran in the
Los Angeles Free Press, a major alternative newspaper that received wide circu-
lation among political activists and counterculture hippies (Jones 1970; Steele
1972; Kaufman 1970). The articles portrayed Scientology as an organization
and a philosophy that fostered artistic creativity, which was a cherished value
among political protesters and countercultural hippies alike. In one article,
which appeared on December 11, 1970, the journalist gave a generally positive review of the performance of a Scientology-inspired improvisational
group of actors called the Key Out Players, who operated out of Scientology's
Celebrity Centre (which Hubbard had founded with the purpose of creating
"a higher civilization").[9] The performances themselves built upon "commu-

9. Actually, Hubbard's reasons for establishing Celebrity Centres are more complex. In
1955, Hubbard initiated "Project Celebrity," which aspired either to convert celebrities and
other prominent people to Scientology or at least to make them "aware of the benefits of Scientology" regarding social concerns. As "prime communicators," celebrities are people "to whom
America and the world listens, and so "it is obvious what would happen to Scientology if prime
communicators benefitting from it would mention it now and then" (Hubbard Association
1955, 2). In 1963, Hubbard published a policy letter indicating that the organization could
achieve "rapid dissemination" of its doctrines "by the rehabilitation of celebrities who are just beyond or just approaching their prime. This includes any person *well* known to the public and well
liked but who has passed his or her prime, or any rising figure" (Hubbard 1972, 7:509). In Feb-

nication" between the actors and audiences, and once this communication link was established, "the better, saner world, according to Scientologist Hubbard, is that much closer" (Kaufman 1970, 61).

Another social position that Scientology emphasized in the early 1970s that appealed to disillusioned youth was its opposition to the reputed monopoly on healing held by the American Medical Association (AMA). Among these youth, opposition took many forms, including the establishment of medical clinics that offered free treatments, a boom in herbal medicine books, interest in alternative practices such as acupuncture, and interest in folk remedies from other cultures. Scientology's hostility to the AMA traced back to the early 1950s when medical doctors (including psychiatrists) scorned Hubbard's *Dianetics* in book reviews.[10] Furthermore, early Dianeticists in at least three American cities—Elizabeth, New Jersey; Detroit; and Phoenix— were charged with practicing medicine without a license.[11] These charges related to the healing claims that Hubbard made for his early Dianetics auditing techniques (Kent 1996, 30–33).

When the *Los Angeles Free Press* carried a Scientology attack against the AMA in July 1972, the article was accompanied by a cartoon (reprinted from the *Ann Arbor Sun*) entitled "People's Health by the People," which also carried a caption underneath reading "Barefootin' Doctor." The barefoot hip-

---

ruary 1970, Hubbard indicated that the Celebrity Centre was to be a "full Sea Org organization. It is responsible for ensuring that celebrities expand in their area of power." Moreover, he envisioned that it "will bring people into aesthetics and speed the forward drive of creating a new civilization," run according to Scientology policies (Hubbard 1970). Appropriately, the name "Key-Out Players" referred to a technical Scientology term: "Key-out" (which can function as a verb, noun, or adjective) refers to a release or separation from that part of the mind in which negativity or spiritually limiting thoughts emerge. For other Scientology definitions, see Hubbard 1975, 222.

10. For example, one 1951 review in *Clinical Medicine* decided that "if the present signs are not deceiving, we are up against a new system of quackery of apparently considerable dimensions" (Stearns 1951). I discuss more fully the medical community's reaction to Dianetics in Kent 1999a, 107–8.

11. *Elizabeth Daily Journal* 1951a, 1951b, 1951c; "Dianetics Pair" 1953; Karie 1955. The two Dianeticists who were arrested "were let off with $50 fines when authorities were unable to decide what the charges against them should be" (Mann 1963, 4A).

pies in the cartoon were strutting out into the world in order to practice their alternative health care techniques, uttering slogans such as "Stay High," "Share what's in your head," "Know your self and your body," and "Watch dem tokes with a cold." In a classic phrase from the period that reflected both counterculture beliefs and the protest subculture's shift toward inward reflection, one barefoot cartoon hippie instructed readers: "Raise the standards of medicine with the rising of your consciousness" (see Adkins 1972, 4).

The article itself was prepared by Scientology's Los Angeles Committee on Public Health and Safety, which had "been doing research on both the American Medical Association and the Food and Drug Administration." It was a sustained attack on the alleged monopolistic operations of the AMA, which (the article claimed) had dire consequences for the health and well-being of the nation. During the early decades of this century, according to the article, the AMA "blossomed out into a monopoly-minded society, determined to suppress all opposition to their policy of 'free enterprise,' by which they mean the well-paid private doctor free from any governmental restraints on the amount he may charge for his fee" (Adkins 1972, 4). Not surprisingly, the article made no mention of Scientology's agenda against established medicine. Nor did it mention that the Food and Drug Administration had initiated two major actions against Scientology: in 1958, when it destroyed vitamins that Hubbard claimed could prevent and treat radiation sickness, and again in 1963, when it confiscated E-meters (Atack 1990, 142, 154; R. Miller 1987, 228, 247–48; Wallis 1976, 190–92). Thus, given the countercultural climate of the times, readers would have located the article's criticisms within the context of other attacks on establishment medicine rather than perceiving Scientology's own specific agenda.[12]

Scientology's agenda also fueled *Los Angeles Free Press* articles against the

---

12. Hubbard had made the same argument almost a decade earlier: in 1963, he blamed almost all of Scientology's bad publicity on the AMA, which he believed "wanted to cause maximum harm to the movement in order to protect its private healing monopoly" (R. Miller 1987, 249). It is entirely possible that mention of the "research" that the Scientology organization had undertaken on the AMA was an allusion to the infiltration (beginning in 1972) of the medical association by Scientology operatives from its Guardian Office and their subsequent removal of documents; see "Sentencing Memorandum" in *United States v. Mary Sue Hubbard, et. al.,* U.S. District Court for the District of Columbia, criminal case no. 78–401 (Dec. 3, 1979), 47–49.

international police agency Interpol and its alleged connections with the nemesis of activists and radicals, J. Edgar Hoover, director of the Federal Bureau of Investigation (FBI). A series of articles insisted that Interpol had been taken over by the Nazis during World War II and that after the war many Nazis remained in it or became affiliated with it, with the clear implication that Interpol was operated by fascists with whom Hoover closely associated.[13] Once again, few if any readers could have known about Scientology's own battle with Interpol since March 1973, when the police agency passed along what Scientologists insist was inaccurate information about Hubbard that had originated with the FBI (Atack 1990, 227–38 passim, 297; Kent 1999b). Likewise, when the *Los Angeles Free Press* published three articles by Scientologists attacking the Internal Revenue Service (Thompson 1974a, 1974b; Jentzsch 1974), only a few readers would have remembered Scientology's battle with the tax collectors after the government's revocation of the Church of Scientology of California's tax-exempt status in 1967 (Atack 1990, 166–67). In sum, the prominent Scientology-backed articles that appeared in the Los Angeles area's major alternative newspaper attacked the organization's opponents at the same time as they enhanced its image with the disillusioned youth of the late Vietnam War era.

A person who had been on staff in the Berkeley Scientology mission in the early 1970s spoke with considerable insight about the appeal that the organization held for the politically conscious but frustrated youth of the late Vietnam War era. Jennifer Osborne (a pseudonym) began our discussion in 1987 in her home in the eastern U.S. by highlighting elements of the counterculture that fed into people's interest in Scientology:

> So we've got a melting pot of several different factors coming into Berkeley; we've got psychedelic drugs, Leary, and Aldous Huxley, and Alpert, with *The*

13. The actual relationship between Hoover and Interpol was far more antagonistic than the Scientology article indicated. In essence, Hoover had grave reservations about the FBI's participation in Interpol because many of its member countries were communist. He withdrew the FBI from the organization in December 1950, and for years afterward the FBI's relationship with Interpol was tenuous at best (Bresler 1992, 107–18).

Doors of Perception, and Tibetan Buddhism.[14] We've got professors . . . who are also sort of sickened with mundane education, who are avant garde themselves, who are open to new ideas. We've got the war in Vietnam going on, which is not a popular war—nobody agrees with, nobody sees the reason for. And out of all these young people, they're the ones that are going to go [and] have to fight this silly war, and they—for which they see no reason. Always before we had a reason for a war—at least we thought we did. And this is one war nobody could understand. So we've got a social climate that is in chaos and upheaval, with a large amount of disagreement. We've got psychedelic drugs and the experiences that people have had, hooking into Eastern religion and the fact that there are spiritual experiences possible on a spiritual plane that we exist on.

And along comes Scientology. Now Scientology had an Eastern flavor with a Western technology. So you—it suddenly combines two very important things for young people at that time. They didn't have to go to India and sit in a cave and meditate for twenty years to get enlightened. They could come into Scientology, they could get enlightened—a series of enlightenments. They could do something about—also as a Western man who wants to be an active rather than a passive member of society, they could do something about society. They could bring about social change and reform with a technology that they could learn, they could teach others, and they could communicate about. That would make more sense than sitting around and talking about Eastern philosophy that was much more passive.

The Berkeley Scientology mission drew in people from local college campuses by distributing tickets every week to free introductory lectures. Probably the people who attended those lectures were individuals who wanted to improve themselves at the same time as they addressed pressing social issues. Osborne recalled that "a lot of people that came in that were politically active at that time, I think they also realized that . . . a certain amount of work had to be done at home, meaning with themselves, in conjunction with working towards big issues. The people that just wanted to riot . . . just to riot and—

14. Beidler 1994 gives convenient summaries of these and other authors and works in the 1960s context.

and that was all they wanted to do, normally didn't come in." In addition to the lectures discussing how society could achieve a world without criminals, insanity, or war, the mission also promoted Scientology "as a solution to the problems of an individual's life."

Osborne went on to highlight several specific aspects of Scientology that she believed added to its attraction. One of these aspects was Hubbard's claim that the technology could end war: "One of the things that I think attracted people to Scientology was that we had a plan for world peace. We had goals to have a civilization without war, without insanity, without criminality . . . in addition to that, there was a plan for world peace that was more extensive than that. So that appealed to people." The plan for world peace to which Osborne referred involved a series of ideas that Hubbard had published in 1964 and spoke about to his followers in a tape entitled "International City." It entailed the construction of a city comprised of the capitals of all nations, with Scientology controlling the area's mental health practices. Structured in this manner, Scientology would control mental health practices around the world (Hubbard 1964a, 1964b).[15]

Scientology's Communication course also held a special appeal to confused and disillusioned youth. Osborne recalled:

> One of the first things that one experiences coming into Scientology is a Communication course. And most young people at that time saw that there was a tremendous communication breakdown. There was a communication breakdown with their families, usually. There was a communication breakdown with their government. There was a communication breakdown with their president, their congressmen. And so there were—there was a real communication breakdown, and they had experiences of a spiritual nature which were very difficult for them to talk about, except with their peers who had also had those experiences. So there was a language that was waiting to be formed for people to be able to communicate what they had experienced.
>
> And Scientology gave them that kind of language. And it also gave them skills in communication that they felt could help them mend these broken

15. For more on Hubbard's plan and on what it reveals about his global aspirations, see Kent 1999b.

communications that had occurred with their families. And, you know, to extrapolate that then to a wider sphere, to their societies, to their government, etc. So it was—rather than a strictly reactionary protest method of fighting back, it gave them a positive approach to bring about necessary change through this technology, and first—starting first of all with communication.[16]

Thus, many young activists and radicals who became involved with Scientology during this period likely believed that the Communication course provided some practical skills that might help them in their efforts at working with others toward massive social change.

A final set of circumstances that Osborne believed made Scientology attractive to protesters and reformers in the Vietnam War era was a practical one. Staff members working in the Scientology mission could earn a decent wage: "At that time I earned three, four hundred dollars a week in Scientology, which was—which was a good wage back in the 1960s. And people were earning more than that. And probably a lesser paid person would earn maybe a hundred, which was still—you could still live on it. You weren't going to, you know, have a fancy car or anything, but you could live on that. So people could fulfill their human needs. They were fulfilling spiritual and social purposes they had." In sum, Osborne believed that practicing Scientologists saw themselves as working toward social change by learning and using Scientology technology. Some persons even made acceptable wages teaching these techniques to others. During an era when "people were looking for a banner to wave, a cause to move [i.e., act] on. . . . Scientology was there, and fulfilled that need."

One person who fit the pattern that Osborne described was a friend of hers whom I will call Joshua Jacobs (b. 1945), with whom I spoke by telephone in early March 1993. Jacobs was an intellectually gifted student who

---

16. The Communication course comprised such activities as learning not to react to insults, sitting perfectly still for up to two hours in front of another individual, repeating lines from Lewis Carroll's *Alice in Wonderland,* and giving, verbally acknowledging, and following instructions for various speaking drills (Atack 1990, 14–16). Not all people who took the Communication course felt it was as worthwhile as Osborne apparently did.

graduated from high school at age sixteen and won a scholarship to the University of California at Berkeley: "I left [home] as a clean-shaven, very good boy who everybody thought would be the first college graduate in the family and become a doctor or lawyer and instead, within two months, I was radicalized. I walked into the campus and this was in 1962 and the civil rights movement was in full gear." He became "outraged" by U.S. restrictions on the travel of its citizens to Cuba; he became morally committed to the civil rights movement; he became troubled over the possibility of nuclear war; and he became deeply involved with the Free Speech Movement.

As Jacobs interpreted events from late September 1964,

> locally of course what became the premier political event of my young life at the time was the Free Speech Movement in Berkeley when a ban was put up against putting up card tables to solicit contributions in Sproul Plaza aimed at soliciting support, and the police tried to arrest a former student and spontaneously several hundred students sat down around the police car and wouldn't let it move. And for the next two or three days there were speeches more or less around the clock. And I . . . took off my shoes and climbed up on top of the police car and made my impassioned defense of—I remember one point I made was, which was not a bad point—was, if we keep letting little freedoms erode, one day we will not have the big freedoms, and the line has to be drawn somewhere and a stand has to be taken.[17]

A few months later, on December 2, 1964, Jacobs accompanied student leaders as they and about a thousand students occupied Sproul Hall. The next day he was among the 773 students arrested, and in March 1965 he was convicted on three counts of resisting arrest.[18]

Between his arrest and his conviction, however, Jacobs began having doubts about the efficacy of political protest. Despite the fact that 55 percent of students and a stunning majority of professors (824 to 115 in a faculty sen-

17. Students began giving speeches from atop the surrounded police car on Oct. 1, 1964. Students and administrators reached an agreement that freed the car in the evening of Oct. 2 (Rorabaugh 1989, 21; Goines 1993, 161–236).

18. I verified some of this information in a standard source on the Free Speech Movement, but I will not be precise about my verification in an effort to preserve Jacobs's anonymity.

ate vote) supported the protesters, little seemed to have changed: "I thought, 'Gee, if we could reach this critical mass in this small little universe and couldn't change anything more than we'd been able to, what hope was there to change, bring about world peace?' "[19] In sum, the harsh political realities of campus politics quickly taught Jacobs a lesson about an institution's stubborn response to popular demands for change.

Coinciding with this growing political cynicism was Jacobs's experimentation with drugs. During his first year in college, he smoked marijuana; more important, in March 1965 (the same month that he was arrested) he took LSD.[20] Around the time of his first three LSD trips (which appear to have happened back-to-back), he concluded that "the political solution isn't working." For him, it was an important conclusion, because "a major philosophical question at the time on the campus in the circle I worked with was, 'Should you live an artistic life or an activist life?' "The LSD experiences, however, helped him to resolve the question for himself, which involved leaving politics and launching into a spiritual quest:

> After my first of three LSD experiences . . . [they] changed my life forever. I could no longer look at the universe as a simple cause and effect mechanistic kind of place. It was very powerful. I sat for, with my friend guiding, I sat for twelve hours without moving and he read me, as I would go through the different phases, he read from the *Tibetan Book of the Dead* as interpreted by Timothy Leary, which—it's a little difficult to tell [about]. At first, on the one hand, I can interpret it as it helped guide me through what was a wholly, you know, unprecedented experience for me. On the other hand, it's also possible that it programmed me to interpret the experience in certain ways because I think you're in a very vulnerable state then and hearing, you know, being read directly at that level, it's hard for me to sort out which is which.[21]

19. Jacobs could not remember precisely the numbers of students and faculty that supported the protesters' position, but his memories were close. I obtained these exact figures from Rorabaugh 1989, 33, 34.

20. Here and elsewhere, I occasionally have had to adjust some of the dates that Jacobs gave from memory, using various sources.

21. The full title of Leary's guide to the *Tibetan Book of the Dead* is *The Psychedelic Experience: A Manual Based on the Tibetan Book of the Dead* (Leary, Metzner, and Alpert 1964).

Even though our interview was nearly thirty years after these trips, Jacobs still spoke of them as transformative experiences that set his life in new directions.

Already feeling alienated because of the failure of social protest to cause desired changes for localized issues, drugs drove him even further away from politics. After hearing Timothy Leary present a lecture, Jacobs dropped out of school for four months and went to Europe. When he returned, he tried college for one more semester, then departed for good. In his words, "I just couldn't find meaning anymore. I couldn't. I wasn't drawn to the politics, the academics . . . seemed peripheral." For reasons that even he does not understand, Jacobs moved across the country to the East Village in New York City. While living there he became involved with a charismatic individual who brought together people at his Vermont farm to explore ways of achieving personal growth, utilizing various techniques including psychodrama, psychedelics, and what Jacobs later realized was Dianetics and early Scientology auditing. At one such gathering, this individual handed Jacobs a copy of *Dianetics,* and almost immediately upon reading it Jacobs felt that "I was being given a model to . . . explain some of the things I was feeling—the different types of emotions." Impressed, Jacobs and some friends went to the local Scientology organization back in New York City. He took the Communication course (probably in March 1966), and in it he was forced to confront his apparent problems with formulating, and then verbalizing, his own thoughts. Not long after taking this course, Jacobs learned that the stated aims of Scientology involved aspirations for a world without insanity, criminality, or war. These aims profoundly affected him: "I thought I had to make a choice between 'Would I be a political activist or an artist—an aesthetic interpreter, a spiritual person?' Suddenly Scientology was telling me I could do both. . . . It [Scientology] was just so attractive to me—it was irresistible." After taking a few more courses, he and a friend (the person whom I am calling Jennifer Osborne) headed for California, and they ended up at the Berkeley mission.

On their way to California from New York, the two friends visited Washington, D.C., specifically to meet John McMaster, the person whom Scientology was calling the world's "first Clear." For Scientologists, this label meant that, among other things, McMaster was "someone who could confront anything and everything in the past, present and future" and who "has lost the mass, energy, space and time connected with the thing called mind" (Hubbard 1975, 75).[22] Jacobs posed a question to him "about psychedelics," and, in reply, McMaster "said something like that it was temporary and what 'Clear' gave you was a permanent state." The answer had an impact upon him, and when Scientology required him to sign a statement promising to stop using drugs, "I was totally ready. I had no resistance to it, and again, it seemed to be something that was beneficial in my life."

Just as Jacobs turned away from mind-altering drugs in the belief that he had found a more beneficial way to strive for a continuous expansion of consciousness, so too did he abandon active political protest in the belief that he was engaged in more essential work. When explaining to a cousin during the mid-1960s why he apparently had abandoned "a political course for changing the world," Jacobs insisted that Scientology "was a whole different paradigm of how to create planet-wide change that could never be done, should never be done in time if we just used traditional political means. We would destroy ourselves before that could happen." He and his wife became so convinced of Scientology's self-proclaimed mission to save the world that they signed billion-year contracts with the group's elite Sea Organization (or Sea Org).[23] He

22. These two phrases come from definitions 2 and 3 of "CLEAR." Actually, the first person (then in Dianetics) whom Hubbard called the "world's first clear" was Sonya Bianca, whom he claimed to have "full and perfect recall of every moment of her life." On Aug. 10, 1950, Hubbard presented her in front of an audience of several thousand people in Los Angeles, who had assembled to hear him speak about his new Dianetics "discovery." When she failed to answer any of the memory questions that audience members presented to her (including one about the color of Hubbard's tie), the presentation turned into a debacle. On this event with Hubbard and Bianca, see R. Miller 1987, 163–66.

23. At the time that Jacobs was a Scientologist, Hubbard proclaimed: "I formed the Sea Organization of OTs ["Operating Thetans," Scientologists who have passed a certain upper level course] in order to have an area where a Scientologist could come, who could safely then walk through this last Wall of Fire [an event that people read about in the course]. . . . Objections to learning the ultimate truth of this universe, and what happened to it and why, are so deeply implanted in people that it is necessary to any extremely advanced level to be relatively out of the common area and not planted on the crossroads of the world. Therefore, the Sea Organization is simply organizing bases which are off the main track of Man, and in these bases we will be able to push people through, and also to handle situations with regard to Scientology, to help it get in ethics on this planet" (Hubbard 1986, 3). However, the less lofty reason behind Hubbard's es-

remained in Scientology until about 1981 and was so committed to its mission that he even endured long stretches (up to a year) in the group's forced labor and reindoctrination system, the Rehabilitation Project Force (RPF).[24]

Jacobs's belief that he was on a mission to save the world helps to explain why he endured for so long the grueling life of a Sea Org member. Hubbard had convinced him and other Sea Org members that the fate of humanity rested upon their efforts:

> I remember very vividly he wrote that we were watching the beginning of World War III with the oil embargo and, you know—so in other words, throughout it there was a pseudopolitical link and the message was repeated for years in one variation or another that we only had—he estimated we only

---

tablishment of the Sea Org was that he had encountered opposition in the United States from the Food and Drug Administration and the IRS, from the governments of Australia, the United Kingdom, and Rhodesia, and from various media sources around the world, which motivated him to set sail on the high seas and thereby escape the control of any nation-state (Hubbard 1986 alluded to some of these problems, but see also Atack 1990, 153–71; R. Miller 1987, 228–64). Because of the opposition that he had encountered, Hubbard realized "that on an international basis one has to get in Ethics before he gets in tech" (Hubbard 1988, 4); in more understandable terms, Hubbard realized that he had to get Scientology's ethical system in place around the world before he could introduce Scientology's techniques. Scientology's ethical system punishes people who oppose or hinder the organization's operation or expansion, or as its dictionary states, it "remove[s] counter intentions from the environment" (Hubbard 1976b, 179). Consequently, Hubbard envisioned the Sea Org as the corps of elite, dedicated members who would establish Scientology ethics around the world so that then he could introduce Scientology "tech" in a successful manner. Jacobs appeared to have been unaware of these pragmatic reasons behind Hubbard's creation of the Sea Org.

24. An accessible description of RPF says that it "becomes Scientology's equivalent to imprisonment, with more than a tinge of the Chinese Ideological Re-education Center. In theory the RPF deals with Sea Org members who consistently fail to make good. They are put on 'Mest work,' which is to say physical labor, and spend several hours each day revealing their Evil Purposes." After reproducing a former member's account of the RPF experience, Atack concluded that "this careful imitation of techniques long-used by the military to obtain unquestioning obedience and immediate compliance to orders, or more simply to break men's spirits, was all part of a ritual of humiliation for the Sea Org member" (Atack 1990, 206). The most extensive analysis of the RPF is Kent 2000.

had five years left if we were going to save the world from destruction, from destroying itself, from the nuclear holocaust. And so, you know, this kept a group who really wound up often being exhausted or burned out, just finding that extra somehow resource to rev itself up again saying, "The world's in our hands. It's not for ourselves we're doing this."

In essence, Hubbard's dire predictions about the imminent destruction of the world kept Jacobs, and probably others like him, working for a cause that they believed was humanity's only hope.[25]

In our interview, one of the historically interesting observations that Jacobs made about Scientology in the late 1960s was that "there was really no sexism in it." Although this claim may not be true—the organization's highest positions are filled by men[26]—Jacobs's perception helps to explain the conversion of women's activist Joan Ford to Scientology in 1971. Ford related her account to me in her California home in mid-December 1992. She attended the City College of New York from 1962 to 1967, and while there she participated in almost every major demonstration that occurred in the city. She also traveled to Washington, D.C., for protests, including Martin Luther King Jr.'s famous demonstration and speech at the Lincoln Memorial in 1963. She also participated in one of the marches to the Pentagon. Her

25. Neither the rigors of life in Sea Org nor the relentless demands of RPF allowed Jacobs many opportunities to discuss people's preconversion lives, but he did discover that another RPF inmate "had been on a freedom ride in Mississippi and had been chased into [a] swamp and had to hide for his life."

26. Critics might argue that Hubbard also exhibited sexism by primarily choosing teenaged girls to serve in the Commodore's Messenger Organization and by dressing them in white, high-heeled boots, miniskirts, and halter tops tied in a knot between the breasts. Their functions involved attending to his personal needs (including washing his clothes, helping him dress, and catching his cigarette ashes) along with conveying messages from him to others. Descriptions of the Commodore's Messenger Organization appear in Atack 1990, 245–47; Corydon 1996, 33–34. Also worth noting is that, in 1951, Hubbard asserted in a discussion about the importance of childrearing that "the historian can peg the point where a society begins its sharpest decline at the instant when women begin to take part, on an equal footing with men, in political and business affairs; since this means that the men are decadent and the women are no longer women" (Hubbard 1951, 1:119).

temporary job with *Newsweek* in 1965 exposed her to the pictures that the magazine's photographers were sending from Vietnam, reinforcing her strong antiwar sentiments. Ford also involved herself in the women's rights movement:

> We marched down Fifth Avenue arm-in-arm with Gloria Steinem and Betty Friedan. We couldn't get a parade permit so we were on Fifth Avenue without one, burning our male bosses in effigy. It was probably about 1968 but there was—when you're marching in a group of 100,000 people on the United Nations [Plaza?] singing peace songs and arms linked, you know you're going to have an effect on the world and there was this wide-eyed enthusiasm. And I still feel that the youth of that date did have an effect in making [President Lyndon] Johnson pull out of the presidency eventually.

To the extent that she shared with others of her generation "this wide-eyed enthusiasm," it probably contributed to her eventual conversion to and involvement in Scientology. In any case, she was involved in the Congress on Racial Equality (CORE) and the National Organization for Women and was "a founding charter member of *Ms.* magazine when it came out and knew Gloria Steinem."

A friend of hers—a person with whom she had attended marches and especially civil rights demonstrations—first introduced Ford to Scientology some time around 1970. Her involvement with the organization came slowly: "It took me a while to get involved in Scientology. . . . I was given books to study. I read all the books of Scientology numerous times and had a very good grasp of the philosophy, and what interested me were things like study tech, education, an ability to get people off drugs. The large social programs appealed to me, coming out of the sixties." Moreover, she believed that, as a group, Scientology had power, which greatly increased its programs' likelihood of success.

Part of her hope for Scientology was that the group would be able to send its trained people throughout society and beyond:

> If those people went out into society and carried out various Scientology social programs as sane, less aberrated [encumbered] people—see, that's how I

felt Scientology could improve the world. Not only would some of the things that they used such as education—that's the tie-in I'd like to make. It was the—really a double appeal to the idealism of the sixties which when Hubbard talked about his tie to Eastern religions, not having studied it other than a glance, I thought, "Well, this is great" because there had been a lot of interest by people in the peace movement into that, into "Eastern religions and peace" and "Buddhism and peace" and so forth. So, again, if you went up the "Bridge" and you became operating as a spiritual being and you were active in using Scientology to create a better world, then this obviously answered everything an individual could want.

Like Jacobs, Ford was attracted to Hubbard's statement about peace: "Hubbard promised to rid the world of criminality and war, you know. I thought, 'Sure, I can attach to this.' " She remained in the organization until late in 1984.

Unification Church

Another movement that contained both Eastern and Western symbols was the Unification Church, founded and led by the self-proclaimed Korean messiah Sun Myung Moon. Moon claimed that, at age sixteen, Jesus visited him and conveyed that he was to complete God's mission of Edenic restoration on earth—a mission that Jesus' enemies had cut short by his crucifixion (Barker 1984, 38, 79–80). An essential part of that restoration was the creation of God-centered families, over which Moon and his current wife reign as members' True Parents (168, 195, 210). The first Unification Church missionary to North America enrolled in the University of Oregon at Eugene in early 1959, but the organization's recruitment successes were modest until it attracted increasing numbers of young, single people during the late 1960s (49).

A victim of Communist imprisonment during the Korean War, Moon constructed a theology that was virulently antagonistic to his godless former oppressors. Moon's anticommunism made him a supporter both of the Vietnam War and of the president who waged that war in the late 1960s and early 1970s—Richard Nixon (Barker 1984, 52–53, 62–63). In fact, the group received national attention in December 1973 when more than a thousand of Moon's followers (popularly known as Moonies) demonstrated their support for the embattled president during the annual lighting of the White House Christmas tree (Barker 1984, 63).[27] Contrasting this unflinching support of Nixon, however, was the fact that in June 1971, one segment of the larger Unification movement, the International Re-Education Foundation, had received permission from the Selective Service System to establish an alternative service program for conscientious objectors.[28] Indeed, despite the Unification Church's overriding anticommunism, I was surprised to find a number of former radicals and activists who had converted to the organization and whose conversion patterns replicated ones that I had observed with other new religious groups.

Two of my interviewees illustrate the journey from SDS to the Unification Church, replacing politics with religion after becoming disillusioned with political efforts to achieve massive power restructuring. I interviewed the person whom I will call Sharon Reeder (b. 1949) in 1989. While a student at the University of Michigan in late 1967 or early 1968, Reeder was inspired by the first Vietnam War teach-in that she attended and soon became an organizer of similar events. Around June 1968, she participated in a three-day take-over of the campus ROTC building,[29] and by 1969 Reeder was attending SDS meetings. On campus she was becoming known "as being part of the group of people that was . . . orchestrating some of the radical politics at Ann Arbor." Although she was never arrested in Ann Arbor, she was thrown in jail (apparently more than once) in Washington, D.C., for various protest-related activities.

Through her psychology studies, Reeder became skilled at running "T-groups" or "sensitivity groups," and her interests expanded to include wilderness survival training. Some of her sensitivity group friends invited Baba Ram

27. I am not certain how this figure of more than a thousand Moonies coincides with another one that Barker mentions from a former high ranking member, who claimed that the movement had only 500 members in 1973. In any case, the December 1974 membership seems to have been close to 3,000 (Barker 1984, 64).

28. Letter from Bill D. McCann, chief of the Conscientious Objector Division of the Selective Service System, California Headquarters, to the International Re-Education Foundation (June 7, 1971). I have a photocopy of this letter in my files, thanks to the assistance of Michael Mickler, who mentioned this letter in Mickler 1980, 142.

29. In our interview, Reeder gave the date of the ROTC takeover as June 1967, but she almost certainly did not enroll at Michigan until September 1967.

Unification Church member Dale Garrat stands in front of other members at the post office in Hempstead, Long Island, N.Y., as they spread their message in June 1974. The photograph, taken by Jim Nightingale, was first published in Newsday with the caption "The only answer [to problems in America] is to come back to God." (© Newsday, Inc.)

Dass to stage a local event, and while following his instructions at the event she "had a spiritual experience, almost a conversion experience in a sense." Reeder later reflected that

> it was a very simple experience. I don't know what induced it. I know I wasn't taking drugs at the time but we were all sitting on the floor and we were chanting or something like that and all of a sudden I felt like somehow I knew that God existed. It's like I rea—, it's like a, a realization that God existed. It was very simple and, for me, it was very, kind of, earth-shaking and in a sense almost disturbing. . . . What happened after that kind of in a way, I think . . . pushed the path of my life in a certain direction because, when I came out of that encounter, I was sitting on the steps of [the] auditorium and I met someone who was a person who had been very involved in the spiritual

kinds of movements and, he, he became a good friend and also . . . kind of a charismatic—almost central point in a way for a number of people from Ann Arbor to become more involved in spiritual things. We began attending yoga classes.

Having grown up in an agnostic home, Reeder was headed into new realms of exploration.

For Reeder as for other youths of the era, politics and religion were co-mingling. For example, in the house in which she lived, "we had our gas masks sitting at the door, so were involved in all the local events." By 1970, however, "the whole inspiration began to hit people that . . . the way to . . . achieve our ideals as community would be to live in the woods, to get back to nature." Pursuing their insight, she and about twenty friends "got in a school bus and we drove across Canada . . . looking for land" on which they could found a commune. The friends' attempt to form a commune *outside* of the U.S. indicated "a real rejection of the political involvement that we had had in the past." Clarifying her comment, Reeder emphasized that

by "rejection," I don't mean that we rejected the values. We were all still op-posed to the war in Vietnam and we certainly were left-wing thinkers. But I think that we were disappointed with the political movement as a whole and we began to feel that the people who were marching didn't really mean it anyway and that somehow, on a level of . . . consciousness that people had in the political movement wasn't really enough for them to achieve their goals anyway. . . . Somehow . . . the change had to happen in ourselves to see if we could live in community.

Disillusionment with the perceived inability of the political movement to reach its goals drove Reeder to explore new means to achieve similar ends.

Much of her disillusionment with the political movement at Ann Arbor came from observing the "back-biting" in the very organizations that were demanding social transformation:

I used to have on my wall Eldridge Cleaver's statement, "If you're not part of the solution, you're part of the problem." And I remember sitting, . . .[in]

one of the last political movements in Ann Arbor, sitting there listening to people bicker over things and kind of stepping back and saying to myself, "This is just like Washington. There is no difference," and feeling that something in human character had to change for political changes to really—to be made anyway.

Reeder elaborated more on these points a short time later in our interview:

You kind of get down to the realization that the changing of the world starts with changing myself and a lot of us were starting to realize that kind of level, looking for that kind of transformation. But the point I'm making which I think is true of many people . . . [according to] my memory anyway, is that at that time, the political movement started waning in Ann Arbor. The, the support it had was really waning anyway but I felt like a lot of people were asking those same questions. You know, like, "We can't seem to work together. We can't seem to love each other, even here. What is it we're really looking for anyway. . . ?" If we can't do that, even if the people in SDS can't love each other, then they really don't have anything to give to the larger society. Then what are they proposing?

Disillusioned, Reeder was drifting away from direct political action.

She and her friends purchased land in Nova Scotia, where she lived for a time. Returning to Ann Arbor to finish her degree (in, I believe, fall 1971), she and a girlfriend lived in a teepee community outside of the city. In December, three old friends phoned her, wanting to visit and talking about a church that they had joined in California:

The next morning, you know, they all came trotting down the walk and I was really shocked to see them. The last [time] I saw Matthew [he] had a pony tail down to his waist practically and here he was looking like a Mormon missionary and I thought, "These guys joined the Mormons." And all they needed was their bicycles. And, they came in and . . . I don't have such a clear memory of what we talked about but I remember being very moved by their spirit and, you know, Matthew said, "[Sharon], you should just—don't go to Nova Scotia, just come to California with us." I said, "Matthew, that's crazy. I can't do that, you know."

She could not have known at the time that soon she would be joining the same church as had her three friends.

On her way back to Nova Scotia, Reeder learned, to her horror, that one of her friends had died on their land. Consequently, she changed plans and traveled instead to New York for his funeral. In the deceased friend's funeral service, she had what she believed to be a spiritual experience when she realized that her life was empty because she did not love anyone. This realization so moved Reeder that she went to Nova Scotia, wrapped up her affairs, and headed for her friend Matthew's church commune in California. As she recounted, "I started hitchhiking for California and I had no idea what I was joining or where I was going."

Her friend's church commune was the Unification Church. She heard the group's teaching (called *The Divine Principle*)

> and I was very moved and . . . I honestly think that the thing that most moved me about Reverend Moon and about everyone in the movement is that they were very careful to live the things that they believed in and it was very pure in that sense and that was very important to me. . . . When I look back over the time I've been in the Church, I really feel like it's very simplistic in a way but that desire to really feel love for people has been something that God has given to me in my life, you know, in, in a way that I'm very grateful for.

Summing up her life in the Unification Church, Reeder reflected, "I've been in the Church almost nineteen years and some of it has been very painful. Our church has gone through a lot of painful things . . . but I wouldn't trade it. I'm happy to be here, you know."

Another Unification Church member interviewed in 1989, whom I will call Kathy Montgomery (b. 1946), was a few years older than Reeder and also had undergone the odyssey of politics to religion. Montgomery recalled being idealistic even as a child. At twelve years old, she determined that she wanted to work for the United Nations in order "to help bring about world peace," and she maintained her desire to work for humanity's betterment when she enrolled at Ann Arbor in 1964. As a student she won several prestigious awards, and she also received some national attention when (as a sophomore in 1965) she appeared on a television program about the sexual revolution.[30] Eventually she attended a few SDS meetings and participated in demonstrations. After graduation, Montgomery "went to Berkeley specifically to demonstrate, to be involved, as a graduate student. I mean, I could've gone to graduate school at other universities, but I chose Berkeley because Tom Hayden went there and some of the other SDS people came in '68 to Berkeley."[31] At Berkeley, however, her frustration only grew over her inability to discover how to make a better world.

Even while moving on the periphery of SDS circles in Berkeley, Montgomery felt uncomfortable about the violent strains within the New Left. Moreover, she was unimpressed with the extensive infighting that she saw in SDS meetings. In one instance, her disillusionment with SDS boiled over: "I stood up in a meeting one time and said, 'Even if we did take over the administration building, we would argue about who was going to empty the wastebaskets.' Because I felt like the New Left had it so little together, in terms of personal relationships and a way of being, that it would be a disaster if we took over anything." At the same time that her frustrations were increasing with the New Left, Montgomery was losing interest in her graduate research in psychology. She finally left the program, although the university awarded her a master's degree for the work that she had completed.

She departed for the woods alone, living outside for six or seven months in Mendocino, on the northern California coast. When it rained, she sought shelter in a hollow tree. As if her lifestyle during this period were not difficult enough, she put herself through ordeals that pushed her levels of endurance. Once, for example, while on a trip to Oregon, she made a raft out of logs that she lashed together and went out on it into heavy ocean surf. On another trip to the same state, she apparently slept in the snow simply to place herself in a life-threatening situation. While in the snow, however, "I got this feeling, this voice came right into my mind and said, 'Go south to Booneville.' And . . . I didn't know where Booneville was." Perplexed, she hitched a ride down the

---

30. Montgomery indicated that she was selected to be on the show because she "was active in some of the campus groups," but I cannot determine to which groups she was referring.

31. Hayden 1988, 328, talks about his move to the Berkeley area in 1969; presumably Montgomery is referring to this period, but I cannot pin down exact dates.

highway and found her way to Booneville. A few months later, in June 1970, she encountered Unification Church members there. For three months Montgomery argued with them, but over the Labor Day weekend when she heard the group's lectures, she converted. Eventually she was responsible for converting about a dozen people from Ann Arbor to the Unification movement. All of these converts had been involved (to some degree) in demonstrations, and all of them "felt like they wanted to make a better society." [32]

When queried about the apparent contradiction between the preconversion Marxist views of many converts (such as herself) and the Moonies' strident anticommunism, Montgomery answered without hesitation that "the Marxist ideology was talking about a single classless society. So in a sense it's a similar vision of an ideal world as the Unification movement. The major difference is that there is a hope of a genuine transformation through the love of God as opposed to simply just more violence and more violence." In her eyes, and in the eyes of many other converts, conversion into the Unification Church from the New Left provided new opportunities to transform the world—opportunities that, from their perspectives, did not require violent upheaval.

Montgomery's interpretation of Unification theology's aspiration for peaceful world transformation conforms with the position that David S. Endo, the director of the International Unification Church, conveyed in a letter to the chair of the San Francisco draft board on Oct. 17, 1973:

> The Unification Church, organized as the Holy Spirit Association for the Unification of World Christianity in 1954, views "salvation" and social reform as a matter of ideological and moral education, not war or force.
>
> Our teaching, the Divine Principle, brings us to strongly believe [that] God's providence of salvation (restoration) is focusing now in America. The spiritual and moral crises of this nation are at a crucial point. No matter what kind or amount of military, economic, or political power we may have, if we fail to rekindle the morality of this generation, our country will decline and

32. I do not know whether Montgomery and Reeder knew one another at Ann Arbor, but apparently they at least had mutual friends.

fall. Therefore, we are zealously looking for "soldiers" for God and Christ, not soldiers of war. In essence, we are working to end war and suffering in the world.[33]

From the vantage point of the members themselves, Moonies in the early 1970s were continuing the leftist struggle for a transformed society, but they were doing so without the Marxist insistence that it would arrive as a consequence of violent upheaval. Conversion, not confrontation, was the path to a new society.

Although the Unification Church claimed not to be looking for soldiers of war as part of its mission, one former soldier of war—whom I will call Fred Smith (b. 1942)—discovered and converted to the Unification Church.[34] Smith related his extraordinary conversion odyssey to me during an interview in New York City in late 1987. As a U.S. army medic in early 1965, Smith was spared service in Vietnam by an assignment to Germany. His ability to speak German allowed him

> to hang out with the local people, and meet a lot of German students who were quite vocal in their opposition to what the U.S. was doing in Vietnam. I at first defended U.S. actions, but found that when I went to my superiors and asked them questions about the war, they were unable to justify it to my satisfaction, and I eventually underwent something of a political conversion at that point, and began opposing the war. I was also fascinated with things that I was reading about, the . . . the civil rights movement, and Gandhi. And the conversion sort of turned me into a Gandhian nonviolent resister.

With only one month left in his German assignment, Smith's troubles began. Willfully disobeying a military curfew order for enlisted men on the grounds

33. Thanks go to Michael Mickler for providing me with a copy of this letter for my files.

34. This person also appears in Fichter 1987, 203–14, under the name "Walter." Although Smith and I agreed to assign him a pseudonym, he consented to allow me to cite newspaper articles concerning him. When citing their titles, however, I will substitute his pseudonym (in square brackets) for his real name.

that it was discriminatory, Smith subsequently served six months of hard labor as punishment for his refusal.

After being released to reserve status, Smith enrolled at the University of California at Berkeley in 1966—the very time when, as he would recall, "the antiwar movement was coming to a boil." In 1967, he refused to attend army summer camp, and in February 1968, he failed to appear for the forty-five days of active service demanded as punishment for his earlier refusal. On April 11, 1968, military police arrested him, charging him with desertion. When he refused an officer's order to put on his uniform, he also was charged with willful disobedience. His jail cell in the Presidio Stockade was six feet eight inches long, five feet wide, and eight feet high (Turner 1968; Young 1968). In the stockade, he persisted in his refusal to wear a military uniform, and so he spent the next four months wrapped in a blanket wearing only his underwear.[35] If convicted for his actions, he faced up to eight years of hard labor ("Late-Blooming" 1968).

The army advised him to apply for conscientious objector status, but Smith resolutely refused. He held his convictions against the Vietnam War so strongly that he stated: "I will not perform such [military] duty if forcibly taken; will not report for any further duty with the U.S. Army; nor will I dress myself in military uniform, nor submit to military orders, under any circumstances whatsoever . . . as a human being, I absolutely refuse to associate with an organization whose primary business is murder" (Young 1968, 1, 12). In a plea bargain worked out with the army, Smith pleaded guilty, received a dishonorable discharge, forfeited pay and allowances, and received a year prison sentence in Leavenworth penitentiary ("Reservist Guilty" 1968).

After completing his sentence, Smith resumed his studies at Berkeley. He remained active in the antiwar movement, writing articles for the antiwar GI newspaper *The Ally*, which soldiers received in Vietnam. Partly because of his "nonviolent convictions," however, and partly because he was on a parole-like

35. For corroboration of Smith's account, see Turner 1968; Young 1968, 12; "G.I. Allowed" 1968. Smith's estimate of serving about four months in the Presidio Stockade seems accurate because he was arrested on Apr. 11, 1968, convicted on June 17, 1968, and transported to Fort Leavenworth prison in Kansas on or around Aug. 1, 1968 ("Late-Blooming" 1968; "Reservist Guilty" 1968; "Former Student" 1968, 1).

release, he refrained from the violent demonstrations that rocked the university community during this period. "And in fact," he recounted, "I was appalled by them. I felt the movement had degenerated, and there was a lot of rock-throwing and provocation of police and just a lot of violence." He grew increasingly disillusioned both "with the violence of the antiwar movement, and [with] the heavy Marxist influence." Consequently, when he completed his bachelor's degree in 1970, he "headed for the hills" of northern California.

For the next several years, Smith "lived on communes, or built cabins, or lived in small towns," taking jobs in hospitals or doing carpentry work. He also became interested in religion, and began "fasting, praying, meditating [, and v]isiting traveling religious teachers." He saw Guru Maharaj Ji on a number of occasions, and he "met plenty of his newly converted followers, some of whom had been my associates in the antiwar movement." He personally met the California philosopher Alan Watts several times, through the latter's daughter (who lived in the same commune as Smith); and he briefly visited Jim Jones's People's Temple in Redwood Valley, California. In 1973, he heard Reverend Moon speak on the Berkeley campus.

At the time of Moon's speech, Smith also visited a Unification Church house in the Berkeley area: "At the house that I visited, I was impressed by the enthusiasm, the friendliness, the high-mindedness, the sort of idealism. I was put off—because I was sort of living in a cabin in the woods at the time—I was put off by the crowded conditions and the highly structured lifestyle. And I was not tempted to join" (Smith 1987, 10). Similarly, some aspects of Moon's speech left an unfavorable impression on Smith, while he regarded other aspects more positively:

I was put off by his style of delivery, which was sort of . . . that of a karate expert. Those were the days when he would sort of chop and stab at the air and, you know, stamp his feet and whirl around and—it was just very bizarre. And very interesting, but bizarre.

The two things that impressed me: first, was the content of the speech—which was really quite American. It was about how God had been with the pilgrims, that they had come to America to establish God's kingdom, which I think has a lot of historical accuracy to it. And that the lesson to be drawn from that is that America does not exist for itself, but exists for God, and that

America has prospered with God's blessing for a higher purpose, not so that it can selfishly consume its own productivity at the expense of the rest of the world . . .

And I was also impressed with the way he handled the crowd. I mean, I had seen an awful lot of crowd behavior up till that point in the last six or seven years. This crowd in Berkeley at Reverend Moon's speech was, I would say—three-quarters of the people there listened politely, and about one-quarter were obnoxious to the point of being almost violent. And the people who were opposing his speech were an interesting alliance of fringe leftists and fundamentalist Christians. And what united them was their opposition to Reverend Moon. And that intrigued me.

In retrospect, Smith was moving toward a conversion.

In 1974, while traveling across the United States, Smith visited a Unification Church center in Huntington, West Virginia, near Marshall University. After hearing "a series of lectures on the doctrine of the [Unification] Church," he agonized over the possibility of converting. Over the next three to four months, Smith put his affairs in order, ultimately joining the church. Since becoming a member, Smith's interests have shifted away from politics and more towards science, although he did work on the Reagan campaign in 1980. Ironically, the Reagan administration would successfully prosecute Moon on a tax evasion charge.[36]

Smith had experienced directly the demands and the constraints of the American military.[37] Another convert, whom I will call Gregg Schultz (b.

36. Moon's appeal of his tax conviction case upheld charges against him both of "aiding and abetting" false returns from 1973 to 1975 and of conspiring (with associate Takeru Kamiyama) to do so; see *United States v. Sun Myung Moon and Takeru Kamiyama*, 718 F. 2d 1210 (U.S. Court of Appeals 1983).

37. I also interviewed another veteran, whom I call Kyle Moore. Moore enlisted in the army in order to avoid what he thought was an impending drug charge (an arrested friend had given police his name). Rather than feeling anger at his betraying friend, "my rage focused against the system. And the political activists offered the only solution, which was 'smash the state.' Smash— just smash it; pull all the pieces apart and start all over. It's always such a simple solution. Just destroy. Don't—don't think about it; just destroy first, get the facts later. Going into the military, making that decision, 'cause I didn't want to leave the United States really [and go to Sweden], I hoped that I could just be out in two or three years. Getting into the military, I saw myself almost

1952), experienced them indirectly—through his father, who was a high-ranking officer in the U.S. Marines. Thus, Schultz's political protest activities had immediate familial implications, which he explained to me in his West Coast home in August 1988. Literally, Schultz's protests brought the war home.

Schultz's radicalization began in the German and Italian high schools that he attended in the late 1960s: "It was the age of rock'n'roll and drugs, and in Germany we had our share of hash and acid and stuff." Drug exploration and music coincided with his political awakening, and as a high school senior in a military school in Germany, Schultz involved himself in a demonstration calling for a moratorium to the war in Vietnam. At the same time, Schultz was applying for a naval ROTC scholarship—about which he had dramatically contradictory feelings. On the one hand, he always had seen himself as becoming a marine officer like his father. On the other hand, "I felt quite rebellious. And I—I felt like the war was wrong, and I wasn't sure if I wanted to participate in that war." Consequently, the night before his ROTC scholarship interview, he dropped acid and spent the entire evening tripping. Not surprisingly, he failed to get a scholarship, but he still was accepted into the ROTC at Marquette University in Milwaukee.

Soon after he arrived at Marquette, Schultz was supposed to sign up for his ROTC courses. Instead, he dropped them. His consciousness was being shaped by Gandhi and Thomas Merton, and "at the end of two years . . . at Marquette, and a healthy dose of liberation theology and the theology of nonviolence and the antiwar movement on the campus and some involvement with the People's Committee for Peace and Justice at Marquette, I was strongly against the war." By 1972, his opposition to the war was so strong that he both participated in protests at the Capitol in Washington, D.C., and

---

as an agent." While serving his tour of duty in Korea during the Vietnam War, he hung a Ho Chi Minh poster in an area where arriving Vietnam pilots would see it. Apparently he also participated in illegally selling American equipment, and once seems to have participated in burying surplus supplies. He had, however, a number of mystical experiences before and during the army, and a sergeant buddy of his introduced him to a persuasive Unification Church member who converted him. He converted to the Unification Church after a number of intense (and in one case, dangerous) religious experiences.

burned his draft card at the Pentagon. The latter act had poignant symbolism for him: as he burned his draft card, his father was inside the building in his capacity as a senior planner of the Vietnam War for the Joint Chiefs of Staff:

> At the time my sense of the war had developed to a point where I felt that I needed to sacrifice myself. I had to place myself on the line for my convictions. And in a way . . . I did that, even though my draft card number was 363—I didn't need to worry about the draft. I did it because I was raised in a tradition of public service. I was raised in a tradition of . . . you know, my . . . father was a marine who—who risked—risked himself. And I think that was very much a part of me.[38]

With some amusement, Schultz pointed out in our interview that when he was arrested and taken to a federal prison, he was not charged with draft card burning but rather with trespassing. His father refused to post his bail, and his sister had to do so with Gregg's own money.

After his release from prison, Schultz decided to move out of his parents' house for the summer. He moved into a garage, took a job at a golf course, and initiated his own spiritual discipline of prayer and psalm-reading: "And I remember taking my Bible and reading the passage of Christ saying, you know, leaving all things to follow him, and telling Jesus, 'I—look, I've left everything to follow you. I'm giving up my family, I'm giving up everything because I—I believe that what I'm doing is right. And I'm doing it for you. And . . . so, take my life. Use me.' " Fully aware of the growing role of spirituality in his life, Schultz also

> felt that what I was doing was a political statement . . . in the sense that I felt I was preparing myself to make a more pure political statement. . . . Basically I had the view that . . . the problem that brought about a war like Vietnam, or the problem that brought about political turmoil, was the problem of sin in the world. And unless I confronted that sin in myself and mastered my own sin, and—my own sinfulness to the best of my ability, at least began the

38. Protests at the U.S. Capitol took place on May 21, 1972 (Zaroulis and Sullivan 1984, 387).

fight against that sinfulness—then I had no ground on which to stand and criticize others.

As had other people of his generation, Schultz had come to believe that the initiation of political transformation began with the transformation of oneself.

Rather than returning to school, Schultz entered a Trappist monastery with the intention of staying there for a year. As with his other spiritual disciplines, he "saw myself entering the monastery for the purpose of gaining . . . a spiritual discipline—gaining the training that monasticism traditionally gave its novices—as a means of making myself a better political activist. And I approached it that way, but I also approached it as . . . want[ing] to find God's will in my life." He remained in the monastery for nine months.

After leaving the Trappists in late spring 1973, Schultz volunteered in a Catholic Worker house, Casa Maria, in Milwaukee. He became involved in protests on behalf of the United Farm Workers, and he continued his antiwar protests. Gradually, however, he began distancing himself from the New Left for two reasons: he distrusted the atheistic ideology behind Marxism, and he felt that Christian principles dictated that Nixon should have been forgiven rather than almost impeached. After publicly challenging a Casa Maria official over the issue of Nixon's probable impeachment, Schultz severed his ties with the house and with the Catholic Workers organization and returned to Washington, D.C., with plans to reenter the monastery.

Before Schultz departed for the monastery, however, events occurred that forever altered his religious life. First, he had a dream involving "God the Father, Jesus, and an Asian man. . . . I had never heard of Unification Church, never heard of Reverend Moon, never—I don't think I've seen his—I had ever seen a picture of him. I knew nothing about the Church." Then, on three different occasions while praying in his room, Schultz felt compelled to go outside. On the third occasion, he

walked out, and I saw this girl walking up the street carrying a bucket of flowers. And I thought, "My God, I've—I've got to talk to her about Jesus. That's why—that's what this is all about. Someone wants me to talk to her about Jesus, God wants me to talk to her about Jesus." So I walked up to her, and I said, "Have you been thinking about Jesus today. . . ?" The woman looked at me like—you know. It just—I just blew her away, and she goes, "Yeah, you know, I've been thinking about Jesus all day." And I said, "Well, you know, I—I just—I was in my room praying, and I felt I had to come out and talk—you know, I had to see someone out here," and I just began to talk with her. And she said, "Well, we . . . I'm a member of a religious group, and we have workshops on the weekend"—and that was on a Thursday. And she goes, "If you want, you can come to our workshop at our house Saturday morning. And . . . and you can stay the night there, and you can . . . hear our teachings." And I said, "Oh, okay—that sounds good." Actually, when I talked to her, I felt like this is what I have to do. I felt it very clearly. I felt I've got to—I've got to do this. And it was a—it was a rock-solid certainty.[39]

Schultz had met his first Moonie, and after the weekend lectures on Unification theology, he converted.

Summarizing his earliest days in the Unification Church, Schultz commented:

We studied constantly. We would get up in the morning, and it was very monastic in a way. You get up early, and you pray and you read and. . . . The only difference was then we'd—it was during the Watergate time, and Reverend Moon had started a program, "Forgive, Love, and Unite." And I was out doing that, and I felt very comfortable doing that, because in Milwaukee I had gone through that struggle [over forgiving rather than endorsing Nixon's probable impeachment]. . . . The political activist in me was still plugged in. And . . . I saw my work as saving America. And that was a way of political activism for me throughout my life in the Unification Church . . .

The political—the activist part of me was being fulfilled by the theological part of me, in a way. And so for me, the spirituality and politics melded. And I saw my—my spiritual purpose as being at one with my political purpose. And all the rebel in me actually never left. You know, in a way, I was—I was there making revolution. But my concept of revolution was that revolution was a return to the source.

39. I found this account to be so improbable that I specifically asked Schultz whether he might be reconstructing his own autobiography in light of his subsequent Moonie involvement. He assured me that he was not doing so and that this incident actually happened.

As did thousands of other young former activists in the early 1970s, Schultz had come to believe that making revolution involved following the dictates of a religious leader.

Another former-protester-turned-Moonie, whom I will call Jim Douglas (b. 1953), began his activism while still in high school. As he related in an interview in a West Coast Unification Church house in 1988, Douglas came from a Quaker background, and in his junior high he participated in a Vietnam War moratorium march on Long Island, New York. Before graduating in 1971, he skipped school to march with half a million people in the April rally in Washington, D.C.[40] Over a week later, he was among the thousands of people who were arrested during May Day protests. His particular arrest came on May 5th, when 1,146 people were arrested on the steps of the Capitol (see Zaroulis and Sullivan 1984, 363). This first arrest "just solidified my opinion that . . . the government was just blatantly suppressing opposition. I thought we had a right to say what we were saying. And that they didn't have a right to arrest us."

His next arrest came in August 1972, when he and over a thousand protesters got picked up during the week of the Republican National Convention in Miami:

> In that particular demonstration, I had decided to get myself violently involved because I was becoming radicalized, and I thought that drastic measures needed to be taken. And we had to be willing to make certain sacrifices, so I was—
> [Kent:] Sacrifices for what end?
> [Douglas]: To stop the war, to stop the system that was perpetuating the war—that was my consciousness. I didn't have any deep strategy. But I just thought we had to get involved. (For more on the Miami convention protests, see Zaroulis and Sullivan 1984, 391.)

The Miami protest and arrest constituted Douglas's last political action before he entered four years of what he called "drugs, sex, and rock'n'roll." After this period, however, he reentered politics, and in 1976 he participated

40. For a discussion of this march, see Zaroulis and Sullivan 1984, 358–59.

in what would be his final protest. In a campaign led by Father Daniel Berrigan called "Disarm or Dig Graves," Douglas was passing out leaflets at the Pentagon when he had a momentary but transformative encounter:

> I was deeply affected by one confrontation I had with a career military gentleman who was walking out of the Pentagon. Other—like, soldiers would walk by and say, "Yeah, right on," and other career people would walk by and say, "You guys are crazy." Just flatly like that. But then there was this real hard-charging looking guy who's just marching across the parking lot, and I thought [*sighs*], "This is getting tiring, you know, handing out these leaflets and . . . it doesn't look like this guy's going to want to take one." And as he walked by me, I handed out a leaflet and said, "Could you take a leaflet, sir?" And he stopped—he was walking by me but he stopped dead in his tracks and he looked at me, straight in the eye, and said, "Son, I've fought in three goddamn wars so you could protest, so you go right ahead." And then he turned around and walked on.
>
> And that really hit me. Because what he said was so right that I couldn't deny it. I just kind of like stood there stunned, feeling like my feet were sinking into the cement as he walked away. . . . But that really affected me deeply, and it kind of stuck in my heart for a while. 'Cause I had to admit that whereas war was wrong, some of these people fighting against Nazism and the imperial Japanese and . . . things like that have . . . you know, I couldn't deny that all of our freedom is being preserved by these people who are willing to go out and risk it, and I had to respect that.

His absolute belief in pacifism began to crumble.

In January 1976, the focus of Douglas's energies for the previous four years—his rock music band—broke up. He continued his interest in music by attending Grateful Dead concerts, often while tripping on LSD. At a Dead concert on May 8, 1977, he had his sixty-fourth LSD experience. Soon afterward, he hitchhiked from New York to San Francisco, where he met a Moonie in a men's room at Berkeley's Sproul Plaza. After attending lectures and workshops, he joined. As he later recalled, one of the reasons that he joined was because Unification theology helped to answer a political question that had been troubling him:

At my last Grateful Dead concert, I was wondering, "Why are there H-bombs in this world when all anybody wants to do is just gather together and have a joyful time?" That was a very basic question. And . . . that was answered in the lecture about the fall of man, which was the origin of sin and where that came from. That answered to me—that described to me how it was possible, if God created man, then how—how men could actually wind up hating each other the way they do.

Not all issues, however, were resolved so easily. At first, Douglas had "hesitations" about the Unification Church's adamant opposition to communism. By the time of our interview in 1988, however, he had reconciled his own position on the subject with that of the Church:

I had decided that I am anticommunist during the course of my education in the Church. But only because I learned that the results of communism were the same as I viewed the results of . . . Nazism, or what I thought was an oppressive . . . barrage of artillery on Vietnam, and napalm and things like that. Communism was doing the same things. And in my political fervor, I had forgotten that. I had forgotten that there was an Iron Curtain, I had forgotten that there was people who were being sent to labor camps in Siberia every day.

Douglas connected his Unification life with his antiwar activities by concluding that "my conscience compels me to be against communism now as it compelled me to be against our involvement in Vietnam."

I interviewed a final activist-turned-Moonie, whom I will call Bruce Jackson (b. 1954 or 1955), in his house on the West Coast in 1988. Like Douglas, Jackson had a history of protest that began in high school. [41] He worked in an organization calling for student representation on school boards (to make them more relevant to contemporary issues), organized voter registration drives and student-participation-in-government days, was elected to the student council, promoted draft counseling for students, and on one occasion

---

41. Another account of a Moonie who had been involved with demonstrations, in this case at Harvard, appears in Fichter 1987, 79–80.

traveled to Washington, D.C., to participate in an antiwar rally. Reflecting upon this youthful period in his life, Jackson commented: "I felt like I was interested in promoting peace in the world and promoting better families and better relationships between people, and that I wanted my life to stand for those issues, and I didn't want myself in a position to hurt or kill people." Shortly after high school, his idealism brought him to George McGovern's presidential campaign.

Work on the McGovern campaign was not a positive experience for Jackson. The disorganization that he witnessed—which he felt reflected the state of liberal politics in America—disillusioned him, exacerbating feelings that he already had about the war "and what happened to some of our great leaders, like Martin Luther King and the Kennedys." He began reading existentialism and Eastern philosophies, and in summer 1974 he hitchhiked from the East Coast to the West, trying to find direction for his life.

While visiting Stanford University, Jackson "found a pamphlet on the campus bulletin board about this organization called the International Re-Education Foundation," which promoted "cultural programs [and] community service programs." The organization's members

> were starting a pioneer academy where they were studying the most critical social issues of the day. They were starting an ideal city project in Mendocino, where they were bringing people together from different races and nationalities and trying to create—break the barriers between those backgrounds and to create more harmony and understanding between those kinds of groups. And this was sort of like an ideal—it seemed like it was an ideal sort of city project, sort of an experiment in trying to create that kind of a situation.

In addition to these lofty attractions, Jackson (who was traveling at the time) added, "they had free lectures and dinners."[42]

His encounter with the International Re-Education Foundation came at a fortuitous moment in Jackson's life. He had concluded that "politics was not the way at the time, and I was searching for another way. . . . I was look-

---

42. On the International Re-Education Foundation, see Mickler 1980, 132–35.

ing to find out whether there was another way or not [i.e., beyond politics], or whether there was a higher truth or not, and I was perfectly willing to accept the possibility that existentialism was maybe the only reality." Within this frame of mind, the Foundation's "programs looked exciting." He did not know at the time that the Foundation's sponsoring organization was the Unification Church.

Jackson went to a lecture and dinner and then to another lecture a few days later. Soon he attended a weekend workshop, after which the organization offered him a job and a place to stay. By this point he probably knew that Sun Myung Moon was the organization's source of inspiration, but it was not until six weeks after joining, while listening to someone read one of Moon's speeches, that he realized that Moon saw himself as the messiah. Because of his particular Jewish background, messianism had little meaning to Jackson, but the organization's members

> basically said, "Well, what does it matter if he's the messiah or isn't the messiah if these principles work to help you come closer to God, to create a better world where we can all live in harmony." And that made a lot of sense to me. . . . And I kept questioning and critically analyzing and trying to figure [things] out, 'cause some of the teachings seemed very bizarre to me. Like [they] were fantasy-oriented, and seemed not having anything to do with the twentieth century. I mean, [Moon] talked about the spirit world, and those kinds of levels. But they kept saying, "Well, you know, if these principles work in actually creating better people and creating a better world, and unless you really give yourself to these principles one hundred percent without, you know, all the criticism, you'll never find out if it really works or not." So that was the thing—that you'd never find out unless you really applied yourself one hundred percent.

After months of struggling over what course to take, Jackson decided to "invest myself a hundred percent" and joined. Thus, in or around January 1975, he found himself promoting Moon's One World Crusade, which involved traveling across the United States with a team of seventy-five people from eleven different countries. He found this crusade to be "very exciting" and became a fundraising captain before it was over. He remained in the Unification Church for a number of years afterward.[43]

Each of the accounts of conversion described above—whether to Scientology or to the Unification Church—maps a common trajectory. In varying degrees, each person had been involved in political protest against the Vietnam War and other issues related to power imbalances in society and in the world. Each person grew disillusioned with the ability of either liberal or leftist politics to initiate the changes that they felt were necessary to create a just social order. Frustrated with political avenues but still seeking personal and societal reconstruction, each person drifted into a religious quest that involved (in varying degrees) any number of religious messages that were current at the time. Finally, through friends or circumstances, each person came in contact with some aspect of Scientology or of the Unification Church and found hope in what they heard. For others of their generation, however, a similar trajectory led not to syncretic organizations like these but to groups that grew directly out of the mainstream soil of American Christianity.

The Jesus Movement and the Christian World Liberation Front

Unification theology insisted that Moon had to complete Jesus' unfulfilled mission of world restoration. By contrast, more traditional Christian theologies popular in the early 1970s emphasized Jesus as an inspirational model for rebellious youth. Consequently, in several Western, Christian groups, the Movement image of "the Revolution" became attached to a generationally-relevant model of Jesus.

Perhaps the most famous conversion of a political radical to conservative Christianity was that of Eldridge Cleaver (1935–1998), who became a born-again Christian and did some work for Reverend Moon's Unification Church (Cleaver 1978). Cleaver's conversion was by no means unique among activists, however. For example, Anthony Bryant was a hitman for the Black

---

43. I do not have recorded in the interview how many years Jackson remained with the Unification Church, but my impression (from memory) is that he had been out at least several years by the time that we spoke in late summer 1988.

Panthers whose 1969 hijacking of a plane to Cuba (in an attempt to obtain weapons) landed him in jail for sixteen years. After his release in 1985, Bryant spoke with Moon's campus group CAUSA (Confederation of the Associations for the Unification of the Societies of the Americas) about the evils of communism and the glory of Jesus (Barker 1985). Among pop-culture figures, Bob Dylan's born-again experience in late 1978 attracted widespread attention (Mackenzie 1980; Gonzalez and Makay 1983; Shelton 1986, 483–90; Day 1988, 96–109). But a decade earlier he had influenced the conversion of another activist singer, Noel Stookey (better known as "Paul" of the folk trio Peter, Paul, and Mary) by suggesting to Stookey that he read the Bible (Richardson 1986, 42; Plowman 1971, 20–21). Dennis Peacocke, who had participated in Berkeley's Free Speech Movement and then joined the Trotskyist Socialist Workers Party, afterwards became a devout Christian (Diamond 1987, 21). Bill Garaway became a Christian after having been a draft resister, twice prosecuted by federal authorities (Lelyveld 1985, 36). Mike Kennedy, who had helped to establish SDS at the University of Houston, subsequently converted to a charismatic Episcopal group, the Church of the Redeemer (Plowman 1971, 20). Interviews carried out in 1971 with eighty-eight members of Shiloh House, a Christian commune near Eugene, Oregon, revealed that of the forty-two people who reported themselves to have been politically active, twenty-three were radical and nineteen were liberal before joining the religious group, although only two people had led political demonstrations (Harder, Richardson, and Simmonds 1972, 110; "Jesus Communes" 1973, 16). To these former activists and radicals, Jesus became the exemplary revolutionary, the antihero of the modern, chaotic American world.

This motif of Jesus as antihero, as it appeared in popular youth culture of the early 1970s, contained elements deeply attractive to some former radicals. According to one scholar, "The antihero tends to be a figure who (1) is opposed to the law, which is seen as the corrupt tool of those who wish to protect vested interests, (2) is a friend to the poor and gives generously to them out of a sense of justice, (3) is inclined to subscribe to orthodox religion, (4) adopts the role of a 'trickster' vis-a-vis the authorities, and (5) tends to be subject to betrayal by friends" (Heenan 1973, 145, based upon Steckmesser 1966; see also Cooper 1972, 126–38; Ellwood 1973, 11–23). Because of

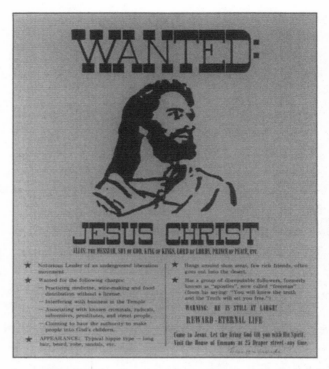

A pamphlet depicting Jesus in countercultural terms, produced by a Jesus movement called the House of Emmaus in Toronto, late 1960s or early 1970s. The House of Emmaus no longer exists.

these images, Jesus the antihero fit almost seamlessly into political protests of the period. As one reporter lamented in 1972, "I don't know how many times I've gone through the routine where I'm on the street and someone walks up and starts talking to me about what a nice day it is, or smashing the state, or something in between and all of a sudden I get hit with, 'Say, do you know Jesus Christ,' and I have to spend the next five minutes shaking off my would-be proselytizer" (Isserman 1972). The location of Jesus freaks (as they were called) in the subculture of political protest was captured in the opening lines of a 1971 article in the leftist publication *Ramparts:*

Swept along in the squall of *Peace on Right Now You-Name-It Against the War* placards at the Spring Offensive in San Francisco waved a flimsy blue poster with drippy red lettering that read *Jesus: A Bridge Over Troubled Waters*. The bearer wasn't a collared cleric or a Youth Fellowshipper chalking up merit points for heaven, but a scroungy, ponchoed, bell-bottomed veteran of the streets. Anyone at all familiar with what is happening in California simply nodded a recognition—ah, a Jesus freak—accepted his tract and plowed on to the polo field. A few stopped and stared, obviously shaken to their Sunday School roots by the very idea of freak evangelism, a fairly new breed in the hip-liberation menagerie. But there he was, marching right-on along with the red armbands, the lavender headbands, the brown berets, the inverted flags, the hardstepping women, the saffron robes and the green earth insignias. And this barefoot boy with his flimsy blue bridge-over-troubled waters certainly did not seem to have come at the wrong time or to the wrong place with this whatever message he had to give America in the Seventies. (Nolan 1971, 20)

No Christian group was more skillful at utilizing political protest and Movement rhetoric in portraying Jesus as the countercultural antihero than was the Berkeley-based Christian World Liberation Front (CWLF). Known as the most "left-oriented of all the Jesus Movement groups" (Richardson, Steward, and Simmonds 1978, 245), the group's indebtedness to popular radical rhetoric was apparent in its use of the phrase "Liberation Front" in its name. The movement that became the CWLF began "in April 1969[, when] three men and their families came from Los Angeles to 'make Christ an issue' on [the University of California at Berkeley] campus, to confront political radicals with an alternative, and to preach the gospel to street people." In order to recruit members, the nascent organization "infiltrated the campus, especially radical student organizations, talked to students, and befriended people on Telegraph Avenue" (Heinz 1976, 143). CWLF publications were laced with Movement rhetoric, as in a pamphlet calling for a meeting on October 8, 1969:

IF YOU ARE A FOLLOWER OF JESUS OR THINK YOU MIGHT WANT TO BE ONE, COME AND JOIN US AS WE DISCUSS THESE ISSUES AND OTHERS AND PLAN ACTION . . .

    1. rent, tenants unions, rent strikes.

    2. war and its control.

3. environmental control.

4. oppression.

5. racism.

6. how we can serve the people.

7. keeping your head straight around here . . .

If you care what's come down around here, BE THERE. (CWLF 1969)

The issues addressed were ones that dominated the political movement of the period, but another CWLF pamphlet suggests that the Christian group's approach to these issues was fundamentally different. Posing the question ". . . AND AFTER THIS WAR?" the pamphlet went on to ask:

Why have violent conflicts continued to plague mankind throughout history, despite numerous and varied system changes?

Will a utopian economy and political system eradicate the seemingly inescapable stigma of social and psychological struggle? . . . In fact, as history insists, no kind of environment guarantees that we will finally realize the beautiful society we so desperately want. It should be obvious—something is wrong with us! The great cop-out today is to blame some impersonal institution or system.

Jesus proclaimed a spiritual revolution to bring about a fundamental change within, to deal with the faulty components of every system—the human components. Accept Him as your Liberator and Leader; then join others of his Forever Family here to change this world.

RADICALIZE THE REVOLUTIONARY MOVEMENT! (CWLF ca. 1969)[44]

CWLF's emphasis on "a fundamental change within" as the means of enacting massive social change is similar to the messages propounded by various Eastern religious groups in the early 1970s, except that Jesus the antihero—not a guru or Eastern mythological figure such as Krishna—was to be the center of emotional and intellectual attention.

Focus on Jesus would be enough, so CWLF members believed, to literally

44. On the copy of this pamphlet that I possess, someone has penciled in the date "1968" in the upper-right-hand corner. Surely this date is incorrect, however, since the CWLF did not establish itself in Berkeley until 1969.

change the world. The process by which such change would come about was spelled out in an eight-page pamphlet (entitled "New Berkeley Liberation Program") in which the CWLF called

FOR SISTERS AND BROTHERS TO FORM LIBERATION COMMITTEES TO IMPLE-MENT [JESUS'] PROGRAM.

These committees should be small democratic working groups of people who have received Jesus. Their aims should be getting to know and understand each other, getting to know God better, and initiating positive action in helping others. They should seek ties with other such committees, helping to build a network of new groups throughout Berkeley. Together as a New Berkeley Liberation Movement, these liberation committees will introduce thousands of others to the new life Jesus offers. (CWLF n.d., [7])

A phrase that the CWLF used to conclude this pamphlet aptly summed up its fundamental philosophy: adapting the popular political chant "Power to the People," the CWLF asserted "POWER THROUGH THE SPIRIT[.] ALL POWER THRU JESUS" ([8]).

Despite CWLF's extreme leftist leanings, its view of the means of social revolution as changing the self through accepting Jesus was the common thread of all of the Jesus movement organizations of the early 1970s (Marin 1972; Fowler 1982, 148–50). For example, the *Augur,* an alternative newspaper in Eugene, Oregon, carried an article on the local Jesus movement in which one adherent proclaimed that

the revolution occurring today is not revolutionary enough! It seeks to change the system, but does not deal with the self-centered attitude of man. We believe that it is not enough to merely end the war; we are also concerned about man's problems of greed; lust; hate; prejudice; anger; anxiety; boredom; bitterness; sexual, social and economic exploitation; dishonesty; purposelessness; frustration; fear; lack of peace; jealousy; strife; envy; impurity; bigotry; intemperance; insolence; materialism; pride; and self-righteousness. We believe that only Jesus Christ has the power to permanently change man from within to produce peace, love, and fulfilment.

The *Augur* summed up the Campus Crusade for Christ's position on political action in words that they could have used to describe the basic political positions of most Jesus movement groups: "The Campus Crusade shies away from political involvement, but [a local staff member] feels that by instilling Christian attitudes into current and future leaders (college students), eventually the political situation will change for the better" ("Christian Activists" 1970, 8). Were it not for the specific mention of "Christian attitudes," the statement could have been made by members of several Eastern and syncretic religious groups as well.

Children of God

The only Christian-based group that rivaled the CWLF in the use of radical political rhetoric for introversionist ends was the Children of God (COG). Founded in 1968 at Huntington Beach, California, by a forty-nine-year-old preacher named David Berg (1919–1994), the group rapidly attracted countercultural youth into its fold (see Davis and Davis 1984 for more on the group's development). Some of the recruits were wayward hippies; others, such as former members of the Jesus People Army in Vancouver, British Columbia, already were involved in Christian missionary activities; and a few of the converts were or had been antiwar activists and radicals. The secrecy of this group during its early years has made research on its initial members exceedingly difficult, as has the practice (which may have been convenient for draft dodgers) of adopting "Bible names" upon conversion (Wangerin 1993, 22). Despite these difficulties, some former activists are identifiable in COG ranks, if only by the stories told about their preconversion activities.

Bill Davis, for example, had been involved in campus protests at Ohio University (Davis and Davis 1984, 132). Although somewhat young at the time, Miriam Williams (b. 1953) had been "a full-fledged social activist" while still in high school and had participated in the spring 1971 antiwar protests in Washington, D.C. (1998, 16, 22–23). Another convert known simply by his COG name, Demetrius, recounted to an El Paso, Texas, reporter in 1971 that "I had a choice: school, get drafted, or go over the border. I was on dope and my morals got so that I was on the point of blowing up buildings, and they'd

Members of the Children of God carried shepherds' staffs, wore sackcloth, and smeared ashes on their foreheads, apparently in the tradition of biblical prophets. On conversion missions, they conducted vigils of "warning and mourning"—such as this one in Houston on Dec. 30, 1969—because they believed that their generation was the last one before revolution would destroy the nation. This photograph first ran in the Houston Chronicle. (© AP/Wide World Photos)

have to kill me. I ran into the group[,] and the first two weeks [that] I had the Lord I count equal to the entire past of my life" (Turner 1971). One of the Weathermen convicted of minor charges for the burning of a Bank of America branch office in Isla Vista, California, met and joined the COG after his conviction but before his sentencing, and for the next ten years he remained on the run from the FBI while in the group.[45] Five members of a California COG team in late 1969 were former political radicals apparently skilled in explosives, and (as one of the team leaders told me) "we were on our way to blow up the Mormon Temple" when they got arrested and imprisoned for disrupting a church service in Sacramento (Whitt 1989). David Berg himself mentioned public relations problems in California caused by the presence in the group of "FRESH RADICALS WITHOUT MUCH EXPERIENCE AND DIPLOMACY AND TACT IN HANDLING THE PUBLIC" (Berg 1976a, 1:377; see also 1:993). Some COG converts in Canada were American draft dodgers, and COG men apparently received ministerial exemptions from the draft (Charity Frauds Bureau 1974, 18–19; Berg 1976a, 1:1062; Davis 1988; Wangerin 1993, 26, 35). The draft was so significant for COG men that Berg devoted one of his *Mo Letters* to it, urged them to call themselves "PASTORS, MINISTERS, OR EVEN REVERENDS WHEN DEALING WITH THE SYSTEM," thereby increasing their likelihood of draft board exemptions (Berg 1976a, 1:961; see also 1:309, 1:473).[46]

The COG's anti-American rhetoric equaled if not surpassed leftist Movement diatribes, with particular derision aimed at President Richard Nixon— "the little Hitler" or "Nitler" as Berg called him (see e.g. 1976a, 1:877; Aagaard 1978). Much of this rhetoric directly borrowed images and themes from the counterculture and from antiwar efforts, which made it easy for for-

45. The Weathermen (also known as the Weather Underground) formed in 1969 as a splinter of SDS. I deliberately do not mention the person's name on request of an acquaintance of his who provided me with this information (Thompson 1988). For contemporary accounts of the incident, see "2 Berkeley Banks" 1970; Kifner 1970.

46. It is interesting to note that Hare Krishna devotees apparently also received ministerial deferments. In early 1969, Prabhupāda wrote a letter to a San Francisco draft board for one of his initiated students who was being trained under him "to become an ordained Minister of Religion in the KRISHNA CONSCIOUSNESS (God Consciousness) SOCIETY." He ended the letter by stating that "SOME OF MY STUDENTS HAVE BEEN CLASSIFIED IN THE 4D CLASS or Ministerial Order prior to this by the Selective Service System" (Prabhupāda 1987, 2:794–95 [letter no. 69-3-34]). Additionally, the Unification Church's International Re-Education Foundation received Selective Service approval (on June 7, 1971) as "an employer of conscientious objectors in the Alternate Service Program," and the director of the International Unification Church wrote a letter of support for a Moonie's conscientious objector application on Oct. 17, 1973 (copy of letter in author's possession).

mer activists who converted to feel continuity with their previous attitudes and activities (Wangerin 1993, 65). In a May 1973 *Mo Letter* (inspired in part by Don McLean's song "American Pie"), Berg presented his interpretation of the contemporary American youth revolution and of the frightened governmental reaction to it:

1. IN THE 1960'S THE KIDS IN AMERICA WERE STILL ROOTING AND RIOTING FOR REVOLUTION and they still had hopes that they could save their country and its freedoms from the destruction, war, pollution and death caused by the diabolical Systems of the older generations and their sins!

2. BUT THE PARENTS BECAME FRIGHTENED that their own children were going to wreck the country and go communist and the older generation would lose its wealth, security and control, and socialize the Nation. Blindly failing to see the handwriting on the wall, the parents desperately got together and quickly elected the would-be Fascist dictators, Nitler, Agony [Vice President Spiro T. Agnew] and their Nitzies to try to save them from their inevitable doom!

3. UNTIL THIS AWFUL ELECTION IN 1968 OF THESE NAZISTIC REPUBLICANS THE KIDS WERE ACTUALLY BEGINNING TO WIN some of the battles, and for a while it looked like the country might even awaken and help its youth win their war against oppression and economic, educational, religious and social slavery! It looked like youth might even begin to have a voice in the Government of America and stop its stupid wars and exploitation of the poor of the world!

4. BUT THE ENEMIES OF CHANGE, YOUTH, AND REVOLUTION, BY HOOK AND CROOK, MANAGED TO KILL AND DISCREDIT YOUTH'S ONLY CANDIDATES, and the reactionary older generation, the enemies of peace and freedom who always resist change, won this tragic election by a very narrow margin, and the kids were licked! In 1969, Nitler and his Nitzies began to crush their youthful rebellion by the most fiendish, brutal, violent and repressive police power ever seen used in America against its own citizens and its own children since the days of the horrible slaughter of the Civil War of just 100 years before!

Berg went on to illustrate his point by alluding to the killings at Kent State and Jackson State universities, to the cancellation of draft deferments (by which he may have been referring to the establishment of the lottery system), and to the American bombing of "the poor helpless populations of the nearly defenseless, backward, agrarian and under-developed nations of the peace-loving peoples of Indochina" (Berg 1976a, 2:1812).

In Berg's eyes, Nixon had crushed the political movement that had persistently opposed an array of governmental policies. Hope for change, however, still existed through the "Jesus Revolution":

> 15. BUT AT THE SAME PIVOTAL TURNING POINT IN AMERICAN HISTORY, as she began passing the point of no return with the election of Nitler in 1968 and the defeat of her youth revolution, God began to bring about a new uprising amongst America's youth, a new and more total and more lasting revolution that will never die, and that not only changed America's youth, but is changing the youth of the whole world: the Jesus Revolution! . . . Violent revolution had failed, but the Jesus war had won! (Berg 1976a, 2:1814; see also Berg 1976a, 2:1855)

Berg offered American youth a new means for achieving their desired goal of revolution: through the lives that they would live within COG after they had been born again (Kent 1994a, 32–33). In a form analogous to the demands placed upon youth who joined other heterodox religious groups in the early 1970s, conversion to COG involved an introspective change of the individual. The "Revolutionary New Life" that Berg promised *"IS A GIFT OF GOD* performed by a miraculous transformation of our lives when we accept His Truth in the love of His Son, Jesus, by the work of God's Spirit. All we have to do is receive Him" (Berg 1976b, 1).

One former activist who converted to the COG, Marylou Hiebert (b. 1947), appreciated the connection between her earlier political attitudes and the radical, even apocalyptic rhetoric that Berg used. In an interview in 1989 in British Columbia, she observed:

> One thing about the leader and his writings is [that] he was virulently anti-American, [and] a lot of us were fairly anti-American also just because of the war in Vietnam. It was just the climate of the times but he made a whole the-

ology out of it. Many of his writings, [his] early writings, were—"The Amerikan Way" was one [*Mo*] *Letter*, A-M-E-R-I-K-A-N. "The Amerikan Way." He had another one called "Nitler," which was about Nixon. You know, in '72, we were all told to leave [the United States]. That's the first time we were told to leave America. . . . [T]he horror of *Revelation* is America, and its materialism and its money is the horror of Babylon. . . . America is Babylon. [The group's] politics were just totally anti-American and he was always trying to butter up to other political [figures]. He'd make parallels between himself and even Mao—like his [i.e., Berg's] methods, not maybe his beliefs, but his methods with Mao. He was always emulating or trying to butter up to Gaddafi [of Libya].

In essence, Berg's rhetoric resonated with the attitudes of his youthful followers by the manner in which it transformed anti-Americanism into theology.

Hiebert's account of her disillusionment with political action and of her conversion to the Children of God embodies elements shared with countless others in her generation. In 1965 she enrolled in Trinity University in San Antonio, Texas, and graduated four years later with a degree in sociology. Considering a master's degree in social work, she joined the American service organization Volunteers in Service to America (VISTA). Her year in VISTA made her realize that "I was unsatisfied with my middle-class, comfortable upbringing and existence, and I wasn't sure that . . . the answer for the poor [was to] just bring them up to the middle-class. I had not found that fulfilling." She thus abandoned her thoughts of graduate school. While contemplating her future after VISTA, Hiebert visited a friend in Washington, D.C., in mid-1970, and she wound up staying in the city for nine months. During that time, she stuffed envelopes for a volunteer organization that was preparing for a major antiwar march, but she never connected with the other activists who also were working in the office. After the march, in another part of town, Hiebert was tear-gassed, and the experience scared her. She learned that she was not attracted to confrontational action, but she was not yet ready to turn her back on countercultural politics.

After her time in Washington, Hiebert "dropped out, became a hippie, went on the road, [and] ended up in Knoxville, Tennessee" before moving on to New Orleans. In New Orleans she found a "university neighborhood" that "had some counterculture happenings going on, particularly political action, economic/social things, and then there were the hippie dropouts and the runaways, and I kind of drifted into them." She gradually became involved with an ecumenical group that funded and provided space for many counter-cultural groups and their activities, and this involvement allowed her unique opportunities to observe the relationships among a wide number of community groups. Her observations led her to conclude that neither the counter-culture nor the political culture had succeeded in creating a new society:

> Even the counterculture was becoming, well—the drug scene was turning bad. We could see [that] . . . the factions within the community—the political faction, the different groups of different interest groups within the counterculture—were at each other's throats, vying for space, money, grants, and I thought, "Gee, this is just like society. How are we forming a new one when we're—it's turning out to be the same old thing." . . . Things were going sour there and so . . . on every front the avenues we had tried were not working. You know, "Love, where is love? It's not—we don't have it, folks. You know, we've, we've tried. We're in the same basket that the other generation was in, that the society in general was in. Well, where does love come from? I've tried; I can't do it. I can't love. Where is love?"

By late 1971, adrift in a failing counterculture, "I was at a point where everything that I had been working for, hoping for, was at a dead end. You know, I could see the death of the counterculture. You know, it was a sinking ship (. . . if it was ever floating), and I knew I had to find something else." Then, immediately after a fractious meeting of vying political and countercultural groups, a member of the Children of God approached her and asked, "You want to receive Jesus, don't you?" After speaking with this person, Hiebert was hooked:

> I asked him questions, eschatological questions. He had the answer for everything. You know, what's going to happen. Like, even in, in the hippie community people were talking about the end of the world and what would happen—what kind of world would come—and he had the answer for every-

thing. I thought, "Wow, this guy"—"it's all from the Bible" he says. You know, he had the answers [that] I was looking for. I was tired of struggling and thinking [that] we had it and we didn't. Well, here's somebody who had it, had—he had it all—every question he could answer.

This COG member even predicted that Christ was going to return in this generation, after "this system" and the world had come to an end.

Hiebert quickly joined the COG, and the transition from her old life into her new one was easy because of the political and countercultural tone of the group's theology:

> I could still be radical because their philosophy [and] their theology is couched—or was at any rate at that point in time—couched in very political terms—"Revolution for Jesus! Jesus was the real revolutionary . . . we're not trying to change society. We're going to create a totally new one and God's government is the best government," and all sorts of things like this that were very much speaking the language of that generation.
>
> Now, they didn't allow drugs—no drugs, no smoking. Jesus is a better high, okay? The Holy Spirit of Jesus is a better high. You don't need drugs any more.

She remained in the group for nearly fifteen years.

Hiebert, like countless others during the late 1960s and early 1970s, found solace from society in Jesus. As a symbol, however, the Jesus of youth culture appeared almost as a different figure than the conservative representation of him in the churches within mainstream culture. Unlike the conservative, nation-supporting Jesus of many churches, youth culture's savior was long-haired, revolutionary, and apocalyptic. Some observers might argue that Jesus transformed youth culture during this period; others would insist that youth culture transformed Jesus. Probably both positions are accurate. Perhaps, as his followers claim, Jesus saves, but most assuredly he saves different generations through different appeals. As a cultural (or subcultural) figure, Jesus is a pliable symbol, malleable to the particular distresses and aspirations of groups or generations that desperately long for salvation. Disillusioned protesters remade him in their own image, and then worshiped their new creation. Alternatively, leaders of youth groups (such as David Berg) provided the new images of Jesus around which their followers flocked. In both cases, however, Jesus was expected to vanquish the powerful as he implemented the supposedly ideal society for which the "disprivileged" had struggled so ardently. His revolution, moreover, would require total commitment from his flock rather than direct confrontation with oppressors. Stated succinctly, the Jesus Revolution was supposed to realize the social revolution that political protest had failed to achieve.

That expectation of social revolution is the common thread in all of the conversion stories recounted above. Idealistic youth—sometimes propelled by the perceived shortcomings of their own generation, and always compelled by promises of dramatic social change—chose to commit themselves to high-demand beliefs that always rested upon supernatural claims. Most of the beliefs were religious, and even Scientology (with its technology) insisted that it was a new faith. These new faiths gave to their converts what direct political protest no longer could provide—hope for the appearance of a purified world. As the vanguard of this long-awaited, purified world, many new converts worked diligently at purifying themselves, often through arduous if not dangerous ordeals and trials. With their like-minded fellow travelers, converts to the new religions in the early 1970s expected to follow their leaders into a future transformed by their purity.

Alas, they marched ahead to the sounds of very different drummers, and so they often collided with one another as they left behind bewildered and bitter family and friends. Indeed, some of the best and brightest minds of a generation were turned against each other by the cacophony of spiritual messages.

6

Conclusion

Mystical Antagonism and the Decline of Political Protest

despite the diversity of ideological positions among the religiously heterodox groups of the early 1970s, the message that they offered to
politically frustrated youth was strikingly uniform. Each new faith instructed
its converts to maintain hope in the reality of an upcoming revolution—in
particular, a revolution fueled by the purified lives of the devout and spiritually
trained. Direct confrontation with political and social systems had failed to ex-
tract the dramatic changes that Movement participants had expected, so large
numbers of them turned toward purifying themselves and those around them
in an effort to bring about what they so desperately wanted.

Steadfast members of the New Left, however, were deeply distressed by
what they were seeing. The religions to which their former associates were
converting usually were sexist, authoritarian, doctrinally rigid, and millenni-
ally self-absorbed.[1] Social protest involving direct challenges to persons and
institutions in power was being ignored in the name of spiritual purity. Sociologist Edwin Schur expressed the feelings of many change-oriented activists
when he warned that "a seductively appealing, but distorted and socially

---

1. I am aware, however, that issues of power, gender, and emphasis vary among groups. On
the issue of gender, for example, Palmer (1994, 9) divides the groups that she studied into three
categories: sex polarity, sex complementarity, and sex unity.

harmful, ideology of [self-]awareness is rapidly gaining acceptance. If we allow this to go on, unquestioned and unchecked, we will do so at our considerable peril" (Schur 1975, 2).

Apocalypticism and Millenarianism

A motivating factor in converts' ritualistic self-purifications was the widespread but varied belief that the millennium was at hand. Each group viewed the age through the lens of its own ideology, but all agreed that dramatic events of a socially transformative nature were imminent. Cosmic forces at work were about to create a world of peace, much like activists and radicals had demanded in their pamphlets and envisioned in their dreams. For some, it was a time of celebration; for others it was a time of anxiety. Some groups sang with joy; others predicted an apocalypse. All purified themselves in order to be among the chosen participants in the divine plan. An observation about the Moonies by sociologists David Bromley and Anson Shupe held true for all of the youth-oriented religions of the period: "[T]he inducement to enlist in a world-saving movement would be greater if potential converts could be told that they were, for a short time, still able to join in on the 'ground floor' of an enterprise that would soon become enormous and important" (1979, 98).

For example, Scientology's millennial vision held out both the joyful promise of a transformed world *and* the apocalyptic threat of nuclear annihilation. The course that the planet would take depended upon the strenuous efforts of the committed few—specifically, the members of Scientology's own special Sea Organization. In a statement first printed in 1965 but periodically reproduced for years afterward, Hubbard announced

The world has an optimistic five years left, a pessimistic two.

A handful of us are working our guts out to beat Deadline, Earth.

On us depends whether your kid will ever see sixteen or your people will ever make it at all.

A handful of us aren't nattering or dramatizing or whining or waiting. We've got our sleeves rolled up for a twelve hour day and sixty hour week. . . .

We know every minute counts.

And we intend to take out of the road anything we have to take out of the road, no matter how big, to make a civilization that *can* survive.

And won't go BANG!

If we win, you will win. The kids in school will grow up. And we'll have a world without criminality, without war.

We mean it. And the only slim chance this planet has rests on a few slim shoulders, overworked underpaid and fought—the Scientologist. (Hubbard 1965)

One of the former Scientologists whom I interviewed, Joshua Jacobs, specifically remembered Hubbard's five-year prediction from his time in the organization in the late 1960s and the 1970s.

Moreover, Scientology's plan of global salvation moved both inward to the individual and outward to the entire cosmos. Hubbard ensured that his followers identified their own salvation with the organizational effort to save planet earth. In a 1963 *Hubbard Communication Office Policy Letter* (which remained in effect throughout the 1960s and 1970s), Hubbard cautioned Scientologists about their mission by proclaiming that "the prize is regaining self and going free. The penalty for our failure is condemnation to an eternity of pain and amnesia for ourselves and for our friends and for this planet." As if that were not motivation enough, he immediately raised the stakes concerning the costs of failure: "If we fail we've had it. It's not just a matter of getting killed. It's a matter of getting killed and killed and killed life after life forever more. . . . We're the elite of Planet Earth, but that's only saying we're not quite gone in the graveyard of the long gone" (Hubbard 1972, 4:345). More was at stake, however, than merely one's own salvation and the fate of the planet; literally all of creation, the vast cosmos, depended upon Scientology's success. Hubbard attempted to establish Scientology's mission of cosmic soteriology in a *Policy Letter* written in 1965: "The whole agonized future of this planet, every Man, Woman and Child on it, and your own destiny for the next endless trillions of years depend on what you do here and now with and in Scientology. This is a deadly serious activity. And if we miss getting out of the trap now, we may never again have another chance. Remember, this is our first chance to do so in all the endless trillions of years of the past" (Hubbard 1976c, 6:9). He considered this *Policy Letter* so important that his organization reprinted it in 1970 and again (with a small correction) in 1973. Among committed members it reinforced the belief that they were on a mission to save themselves, their loved ones, the world, and the entire cosmos from destruction. No sacrifice was too great, because success depended entirely upon the efforts of elite Scientologists performing their duties within a vast organizational structure.

Another group from the 1970s whose apocalypticism drove believers into acts of selflessness and intensity was the Children of God. At the same time as COG leader Berg preached about the imminent return of Jesus, he warned about a period of terrible tribulation prior to Christ's establishment of his kingdom on earth. Following a pattern of premillennial dispensationalism common to fundamentalist Christians, Berg presented his prophecy of the "end times" in pictures and in words.[2] Concisely, he summarized his millenarian apocalypticism in seven steps:

> (1) 1968–9: End of the Time of the Gentiles.
> (2) 1968–89: Restoration of the Time of the Gentiles.
> (3) Late 70's and/or Early 80's: Rise of the Anti-Christ to power.
> (4) 1985: The Covenant confirmed by the Anti-Christ.
> (5) 1985: Seventieth Week of Daniel begins—Last Seven Years of world history.
> (6) 1989: Tribulation begins.
> (7) 1993: Jesus comes! (Berg 1976b, 943)

From these predictions, Berg concluded: "SO IT WON'T BE LONG NOW!—It won't be long that we, the Aquarian followers of the Lord, have to finish the job of reaching the rest of the world with the love of Jesus!" In essence, the

---

2. Premillennial dispensationalism claims that "God is revealed to humans through a series of dispensations or stages, each with its own narrative sequence that ends in violent disruption in the transition to the next dispensation (the expulsion from the garden, the flood, and so on). . . . Furthermore, the 'premillennial' part of the theory holds that Jesus returns to rule at a point of the transition as human history ends" (Strozier 1994, 9).

Children of God had the self-appointed mission and responsibility of preparing the world for the imminent return of its savior.

As proof of the accuracy of his predictions, Berg wrote about the significance of the comet Kohoutek, which the world was awaiting eagerly to see in the late autumn and early winter skies. His first discussion of the heavenly body was cautious: "18. EXACTLY WHAT THIS HUGE NEW COMET SIGNIFIES we cannot tell, but we've already told enough to get a pretty good idea of what it could signify in possibly portending the end of things as they now are, including present world powers, economic systems, etc." (Berg 1976a, 2:2119). He continued this theme in a second tract, proclaiming that Kohoutek's appearance "COULD BE THE END OF FASCIST AMERICA AND ITS NEW NAZI EMPEROR and the beginning of a new day for the whole world! We pray God this is so, and that the new day will be a better one in the End, as we bid farewell to God's messenger, Kohoutek, and its coming crises! Amen?" (2:2237). In a third tract, Berg reviewed a series of recent natural disasters, solar flare-ups, UFO reports, and astrological projections and concluded: "SURELY THIS SHOULD BE ENOUGH TO CONVINCE YOU, along with the events you are now experiencing that this comet does mean something, has already had calamitous effects upon us and portends even worse!" (2:2277). Even after Kohoutek failed to light the night skies, Berg stuck to his apocalyptic theme, insisting that "we can see its effects everywhere. It seems like the world's exploding!" More importantly, however, he exclaimed that a significant aspect of the comet was that it served "AS A WARNING TO THE WORLD" sent by God. Interpreting the comet in this prophetic manner, "the Lord didn't even have to let the comet appear! HE HAS WARNED THE WORLD BY OUR WORDS!" (2:2355) As God's apocalyptic prophets on earth, the Children of God (or so its leader pronounced) had fulfilled a cosmic mission.

Disappointment about a comet also played a small role in the millenarian fervor of the Divine Light Mission. Apparently many premies expected a comet to blaze across the sky above Houston, Texas, during the organization's Millennium '73 festival in early November 1973. It was to have been "the new star of Bethlehem" above their messianic master, Maharaj Ji (Haines 1973–74, 8). The event's organizing committee announced that the festival's "impact will last a thousand years. And it will change the world" (Van Ness

1973). Expectations among believers were high that the guru would unveil "his blueprints for the realization of World Peace" (Woyce 1973, 4). Part of his blueprints involved the construction of a divine city, and promoters of Millennium '73 stated that details of the plan would be made public at the event (Blau 1973; see also Collier 1978, 177–78). Because space aliens were among the expected guests at the three-day extravaganza, organizers provided a landing area for a flying saucer in the parking lot of the Houston Astrodome (Morgan 1973, 90; Haines 1973–74, 8; Collier 1978, 157, 177, 178).

At the event, a premie architect described the eagerly awaited "Divine City" utopia, which journalist Ted Morgan summarized for his readers in the *New York Times Magazine*:

> It will run on solar energy, and the basic building unit will be a hexagonal plastic shell. Gas propelled vehicles will be banned, and public transportation will consist of computerized monorails and duorails with detachable cars that take you to your building elevator. Simple medical diagnosis will be available by telephone; goods will arrive in your apartment by pneumatic tube; birth control will be by pineal gland cutoff; and teaching machines will teach you four languages in five weeks by tuning in on your alpha waves. Every need has been foreseen, from a place to make movies called Holywood to a toothbrush with toothpaste in the handle. (Morgan 1973, 104)

Morgan reported that the DLM was considering the Blue Ridge Mountains as a possible site location, although a later source suggested an area near Santa Barbara, California (see Snell 1974, 50–51). The city's projected location matters little, however, because Millennium '73 so demoralized and financially burdened the DLM that the entire organization went into decline (Downton 1979, 6, 188, 190).[3] The DLM's fantasies about world peace and a divine city were religiously driven utopianism among politically frustrated

---

3. As Downton discusses, I am aware that organizational and family disputes also contributed to DLM's decline.

and profoundly alienated youth. Having been forced out of the political process, these adherents retreated into a "golden age" of their dreams.[4]

Sexism and Patriarchy

Were any of these utopias to have been realized, women would have fared poorly in them. Indeed, as a group, women usually were among the casualties resulting from the generation's withdrawal into authoritarian religious inner-absorption. Women suffered because of the new religions' retreat into religiously sanctified patriarchalism and resultant discrimination—patriarchalism that exceeded what they likely would have experienced within the dominant culture, curtailing the kind of discussion about gender issues that was beginning to take place within politically attuned segments of the counterculture. With the possible exception of a few groups such as Scientology, the heterodox religious groups in the early 1970s were extremely sexist (Culpepper 1978, 220–21; see also Jacobs 1984). If involvement by former activists in various alternative religions partially served to dissipate the Movement's political energies, it also served to fragment the growing awareness of gender equality issues that were at the heart of the women's movement.

In a study of sex roles in American communes, Jon Wagner distinguished between "corporate" and "noncorporate" communes, concluding that "the evidence for equality in contemporary corporate communes is extremely weak" (1982, 34). Example after example revealed "a clear-cut distinction between male and female roles, and all possess, in some measure, an explicit ideology of female subordination." Although examples do exist of egalitarian and even matriarchal communes, "many of today's 'successful' communes have adopted more, not less, rigidity and inequality than is present in the mainstream society" (36–39; see also Jacobs 1989, 64–70). Ironically, the sexism of communes did not deter some socially conscious women from joining them. For example, the leftist feminist writer Sally Kempton became a fol-

---

4. I take the phrase "golden age" from comments that a premie made to a reporter: "A golden age is dawning. . . . It won't be long until 50,000 people a day a[re] receiving the Knowledge. Guru Maharaj-ji has the power to turn on anybody he wants to" (McAfee 1973, 4).

lower of Swami Muktananda despite his traditional and conservative attitudes toward women (Kempton 1970, 1976; see also Kopkind 1973, 47).

In particular, the Indian-based religions had clearly defined, power-differentiated gender roles, and they reinforced these gender roles with traditional patriarchal assumptions from the host countries. The rhetoric that the groups used to justify these gender distinctions contained imagery that group leaders brought with them from India, but occasionally their rhetoric borrowed phrases directly from the women's movement.

ISKCON—the Hare Krishnas—is the best example of a popular religious group from the early 1970s whose attitudes regarding women directly reflected the traditionalist, non-Western background of its leader. An early researcher on ISKCON realized that "the Vedic position on women . . . relegates the women completely to the charge of men. . . . In the American as[h]rama [spiritual community] the women are under the care of their god-brothers (ISKCON males) until they marry . . . ISKCON women are discouraged from doing anything on their own, so they cannot even walk out of the temple without permission. . . . Ideally, the [married] woman must be completely submissive and a constant servant to her husband" (Daner 1976, 67–68). Prabhupāda himself believed and imported these Vedic ideas, writing to one of his important male disciples that "women are looking for husbands because they feel unprotected" (Prabhupāda 1987, 4:2243 [letter no. 73–2–9]) and announcing in 1975 that women "assist men. They are not as equally intelligent as men" because, he insisted, "the brains of men are 64 ounces. The brains of women are only 36 ounces" (Prabhupāda, quoted in Soll 1975). Demeaning and sexist attitudes such as these may help to explain why (in 1972) men outnumbered women in the organization by a ratio of about two to one (Daner 1976, 68; see also Palmer 1994, 239). An article in Atlanta's alternative press specifically addressed ISKCON's sexism, and the reporter's conclusions were not favorable either to the devotees or to their leader. When Prabhupāda landed at the local airport, reporter Barbara Joye found time during her coverage of the event to enquire, "[H]ow do the women feel about reliving ancient Indian male supremacist culture in the service of God? [One woman replied,] 'We like it! Women are less intelligent than men. So the Spiritual Master teaches the men and they teach us.' " Joye was not impressed, concluding that "for the moment, the rest of us will just have to write them off along with the heroin addicts, Jesus freaks, and the whole straight world of convinced male supremacists" (1971, 6).

One may wonder why there were any female ISKCON members at all, given their extreme (by most North American standards) and obligatory subservience to Krishna men. For some women, however, part of the group's attraction resided in that very subservience. One researcher who wrestled with the issue of why women joined such a sexist religious group concluded that "social movements like ISKCON . . . offer a message extolling the virtues of traditional, private feminine roles" at a time in cultural history when feminists increasingly were challenging those roles. Although ISKCON's lifestyle "may have little or no appeal for many contemporary women, [it] nevertheless provides a traditionalist solution to the marginality faced by women in modern industrial society" (Rochford 1985, 130, 135; see also 126–32; Palmer 1994, 239).

In comparison to ISKCON, the Divine Light Mission's conceptions of women's roles were less rigidly defined, but the organization still thought of women's contributions largely in the context of chores involving housekeeping, motherhood, and selfless devotion to others. For example, when Maharaj Ji's mother, Mata Ji, spoke about women's roles in February 1974, she stressed women's centrality in the family:

> The life of a woman is like a lamp. A lamp burns itself and gives light to everyone. They have so many troubles and difficulties, but always give light to others. In the same way, a mother suffers a lot for the sake of her children. Her whole life is devoted to her husband and children and the family. She bears all the difficulties, faces all the troubles, and thus she becomes great. She spreads light throughout the family, the society, and brings the world into light by her greatness, by her own spiritual upliftment. (Mata Ji 1974, 22)

Directed to selflessly "spread light" into the world through devotion to their husbands and children, women were discouraged if not prohibited from developing talents and skills in roles outside the traditional family setting. Not surprisingly, when the DLM organization wrote its "Ashram Manual," it established the formal position of house mother, whose assignments included "doing the cooking service" and giving a "daily clean [of] the ashram from top to bottom" (DLM n.d.).

The DLM's own group for women, the Women's Spiritual Right Organization, seems to have been a service program of outreach to prisons, mental institutions, and hospitals, and it appears not to have been devoted to consciousness raising of any kind (Messer 1976, 64). Nevertheless, the DLM was sufficiently aware of the women's movement to publish an article on it in 1973, thereby implying to its members that the group was attuned to feminist issues. The article concluded by quoting a woman who stressed the value of love at the core of women's quest for fulfilment: "Women are very much wanting to be able to love everybody. But it must begin at home where the root of the problem is: self-hatred. To erase self-hatred we need self-love, love in ourselves. We need to depend on that" (Best 1973, 52). Thus, as in other publications, the DLM reified the importance of women in an affective and nurturing family role. Moreover, for members of the DLM, the way to cultivate a true self-love even in a family setting was to surrender at the feet of the person whom they believed to be the source of all love, Guru Maharaj Ji.

The role of women in 3HO during the early 1970s is complex. Women's status directly reflected the traditional Indian background of Yogi Bhajan, even though the loosely knit women's organization that he began for 3HO members in 1971 (called the Grace of God Movement) was acutely aware of the secular women's liberation. The most incisive summary of 3HO's attitudes toward women came from a doctoral student who was not a member but who had attended the special summer women's camps that Bhajan ran:

3HO participation tends to limit women's activity within the public sphere by fostering the ideal of the "graceful woman." Yogi Bhajan, viewing American women's freedoms from the perspective of his traditional Indian background, complains that American women try to imitate men, and he advocates, and idealizes, a special form of femininity. Women, he teaches, embody a basic spiritual energy *(shakti)* and are "the highest incarnation of planet earth." Women, he claims, are more intuitive, creative, and compassionate than men and have "sixteen times more patience, tolerance and endurance of pain." Moreover, women are capable of dividing their attention and maintaining awareness of a multitude of stimuli, events, and moods, while men can only concentrate on one thing at a time.

On the other hand, he says, a woman can easily become "uncentered," and overly emotional. . . . She will "lose her vastness" if she competes with men, "lowers" herself to using male tactics, manipulates others, or experiences too much "insecurity." Her psyche is easily duped by men who seek to use and control her. There is much to suggest that she must remain in her own sphere and that she will encounter nothing but trouble and suffering if she dares to step out of it. Thus her empowerment has its boundaries. (Elsberg 1988, 28–29)[5]

Despite the traditionalist strains that ran through Bhajan's opinions about women, a number of female converts to 3HO had been active in the women's movement prior to joining (93), and one 3HO member informed me that an entire women's collective of six people joined the religion in Toronto (Gurutej 1987).

3HO's appeal for some women lay in its "gender-based ideology," which provided them with a special (if unequal) status that had parallels to aspects of contemporary feminist secular ideology. Special 3HO courses, for example, aspired to raise women's self-esteem while overcoming society's negative socialization about them, resulting in women becoming aware of their own divinity. 3HO women even sponsored a candlelight vigil in 1971, parading past strip clubs in San Francisco to protest sexual exploitation (Elsberg 1988, 94–95). These activities shared similar perspectives with the secular women's movement of the day, as both 3HO and the secular movement saw themselves as challenging social activities and socialization patterns that demeaned females in relation to males.

The Grace of God Movement, however, specifically targeted the secular women's movement as one of women's oppressors, arguing that motherhood and family roles (both of which the secular movement diminished in impor-

---

5. Elsberg's analysis is more nuanced than that presented by another Ph.D. candidate—who was also 3HO member—who claimed that "women are seen as and more importantly feel themselves to be equal to men and in some ways, especially in marriage, they may experience themselves as an underlying support" (Khalsa 1982, 18).

tance) were vital areas in which women manifested their power. A 1973 article in 3HO's official publication presented the Grace of God Movement's position on women in a family setting:

> The earliest recorded history shows woman as the one to care for the home, serving her babies and preparing the home for her husband. This early record also shows man as the provider and the protector, assuring woman of food, shelter, and the security for which she longed.
>
> To this day, it really has not changed considerably from the family structure our early predecessors initiated. Woman still is the only one who can comfort her man when he comes home from the battles of the day. She is the one that inspires him through the peaceful vibration she has established in the home. . . . The home is the oasis from the struggles of the outside world and the woman is its guardian. It is her responsibility to make sure the home is pleasing and soothing to her man. . . .
>
> Making sure that his clothes are clean and crisp, a delicious meal, a soothing foot massage, the refreshing appearance of his woman, are seemingly little things. . . . However, those little services play important roles in inspiring a man, because they let him know that someone really cares about him and wants to help him by seeing to it that the little things that he cannot do by himself are done. (Kaur 1973, 28)

Given the parallels between these views and the traditional American cult of domesticity (see e.g. Cott 1993),[6] it is not surprising to see that 3HO occasionally set itself against the secular women's movement on specific points. In 1972, for example, after white-clad 3HO women marched from the Washington Monument to the White House carrying a sign that read "Woman is the Grace of God," they were pleased at a local newspaper article announcing: "WOMEN'S LIB HELD A CONSPIRACY! That's what it is, whether conscious or not it's a conspiracy to remove us further and further from our natural roles and from our fulfillment as men and women. But our GGM [Grace of God Movement] ladies are certainly putting out the vibrations to counteract all of that, for there were almost as many babies at this year's march as there were women!" ("GGM" 1972, 41). Evidently, the primacies of motherhood and of

---

6. I thank Theresa Krebs for this reference.

the family were cornerstones of 3HO's ideology concerning gender roles, for as late as 1986 a male 3HO member wrote that "the woman's liberation movement is right. Our women need to be liberated from our culture and their negative past. But the liberation they need is not [to] an equalization of sexes but to a realization of their inner, timeless truth. The greatest self-redemption possible for the American woman is the realization, 'I am the grace of God' " (Khalsa 1986, 9). In essence, confrontation with political and social institutions that perpetuate gender inequalities was of little importance when seen against the presumed value gained by improving the self to the point that it realizes "inner, timeless truth." 3HO women had adopted the pervasive cultural pattern more typical of the nineteenth century than of the twentieth.

By far the most manipulative use of feminist rhetoric against women occurred in the Children of God. Its leader, David Berg, specifically appropriated the language and images of women's liberation in a manner that subjected women to numerous pregnancies, traditionalistic family roles, subservience to men, prostitution, physical violence, and general sexual exploitation (see Kent 1994b). The sexual exploitation of COG women resulted from Berg's gradual imposition of antinomian doctrines within the group, which involved increasing emphasis on the value and importance of sexual contact among members and with nonmembers—in all cases without benefit of birth control.[7] Berg himself seemed fixated on women's breasts, even writing a poem about them that ran to almost three hundred lines (Berg 1976b, 1363–66). His letter to followers entitled "Revolutionary Women" concentrated almost exclusively on how women should make themselves sexually attractive to men:

> 3. ON THE WHOLE, A WOMAN SHOULD WEAR AS LITTLE CLOTHING AS POS-SIBLE, so as to both partially reveal and yet at the same time partially and provocatively conceal her natural beauty and charm. The revealment arouses his interest and admiration and enjoyment, but at the same time the partial

---

7. "GOD IS OBVIOUSLY DIAMETRICALLY OPPOSED TO ANY FORM OF BIRTH CONTROL whatsoever, even this so-called 'natural' method, which apparently He considered very unnatural, selfish, and even sacrilegious!" (Berg 1976b, 1339).

concealment of certain parts also arouses his curiosity and desire to know the
unknown, which helps to hold his interest with the hopes that he may catch
some otherwise forbidden glimpse of something he hasn't seen before—or at
least he hasn't seen that particular one before! (1317)

In essence, Berg took the secular image of revolutionary women engaged in
political and social struggle and transformed it into an image of women struggling to enhance their sexual allure. Thus, when a previously supportive
mother of a female follower wrote to Berg with concerns about his increasingly sexualized teachings, Berg responded with the advice, "COME ON MA!
BURN YOUR BRA! BE LIBERATED TONIGHT!" (Berg 1976b, 1362).[8] The liberation that he had in mind was strictly sexual—one that would free his flock of
sexual restraints even as it potentially exposed them to sexually transmitted
diseases and the women to unwanted pregnancies. Berg, meanwhile,
"thank[ed] God for the sexual liberation movement [because i]t is beginning
to relieve us from some of our former taboos and inhibitions and abnormal
guilt complexes and frustrations of the past" (Berg 1976b, 1335). Little
doubt exists concerning which sex benefitted most from this sort of liberation.
The sexism within the COG was extreme, but many other Jesus movement
groups insisted that women were to be submissive to men (Harder 1974,
345). These groups and communes followed biblical passages that demanded
female subservience,[9] and they established a rigid hierarchy of male domination. Their ideology was diametrically opposed to that of the women's liberation movement, and they knew it. For example, one Jesus movement
newspaper carried a snide rebuff to women's liberation in a 1972 article: "The
thing with the radical feminists is that they're not satisfied with being equal
with their husbands—to be under his arm and to be protected and near his
heart to be beloved. The new breed is the Woman's Lip [sic] Movement
shooting off at the mouth for headship to rule over all male chauvinist pigs.

8. The association between radical feminism and bra burning stemmed from protests against
the Miss America beauty pageant (a beauty contest) in Atlantic City, N.J., in September 1968.
Apparently, in an effort to attract attention to the upcoming protest event, one of the organizers
told the press that such an incident would take place. Subsequently, many media reported that the
protesters had in fact burned a bra, but apparently they had not done so (Echols 1989, 93–94).

9. Representative passages are listed in Harder, Richardson, and Simmonds 1972, 48.

What's a chauvinist pig anyhow?" (Kerby 1972, 4, quoted in Roberts and Kloss 1974, 43). Such intense hostility to the women's movement on the part of new religions such as the COG led one feminist to speculate that the Eastern and Western religious revival of the early 1970s came about because "man is simply beginning to feel his dominion shaking. He can no longer, for ecological reasons [presumably involving effective birth control], keep woman burdened with unlimited pregnancies and their results"—unless, of course, he uses religion (Fritz [1974?], 5).[10]

Sexism in the Jesus movement drew additional attention in the alternative press after a study of a large Christian commune, Shiloh House near Eugene, Oregon, appeared in the popular magazine *Psychology Today* (Harder, Richardson, and Simmonds 1972; see also Richardson, Steward, and Simmonds 1979, 66, 79, 137–41; Everett and Plowman 1973). Later the following year, *FPS* (of Ann Arbor, Michigan) specifically highlighted the sexism found in the Shiloh study. Referring to "the mountain of crap in the social relationships between men and women" in the commune, the article summed up the Movement's attitude toward Christian sexism by concluding that "it's really quite disastrous that people who are willing to work hard and build communes and economic independence latch on to repressive and stupid belief systems out of the past" ("Jesus Communes" 1973, 16).

Rhetoric, Action, and Mystical Antagonism

The hostility that *FPS* expressed toward the sexism in Shiloh's Christian commune is one of many examples of the deeply felt tension that existed between activists and mystics during the late Vietnam War era. For political radicals who continued to believe in the importance of confrontation with influential governmental and social institutions, the inward orientation of the religious groups was misguided and misdirected. Although the two parties

---

10. Worth mentioning here is Todd Gitlin's observation that "the sea change from politics to personal salvation and the cultivation of personal relations also gave men, at the turn of the decade [1969/1970], a way to cope with women's liberation" (Gitlin 1987, 427). He did not seem to have in mind, however, men's involvement in patriarchal heterodox religions when he wrote this.

shared much rhetoric and imagery, they were at odds over tactics (confrontation versus contemplation) and, especially on gender issues, over goals themselves (equality versus subservience).

In addition to the opposition that many Movement people felt toward the Jesus people's position on women, they felt a visceral uneasiness with the implications of the new Christian message. Atlanta's *Great Speckled Bird* carried an article in late 1971 on the Jesus freaks that contained standard Movement concerns about them:

> The problem is that Jesus Freakism looks so innocent. But everyone should know by now that the churches (religion), supposed protector[s] of the people, have always been the greatest oppressor. People went to the churches in need, and the churches found it easy to subvert their cause, "stay in your place and things will be better when you die." And "Blessed are the meek for they shall inherit the earth." The meek shall be the oppressed, the workers, the peasants and the slaves. They shall inherit the earth with their numbers but the bosses will tell them what they can and can't do on it. The Jesus Freak movement seems to be in those same insidious hands. (Harper 1971, 6)

Although some people in the Movement probably believed that no social and political activism existed among the Jesus people and that the religion was therefore relatively harmless (Weiner 1970, 12), others undoubtedly shared the opinion printed in Eugene, Oregon's *Augur* during summer 1970 that "in the Christian attempts to be apolitical, [there] is a subconscious aversion to the New Left/counter-cultural movement" ("Politics" 1970, 1). These leftist critics of the Jesus people probably were not surprised by the red-sackclothed COG members who picketed Movement events (including anti-war rallies, a talk by Jerry Rubin, and the Chicago Seven trial), simply to "denounce the unrepentant" (Enroth, Ericson, and Peters 1972, 34). Nor were these critics surprised when clashes broke out in April 1970 between Christian World Liberation Front members and Maoists on Berkeley's campus, which led to the torching of the nearby ROTC building and the worst riots the school had seen up until that time (Plowman 1970).

A particular aversion existed on the part of the Movement toward several of the heterodox religions, and the alternative press was not above mockery or ridicule when expressing its disdain. Atlanta's *Great Speckled Bird*, for example, snickered as it described an early 1974 rally that Moonies held in support of Nixon:

> Astride one of the sound trucks which made the Reverend's last visit so obnoxious were three figures: Abraham Lincoln, George Washington, and someone in a Nixon [m]ask claiming to be the President. Arrayed before him in the throng of about a score or so were the flags of the "free world" nations of West Germany, Switzerland, the United Kingdom, the United States, and South Korea. The whole production was quite serious. As agents moved through the thirty some odd press in attendance with soft spoken prayerful ignorance, two "marathon runners" who had just run "180 miles in support of the President" arrived, carrying in their train yet another sound truck with a three piece band. The runners immediately fell to singing and dancing (coaches should take note). ("Moon Comes Out" 1974, 10)

Later in that year, the Moonies were Nixon's "most visible supporters" during the U.S. House of Representatives Judiciary Committee hearings about Watergate:

> For three days during the Judiciary Committee's debates, three hundred and fifty crew-cut, well scrubbed acolytes [of Moon] held a public fast and prayer meeting on the steps of the Capitol, each with a sign around his neck reading, "I am praying for (a member of Congress)." They heard speeches from several of the President's most fervent congressional supporters and one day a messenger arrived with a statement from Nixon himself: "The world has always known the shrill voices of anger and frustration, but what has saved mankind even in the darkest hours of our civilization has always been the voices that are raised in prayer and a spirit of love for one another." When the fast ended, the Moonies filled Washington restaurants, stuffing down fried eggs and apple pie. And now, on Monday, August 5, [1974,] they were back in the House corridors, lobbying for love, forgiveness, and Richard Nixon. (Lukas 1988, 552–53)

Because of the Moonies' political positions (such as their support of Nixon), leftists continued their hostility toward them throughout the remainder of the decade. In September 1976, for example, "the kamikaze unit of YIP [the Youth International Party, a.k.a. the Yippies!]¹¹ staged a smoke-in [of marijuana] in the middle of a Moonie rally in Washington, D.C." ("Moon Goons" 1977).

Even in April 1980, the *Guardian* of New York City reported clashes between antidraft protesters and members of the Collegiate Association for the Research of Principles (CARP), "a new student front group for the Unification Church." In a March 22 antidraft rally in Washington, D.C., CARP members arranged themselves into "tight contingents" and "repeatedly rushed the speakers' platform . . . and propagandized the crowd through their own well-protected sound system." With concern, the article quoted Moon as saying about CARP, "Once we can control two or three universities, then we will be on the way to controlling the certification for the major professions in the U.S." (Manning 1980). In sum, the Moonies' hostility toward communism and anything that their leader perceived to be anti-American irrevocably kept the religion at odds with the political Left. Even as late as November 1983, eighteen CARP members were arrested in Washington, D.C. for attempting to block a march led by then-presidential hopeful Jesse Jackson against President Ronald Reagan's foreign policy in the Caribbean and Central America ("20,000 Protest" 1983).

Like the Unification Church, Scientology also felt the wrath of the alternative press. The *Berkeley Barb,* for example, was angrily aggressive with a boldfaced headline on its May 1970 issue: "SCIENTOLOGY SUCKS!" Apparently the paper was convinced that Scientologist Bill de Carle "has organized, believe it or not, a Committee to Abolish the Neo-American Church" (a group advocating drug use and LSD as a sacrament). As a former member

11. At a 1967 New Year's Eve party at Abbie Hoffman's apartment, Paul Krassner conceived of the catchy name "Yippies!" to represent "an organic coalition of psychedelic dropouts and political activists" who would counter the upcoming Democratic National Convention in summer 1968 (Krassner 1993, 157). The Yippies! engaged in outrageous behavior designed to capture media attention, including running a pig named Pigasus for U.S. president (168). The organization that Yippies! supposedly belonged to, the Youth International Party, also was a Krassner creation (156). The Yippies! occasionally were on the receiving end of police clubs (see Krassner 1993, 164; Gitlin 1987, 237–38).

who claimed that the Neo-American Church caused harm and suffering, de Carle allegedly suggested "using blackmail, by exposing members to police scrutiny." In mocking conclusion to the piece, the *Barb* wondered "if [de] Carle's crusade represents progress toward that state of Scientological enlightenment known as 'clear'?" (Poland 1970, 12).

A year later, in 1971, self-identified "investigative satirist" Paul Krassner grew concerned about "various groups all trying to rip off the search for consciousness." He felt that "Scientology was one of the scariest of these organizations" because, he claimed, it used an E-meter and auditing sessions to transform people into "automatons" who "could become programmed assassins" (Krassner 1993, 192). Consequently, he began researching the organization, and in the process learned about Hubbard's unanswered 1962 letter to President John Kennedy in which the Scientology leader claimed that his religion could give miraculous powers to Americans embroiled in the Cold War. When, under Kennedy's administration, the Food and Drug Administration raided the Scientology headquarters in Washington, D.C., and confiscated E-meters, Hubbard fired off another letter, this time to Attorney General Robert Kennedy, which again received no response. Robert Kennedy's assassination by Sirhan Sirhan thus gave Krassner a "satirical angle—Hubbard's motivation for programming Sirhan Sirhan to kill Bobby Kennedy would be *revenge*" (193). The scenario was fictitious, but Krassner announced in his magazine *The Realist* that he was preparing an article entitled "The Rise of Sirhan Sirhan in the Scientology Hierarchy" (see Krassner 1993, 192).[12] Shortly after the announcement appeared, Scientology served Krassner with a subpoena that accused him of "libel and conspiracy" and sued him for $750,000. Scientology eventually dropped the suit, but Krassner

12. Krassner published excerpts of Scientology's lawsuit against him in the July/August 1971 issue of *The Realist*. Among other allegations, the Scientology suit charged "that the reference to Sirhan 'was published for the purpose of exposing plaintiff to public hatred, contempt, ridicule, obliquy and did cause it to be shunned and avoided, intended to injure plaintiff in the further proselytizing of the religion of Scientology and to heap embarrassment and humiliation upon it through the distribution of the aforesaid statement throughout the United States of America and the world at large' " ("Scientology Sues" 1971).

never published the promised article—partly because he became diverted by tracking down the (actual) connection between Charlie Manson and Scientology (see Krassner 1973, 193–96).[13]

Krassner's antipathy for Scientology remained, and in late 1973 *The Realist* published a long, insightful, and very critical article about the organization, written by someone identified only as "Another Hired Stranger" (most likely a former Scientology staff member). The article's detailed analysis of Scientology's organizational structure and workings concluded by stating that "it is arrogant and high handed beyond belief, and its technology works no better than ordinary medicine. The fact that it exists at all is a sad testament to the spiritual poverty of our age, in which people can become so alienated and starved for purpose that they will attach themselves to such a cause" (Another Hired Stranger 1973, 8). Krassner, who controlled the content of *The Realist*, undoubtedly agreed with this assessment.

In the same year that Krassner had his own run-in with Scientology, 1971, another alternative press publication in Canada concluded a long article on Hubbard and Scientology with the rumination: "[M]eanwhile, that fanciful, possibly mad, man moves on. Whether [Hubbard's] science-fiction dream becomes a world nightmare remains to be seen. But it is presently evident that Scientology is not the world's greatest religion, nor the world's greatest science. It may just be the world's greatest put-on" ("Scientology" 1971, 17). In the same scornful vein, the *Green Revolution* simply referred to a number of circulating gurus in the early 1970s as "spiritual con men" ("Illusions" 1974, 14).

High upon the Movement's list of "spiritual con men"—or in this case, boys—was Guru Maharaj Ji. Caricatured in the *Ann Arbor Sun* as "Fifteen-year-old Perfect Body, Satnudu Haharaz, Jr.," Maharaj Ji's ownership of two Lear jets and three Rolls Royces led Madison, Wisconsin's *Free For All* to label

---

13. Manson "learned about" Scientology while he was in prison, and one study of him concluded that "Manson picked up a fair number of Scientology phrases, neologisms, and practices which he put to his own use when he began to reorganize the minds of his young followers" (Sanders 1971, 29; see also 30; Bugliosi and Gentry 1974, 237). Krassner (1993, 193) indicated that Manson had an E-Meter on the ranch where he lived with his followers in the California desert.

him "Guru Maha Ripoff" (see Haines 1973–174, 8; "Guru Maha Ripoff" 1973, 18).[14] An especially vitriolic attack against Maharaj Ji and premie Rennie Davis appeared in an anarchist magazine in Tucson, Arizona, which spoke about the "hocus-pocus artists" who "are the direct descendants of the carnival rip-off snake-oil sellers and other mountebanks. . . . Some, like two-ton butterball boy 'avatar' Guru Mararaji-Gee-whiz, even have the effrontery to state that since they are 'God' themselves, they deserve to ride in Rolls Royce automobiles and live like kings". . . . The "very vocal barker" for the guru was Davis himself, who "enjoys an extension of his time in the limelight and his role of apologist for the Gooroo and his various enterprises. Some people have an insatiable need for power trips and publicity and the more absurd the proposition, the more challenging their ability to rationalize their involvement and explain it. Anything so long as they are at or near the center of vast attention" (McNamara 1974, 6–7).

Other articles were critical of him in a more ominous tone, as they spoke about the fascism or Nazism that reporters felt within his organization. After noting that the "Guru's pig [i.e., police] force" bore the Orwellian "newspeak" title "World Peace Corps," *Ann Arbor Sun* reporter Steve Haines indicated that, at Millennium '73, "15,000 gurunoids—shouting their praise of the boy-god Groomraji with their arms high in the air—sound just like the Nuremburg [sic] rally flicks of the '30s that used to chill my spine in college" (Haines 1973–74, 9).[15] Similarly, an *Augur* reporter confessed that "his followers alarmed me. I was frightened by the total abdication of self-direction, free will, and thought that they displayed. Like automatons they hook into a chant started by a leader and end with their arms shooting upwards in salute" (Massoglia 1974, 7). A few days after a reporter from Detroit's underground newspaper *Fifth Estate* took inspiration from the Yippies and "pie-killed"

14. Also worth mentioning is that customs agents detained Maharaj Ji at the New Delhi airport in 1972, and they discovered that he was carrying "approximately $100,000 in money, watches and jewels, including diamond rings and a pearl necklace" (Morris 1972).

15. As another example of the guru's "newspeak," I also should note that a 1970 discourse that the twelve-year-old Maharaj Ji allegedly gave about his bringing peace to the world came to be known among his followers as the "Peace Bomb" ("History" 1973, 12). For other examples of critics equating the crowd behavior of premies with Nazism, see Van Ness 1973.

Guru Maharaj Ji, two irate premies shattered the writer's skull with what probably was a blackjack (see Kelley 1973c, 1974b).

In early 1979, writer Peter Marin reproduced a long excerpt from "a good friend of mine, a poet who has always been torn between radical politics and mysticism," and who also was about to leave the Divine Light Mission organization. Marin let his unnamed friend reflect upon the nature of ashram life as a premie in service to "the Lord of the Universe":

> The decision in me to hang it up is the one bright light within me for the time being. Because what is actually the case is that I've lived very much the lifestyle of 1984. Or of Mao's China—or of Hitler's Germany. Imagine for a moment a situation where every single moment of your day is programmed. You begin with exercise, then meditation, then a communal meal. Then the service (the work each member does). . . . You work six days a week, nine to six—then come home to dinner and then go to two hours of spiritual discourse, then meditate. There is no leisure. It is always a group consciousness. You discuss nothing that isn't directly related to "the knowledge." You are censured if you discuss any topics of the world. And, of course, there is always the constant focus on the spiritual leader.

Marin's friend continued by asking, rhetorically:

> What is the payoff? Love. You are allowed access to a real experience of transcendence. There is a great emotional tie to your Guru—your Guru, being the center stage of everything you do, becomes omnipresent. Everything is ascribed to him. He is positively supernatural after a while. Any normal form of causal thinking breaks down. The ordinary world with its laws and orders is proscribed. It is an "illusion." It is an absolutely foolproof system. Better than Mao, because it delivers a closer-knit cohesiveness than collective criticism and the red book. (Marin 1979, 43–44)[16]

16. The "red book" is a reference to the red-covered *Quotations from Chairman Mao Tse-Tung,* which was distributed widely in China and elsewhere during the Cultural Revolution. For an additional criticism of ashram life, see Schafer 1973.

By the end of the 1970s, Marin's friend realized that he had been living within the boundaries of extremist religious constraints, and he could do it no longer.[17]

Earlier in the decade, several reporters also noted the fascist elements in the new religious groups. Writing in Toronto's *Alternative to Alienation*, Bill Holloway observed that "in spiritual groups, we can find the same forms of the authoritarian personality seen in Nazism: the ardent supporters who have found a solution to their ineffectiveness, the followers who would rather join than be alone, and the leaders and sub-leaders who exert control and use invalidation" (Holloway 1976, 20). Louise Billotte, in a piece that initially appeared in the *Berkeley Barb*, realized that "absolute faith in the guru does lead to fascistic manipulation. The best (but not only) case in point are the Moonies, whose religious needs are being exploited by an obvious and blatant political organization. Leftists are also by and large right [i.e. correct] when they argue that religious faith is often an excuse not to deal with the most pressing and difficult social problems" (Billotte 1978, 5). Scientology received similar scrutiny. Once again a Toronto alternative press publication summarized the issues: "Scientology guarantees freedom to its members but domination by the Ethics Officer is so rigid that an ex-Scientologist called his experience 'like Orwell's *1984* arriving 20 years ahead of time.' Thought control during auditing with an E-[m]eter is total. He said, 'They keep asking you the same question over and over again until you tell them what they want to hear' " ("Scientology" 1971, 17). In this view, Scientology was a system of subjugation that used, in Orwellian fashion, the language of freedom.

Beat writer William Burroughs also held the view that Scientology shared vital traits with fascist movements. As an ardent and trained Scientologist with considerable reputation in literary and artistic circles, Burroughs spoke favorably about many Scientology concepts in the early 1970s (Atack 1990, 178; Miles 1992, 172–173, 180, 191; Morgan 1988, 439–44). He was impressed, for example, with Hubbard's claim that negative charges called "engrams" lodged in a part of a person's mind (termed the "reactive mind") and could be

---

17. For another example of a former premie who had become scared by group members' growing social isolation and blind devotion, see Manoff 1973.

erased through proper work on an E-meter (Burroughs and Odier 1974, 40–43, 46–47). He also believed that Hubbard had discovered that the governments of both America and Russia were experimenting with a destructive combination of pain, drugs, and hypnosis in their respective efforts to study conditions fostering human compliance (65–66).[18] Nonetheless, Burroughs also had grave reservations about many aspects of Scientology's management and organization—reservations that he feared would be overlooked by persons reading his comments about Scientology in a series of articles and interviews that were published in book form.[19] In an attempt to convey his reservations to the public, Burroughs wrote an article for the March 6, 1970, issue of the *Los Angeles Free Press* in which—after admitting that he found some of Scientology's techniques to have been "highly valuable and warrant further study and experimentation"—he clearly stated that "I am in flat disagreement with [the group's] organizational policy." Some of his disagreement stemmed from his general position that "organizational policy can only impede the advancement of knowledge. There is a basic incompatibility between any organization and freedom of thought." Specifically, Burroughs was convinced that "organizational necessities . . . have prevented Scientology

18. Hubbard apparently was incorrect in believing that the Russians had a program using "pain-drug-hypnosis" in efforts to alter people's moral codes. In 1953, CIA Director Allen Dulles indicated that the Soviet Union was battling for people's minds "on two fronts: mass indoctrination through censorship and propaganda, and individual 'brainwashing' and 'brain changing' " efforts (Scheflin and Opton 1978, 437). Despite Dulles's statement, "the CIA knew in the early 1950s that the Soviets possessed no secrets of mind control that would permit them to construct 'programmed' agents" (468). Worth noting is that Hubbard himself almost certainly was the author of a fraudulent psychopolitics/brainwashing manual that he and Scientology attributed to the Russian communists and that contained mention of "pain-drug-hypnosis" techniques designed as weapons against target populations (Corydon 1996, 107–17; Kent 2000, 52). In contrast to the almost certain absence of such a research program in the Soviet Union, the CIA operated an "extensive mind-control program . . . from the late 1940s well into the 1970s," often conducting drug experiments on unsuspecting and nonconsenting people (Scheflin and Opton 1978, 466). Because Hubbard never spoke in depth about the "pain-drug-hypnosis" experiments that he said the CIA was conducting, it seems unlikely that he actually knew of them.

19. The book was Burroughs and Odier 1974, which was originally published in 1969. Some of Burroughs's negative comments about Scientology also appeared in a *Los Angeles Free Press* review of the first edition of the book (see Strachan 1970).

from obtaining the serious consideration merited by the importance of Mr. Hubbard's discoveries. Scientologists are not prepared to accept intelligent and sometimes critical evaluation. They demand unquestioning acceptance" (Burroughs 1970, 33).

Burroughs knew about the organization's demand for unquestioning acceptance by the procedure that he himself had had to endure in order to gain access to some upper-level Scientology course material. For twenty-three hours, Burroughs underwent what Scientology calls a "Sec Check" (short for "Security Check"). Wired to a lie detector (which almost certainly was an E-meter that was being used for a non-religious purpose), he had to provide answers to (it seemed) hundreds of questions, including ones about whether he had any doubts about Scientology; whether he had "any unkind thoughts" about Hubbard; and whether he had any contacts with persons whom the organization had declared to be its enemies (called "Suppressive Persons" or "SPs"). Although he incorrectly stated that the organization had ceased giving these Security Checks, Burroughs correctly summarized Scientology's ethics system of punishments (called "Conditions") "for misdemeanors and crimes against Scientology." A "student assigned to an advanced condition must wear a dirty grey rag around his arm, may not bathe, shave or change his clothes, must remain on the premises, must perform manual work, deliver a 'paralyzing blow to the enemy,' admit his errors and petition every member of the center for forgiveness."[20] Returning to his claim that aspects of Scientology were valuable and need to be evaluated and tested, Burroughs concluded his discussion of Scientology's ethics by posing the rhetorical question, "Does Mr. Hubbard seriously expect mature scientists, artists and professional men who have distinguished themselves in their respective fields to submit to this prep school nonsense?" (Burroughs 1970, 41).

Burroughs was equally scornful of Scientology's blanket attack against psychiatry. Actually reprinting in his own article a long Scientology harangue about an international psychiatric conspiracy, Burroughs surmised that the

20. On the prevalence of Security Checks in Scientology (including the use of E-meters in this capacity), see R. Miller 1987, 239, 243–44; Atack 1990, 147, 148, 150–52, 188, 203, 298, 312. As of 1990, "the Sec Check lists of questions written by Hubbard in the 1960s remained, and are still in use" (Atack 1990, 188).

propagation of such ideas "is uneasily reminiscent of the *Protocols of [the Elders of] Zion*," an anti-Semitic forgery from earlier in the century (Burroughs 1970, 41). These diatribes, along with other "overtly fascist utterances," went against contemporary countercultural trends. Consequently, Burroughs concluded that these positions "can hardly recommend [Hubbard] to the militant students. Certainly it is time for the Scientologists to come out in plain English on one side or the other, if they expect the trust and support of young people" (33). Particularly having in mind Hubbard's denunciations of communism, Burroughs concluded this section of his article by asking, "Which side are you on, Mr. Hubbard, which side are you on?" (33; see also Burroughs and Odier 1974, 47–48).

All of these criticisms indicate that surviving members of the Movement and of the New Left could not understand how people who had struggled so fervently against (what they believed was) abusive authority could sit at their master's feet after religious conversion and execute obediently their teacher's every command. They had become co-opted by the very principles against which they had struggled. Even the free spirit Allen Ginsberg remained loyal to his spiritual mentor Trungpa after he learned of a Halloween 1975 incident in which Trungpa ordered and directed his followers to physically and sexually assault a couple who refused to participate in a drunken party that the teacher led. The man, poet W. S. Merwin, cut several assailants with broken bottles as they burst into the room he shared with another poet, Dana Naone. Trungpa's mob led the couple to their teacher, whose racist comments about Merwin (a Caucasian) elicited bitter allegations from Naone (who was Hawaiian) that he was "a Nazi." Trungpa eventually ordered his compliant guards to strip off the resistant couple's clothes. They did, by force. Only one or two people in the crowd spoke out against this violence, and no one called the police. Trungpa himself punched a man who was protesting the assaults. Several months after this event, Ginsberg received a firsthand account of it from Merwin himself.[21]

These assaults contributed to a growing number of criticisms against the

21. See Clark 1980, 23–25; Marin 1979, 51–53; Miles 1989, 466–70; Schumacher 1992, 612–15, 619. The most complete account appears in the now-scarce Investigative Party Group 1977.

Tibetan teacher concerning his heavy drinking, his houseful of maids and ser-vants, and his chauffeur-driven Mercedes Benz. Furthermore, his private guards "had a paramilitary look to them that made some people uncomfort-able. Rightfully or otherwise, the word *cult* slipped into conversations about Trungpa's Buddhist group." Ginsberg, however, "remained loyal to Trungpa" and held "steadfast in his belief that the bulk of ill will was the result of long-held misunderstandings of Buddhism, Trungpa, and Eastern thought" (Schumacher 1992, 633). To be sure, Ginsberg also had an enor-mous personal investment in Trungpa's Naropa Institute, especially its school for poets, and the downfall of the teacher almost certainly would have meant the death of the program.

In a moment of revealing anger in 1978, Ginsberg exploded at a reporter who was attempting to draw analogies between the obedient actions of Trungpa's compliant followers and the mass suicides at Jonestown:

In the middle of that scene, [for Dana] to yell "call the police"—do you re-alize how *vulgar* that was? Allen said. The wisdom of the East being un-veiled, and she's going "call the police!" I mean, shit! Fuck that shit! Strip 'em naked, break down the door! Anything—symbolically. I mentioned pri-vacy before—the entrance into Vajrayana [Buddhist path] is the abandon-ment of all privacy. And the entering on the Bodhisattva path is totally—you're saying, "I no longer have any privacy ever again." (Gins-berg's interview in Clark 1980, 60; also quoted in Schumacher 1992, 638)[22]

22. The Vajrayana school developed between the eighth and the twelfth centuries and in-volved the doctrinal claim that "if the world was non-different from Nirvana, *any* object or action could potentially be used as an entrance to ultimate reality, if the motive and method was right, using skillful means." Proponents of this perspective "were usually long-haired lay-people who lived unconventional wandering lives as crazy-sounding wizard-saints" (Harvey 1990, 134). The term *Vajrayna* translates as "thunderbolt, adamantine, or diamond vehicle" and sometimes refers to Tantric Buddhism (Harvey 1990, 135; Shaw 1994, 211n. 1). The doctrine of the Bodhisattva first appeared in early (Hinayana) Buddhism, but it attained its full development in later (Ma-hayana) traditions. Simply put, Bodhisattvas are beings who postpone their own Enlightenment in order to assist others in obtaining it (Conze 1975, 125–30).

Even though Ginsberg later deeply regretted these words and apologized to Merwin and Naone for his remarks, they nonetheless reveal an incongruity that haunted others who committed themselves to religious paths during the early 1970s. In the face of great improprieties or even small indiscretions on the part of supposedly spiritual teachers, many former activists-turned-devotees had relinquished their ability to challenge abusers of power.

Trungpa, alas, repaid Ginsberg's years of devotion by publicly criticizing the poet's protest actions during the 1960s and early 1970s. In a brief, rare mention of the 1960s' protests during a lecture in early 1982, Trungpa stated to the audience, "I don't want to play down the colorfulness of the early poems of my friend Allen Ginsberg, but when he made poetry out of his reaction to the Vietnam War and other problems that America faced, he could have been contributing to the problems" (Trungpa 1999, 121–22). Meditation rather than poetry, the guru implied, would have been a far better response.

Antagonism between activists and former-comrades-turned-converts was, at times, intense and bitter. The *Berkeley Barb*, for example, berated these converts, and then added a word of caution about them: "In the leftwing quest for spiritual rebirth, as in Left politics, we repeatedly find brothers who are driven to imitate the enemy, to become hard and tight, crewcut lifedeniers, weatherpriests, young authoritarians for freedom—ostensibly in the name of love and liberty. . . . Such people bear watching. As defectors from our scene to The Other Side, they have inside understanding of us which allows them to cause trouble if they wish to do so" (Poland 1970, 12). Strident leftist and editor Paul Krassner certainly felt that Rennie Davis was causing trouble for the Movement, and at the DLM's Millennium '73 in Houston, he challenged Davis to debate the idea "that Guru Maharaj Ji diverts young people from social responsibility to personal escape." Krassner even accused Maharaj Ji of being "either a conscious or unconscious agent of the Government, which was only too glad to see tens of thousands of its critics funneled into devotional activities" (Morgan 1973, 100).[23]

Earlier in 1973, when Krassner rocked the New Left with his suspicions

23. Apparently the debate did take place, given that a picture of Davis and Krassner sitting beside a moderator (reporter Ken Kelley of the *Berkeley Barb*) appears in the photo section of Krassner's *Confessions*. Always irreverent, Krassner played with Maharaj Ji's title as "The Perfect

that Davis himself was a CIA operative, he also repeated William Burroughs's (inaccurate) claim that Scientology had been infiltrated by the CIA and raised the possibility that the federal spy agency was behind Maharishi Mahesh Yogi's trip with the Beach Boys (Krassner 1973, 5).[24] (Suspicions about the connection between Maharishi's "implicit support of authoritarianism" and the CIA had been raised five years earlier by Allen Ginsberg [1968]). Yipster Stew Albert was kinder to Davis when he wrote him an open letter in September 1973, but he, too, was profoundly disturbed by the latter's conversion:

> Right now many Americans are feeling low, down, and impotent. They feel the politics of the 60's have failed, and that all politics must fail. So a lot of young people are looking for Christs, Babas, Swamis, and gurus to pull them out of a never ending bummer. Rennie, I wish these people would realize how much we accomplished in the 60's. It's all a matter of self-confidence, of believing ourselves, the regular flesh and bones of humanity and not the abracadabra of charlatans who want us to feel weak so they can hustle our bread and create a jet-set of Divine Millionaires.
>
> So, Rennie, I have to figure out how an old buddy of mine with whom I have smoked many joints got caught up in something so silly and inevitably dangerous. (Albert 1973, 8)

It is doubtful that Albert ever fully succeeded in understanding why Davis chose this new direction.

Davis's unswerving devotion to his guru drove an irreparable wedge between he and other masterminds of the Movement, including another friend and fellow radical, Tom Hayden:

> Listening to Rennie [recount his conversion story], I thought I was going to be ill. Here was my best friend in front of me, present in form only, his mind gone somewhere else. I believed in mystical experiences and a religious di-

Master" and told Davis that his guru was "the Perfect Masturbator." Davis did not respond to the provocation.

24. The Maharishi's 1968 tour with the Beach Boys was disastrous, with the fans "completely uninterested in hearing the Maharishi." Ticket sales were so low that "the tour was cancelled halfway through, at a loss approaching half a million dollars" (Gaines 1986, 197).

mension of life, but not prostration in front of a fifteen-year old with a taste
for Rolls-Royces. . . .

   We said good-bye that night and didn't see each other again until the
Chicago contempt retrial that October [1973], when there was a last, wild,
and tumultuous meeting of the Conspiracy defendants. We tried political argument, hard denunciation, and emotional pleading to stop Rennie's new
direction. We failed. For several years after that I couldn't spend time with
him because I was too upset. (Hayden 1988, 462–63)

Apparently, Davis convinced another friend and Conspiracy defendant, Jerry
Rubin, to visit the Millennium '73 affair, but Rubin's reaction was almost as
strong as Hayden's. As he left the Astrodome, Rubin muttered, "I see very little positive out of this. Meditation is good for you, but not if it leads to this"
(Haines 1973–74, 9).

   Already plagued by ideological divisions, the Movement now had religious factions tearing it apart. The hostility among various new religious
groups was so intense that one participant-observer lamented: "I could see a
time when we would have religious wars. These people were at each other's
throats. All their energies were being dissipated in battles between sects. A
waste" (Gortner 1974, 133). After leaving Davis at Millennium '73 and head-
ing for the parking lot, Rubin probably had to run the gauntlet of either Jesus
freaks by the dozen or Hare Krishnas by the score (McRae 1974, 4; Haines
1973–74, 9). Both groups outside were protesting against the guru inside,
with Christians calling him the "antichrist" and Krishna devotees offering premies a different path to peace. A few weeks earlier, in late October, the Krishnas had begun their campaign against the Divine Light Mission by
distributing leaflets that "denounced 15-year old Guru Maharaj Ji as a fraud, a
rascal and a small pudgy boy of questionable character" (Cunningham 1973,
8). Eventually, Maharaj Ji's World Peace Corps security force got thirty-five
Krishnas arrested, an act that colorfully illustrates how divisive religious ideology was among various groups that had drawn upon the New Left both for
personnel and for rhetoric. Not surprisingly, many leftists shared the religious
sects' negative judgements of the adolescent guru and his message, albeit for
different reasons. In a rare moment of uncoordinated mutual hostility, "an
unlikely coalition of disgruntled Hare Krishnas, Jesus-freaks, and assorted

leftists" heckled Davis during an October 1973 talk at Portland State University (Isserman 1973).[25]

Similar confrontations took place between diehard leftists and new religionists in other parts of the country. In autumn 1970, for example, "a band of Jesus people made up of members of the CWLF, the Jesus Mobilization Committee of Marin, and other [San Francisco] Bay communes, started such a row at the West Coast SDS conference that they were bodily removed from the gathering" (Nolan 1971, 25). During the two hours of protest speeches outside the July 1972 Democratic National Convention in Miami, the constant Krishna din from chanting was sufficiently loud that "one demonstrator remarked, 'Those dudes are enough to stifle a revolution' " (Delaney 1972). Similarly, members of the COG disrupted a speech by Jerry Rubin at the University of California, Santa Barbara, by pounding their wooden rods on the ground and chanting "Woe, woe, woe" (Enroth, Ericson, and Peters 1972, 34; see Wangerin 1993, 22–23). Perhaps the chant was an appropriate epithet for the dying Movement.

Mystical Conversions and Social (Dys)Functionalism

Sociologists were less critical than activists in their evaluations of the meaning and consequences of sectarian involvement in the late Vietnam War era. Given that the explosion of these groups in America and elsewhere raised the status of the sociology of religion within the sociological discipline, it may be no coincidence that many of the excesses and dangers observed by activist critics received little attention in academic publications. Rather than seeing the shortcomings of these groups, academics tended to concentrate on the ways that they functioned positively both for society and for individuals. As sociologist Thomas Robbins observed about the state of sectarian research,

considering the attention given in the late 1970s and early 1980s to agitation over the depredations of "destructive cults," it is ironic that much of the so-

25. For an additional example of Davis (this time in either New Jersey or New York) being hassled by leftists who turned his talk into "a three-ring circus of verbal confrontation," see Jorgensen 1973, 6.

ciological commentary on [new religious movements] in the early 1970s tended to highlight the "adaptive" and "integrative" consequences of particpation in [new religious movements] in terms of rehabilitating drug users and reassimilating alienated nomadic youth into conventional educational and occupational roles. (Robbins 1988, 28–29)

It is interesting to note that it was these same assimilationist qualities that steadfast activists abhorred.

Researchers identified seven areas in which the sects of the early 1970s supposedly helped to integrate young adults into society. First, many groups had drug rehabilitation programs or at least had decidedly hostile theologies about drug use. Second, many groups discouraged promiscuity among their members. Third, quite a few were politically conservative (in sharp contrast to youth culture during the previous decade). Fourth, several of the new religions developed a work ethic. Fifth, these groups "appeared to provide a kind of haven or asylum from *both* the system *and* the counterculture in which individuals could temporarily sustain the deviant *style* of the counterculture while changing their practical values and behaviors in the direction of the conventional expectations" (Robbins 1988, 29). Sixth, "many young people embark on an investigation of the new religions in an 'experimental' mode, in the sense that the group provides them with an opportunity to 'try out' new concepts of gender and the new modes of relating to the opposite sex" (Palmer 1994, 239). Seventh and finally, many of these sects supposedly narrowed gaps between members and their families and former friends.

Although each of these claims is supported by scholarship on various religions that were current in the early 1970s, dramatic examples also contradict them. More important, however, functional analyses of the religious conversions are at most only half the story. Leftists were correct in their assessment that many of the sects fostered widespread sexism and authoritarianism, but only a few scholars examined these and other negative dimensions of the new religious groups. Likewise, most research left unexplored the tension between the religious groups' wholesale condemnation of drug use and the many testimonies by experimenters from the 1960s regarding the generally positive effects of some drugs. Finally, few if any academic analysts examined the social costs to societies whose well-educated but profoundly alienated middle-class cohorts left politics and the socially conscious responsibilities that political life often involves. Alienated from the wider society, many of the nation's best and brightest people lost themselves in utopian dreams that squandered their talents and depleted their resources. Although these people can claim that their attempts to initiate massive social changes fell on deaf ears throughout much of the Vietnam War, cultural commentators also must acknowledge that their retreat into mystical religion often proved to be personally harmful and socially ineffective. Their religious efforts at orchestrating "revolution" through personal evolution failed to have any significant impact on societal inequality and imbalances in power.

Certainly some mystical religious converts such as Baba lover (now Quaker) Tom Wolfe and Harinam Singh Khalsa of 3HO have utilized their religious bases to contribute to their communities through their businesses. Indeed, 3HO's business clout in New Mexico has made the group a major political player in that state (Hunter 1992). Among other converts whom I interviewed, one had become a writer, one a consultant, one a personal development counselor, one a medical doctor, and two were lawyers. Still another interviewee, Subhananda das (Steven J. Gelberg), departed from his ideologically demanding group (he had been a Hare Krishna devotee for seventeen years) and spoke out publicly about "the offensive attitudes and discriminatory policies toward women" that he witnessed and presumably participated in as a member (Gelberg 1995, 41). Rennie Davis complicated an already unpredictable life-path when he entered into the family insurance business in the late 1970s (Greene 1977), quickly followed by work as a management consultant.

In general, though, a great many mystical converts remained devoted to spiritual masters and their teachings. Operating in the self-contained worlds of gurus, swamis, teachers, and sages, these devotees often relinquished opportunities of actively engaging (and occasionally influencing) the wider social and political world. Sometimes people never reentered that wider, secular world, remaining encapsulated for decades if not lifetimes. Moreover, sectarian religion, perhaps even more than factional politics, isolated followers in ideologically constricted doctrinal camps. Even though these people may have shared similar visions about a transformed society, they nonetheless hotly disagreed over whose godly inspiration was to provide the divine plans. Turning their backs on political confrontation while still using Movement rhetoric to explain their inner quests, activists-turned-mystics marched out of the "protest decade" and into the "me decade," the women trailing behind their men.

Treat Your Children Well

Writing in the early 1980s, Peter Clecak offered a complex and rich argument that emphasized the "thematic and ideological continuities and connections instead of the usual disjunctures" between the 1960s and the 1970s (Clecak 1983a, 5). The "central cultural theme" linking together the two decades, Clecak claimed, was "a quest for personal fulfillment, a pursuit of a free, gratified, unalienated self within one or more communities of valued others." At the same time, he realized that some communities alienated the self and curtailed freedom through their harsh and authoritarian demands. Clecak specifically singled out one group, the COG, as an exception to his central cultural theme of personal fulfillment through community, and he criticized it harshly: "[E]ven tolerant critics lose patience with those who press their exclusive views beyond the elastic bounds of civility, or worse, as in the case of such cults as the Children of God, practice legally questionable and morally unconscionable forms of psychological coercion" (6). He probably had in mind the group's practice of using its members (especially women) to raise money and to recruit members and supporters through what critics called religious prostitution.[26]

Nevertheless, Clecak might be surprised to learn that his harsh criticism of the Children of God (now called The Family) receives independent endorsement from unexpected sources, including both many former members who had converted during the late Vietnam War era and their children, now young adults. The young adults, especially, provide unique perspectives on the activities of their parents, having grown up in the alternative culture that the older generation created. This younger generation experienced the converts of the early 1970s in uniquely intimate ways—as parents, relatives, teachers, role-models, and exploiters. Consequently, they provide strong indicators about

---

26. For the account of one such religious prostitute, see Williams 1998. See also the reproduction of Berg's *Mo Letter* "Heaven's Whores?" in Van Zandt 1991, 202–7.

how best to evaluate the attempts by the converts to change the world by first transforming themselves. Regrettably, the evaluations provided by many of these young adults are damning.

On television, in court, and on the World Wide Web, young adults are informing the public about what life was like for them as children who were born or grew up in the COG during the late 1960s and early 1970s. For example, several young former COG members who posted on the website "MovingOn" (<http://www.movingon.org>) expressed intense hostility toward older adults (even the former members) who were their parents' age. These youth spoke bitterly about what they claimed were inadequate educations, beatings, emotional stresses, and sexual assaults that they and their friends experienced at the hands of adult COG caregivers. Some young adults were so angry that they posted the names of the people who they say violated them. Similar accounts of abuse against COG youth appeared in the written opinion of a British family court judge in London. Judge Alan Ward heard and read testimony from at least eleven young adults (men and women, some of whom were Americans), who spoke about a wide range of sexual assaults that they claimed to have experienced while children and teens (Ward 1995, 91–97). After reviewing extensive and diverse evidence, Judge Ward concluded, "I am totally satisfied that there was widespread sexual abuse of young children and teenagers by adult members of The Family, and that this abuse occurred to a significantly greater extent within The Family than occurred in society outside it" (111). In addition, he heard and read sufficient evidence about medical neglect that he concluded, "The Family's history leaves me with festering doubts about the organization and its order of medical priorities" (133). Educationally, the group's continued emphasis on the apocalyptic "End-time . . . is a limitation on the full development of the child" (146). Specifically writing about a COG facility in Macau designed "to bring about changes in the habits and attitudes of the teens who had reacted against the Family way of life," Justice Ward concluded that the means used against COG youth who were there "was a form of physical and mental atrocity mercilessly dished out to young, often already emotionally damaged children" (162). Regarding physical punishments, some teens received "savage beatings with paddles" (181). In essence, converts to the COG in the late Vietnam War era may have set out to transform society by preparing the world for the return of

Jesus, but instead they created a closed social environment that was physically, emotionally, and sexually dangerous for their offspring. Out of their utopian dreams, they created a dystrophic nightmare.[27]

Tragically, so did the idealists in the Hare Krishna movement. Public allegations of child abuse in Krishna facilities date back at least to 1986, when the *Los Angeles Times* carried a story about a caretaker at a Krishna child-care center who was convicted for molesting four children (Enriquez 1986; see also Franklin 1987, 32). Additional child abuse allegations trickled out over the years and several convictions occurred;[28] however, it was not until November 11, 1996, that former students from the organization's school system began speaking out collectively on their own. Opening a website entitled VOICE (Violations of ISKCON Children Exposed), an undisclosed number of former "Krishna kids" wrote an analysis of the abuses that they had suffered in the Krishna schools and printed excerpts from young people's own accounts of abuse. When discussing their parents' generation, the designers of this website realized the social and political climate in which (the now older) adults had converted: "In the 1960s," one posted essay began, "there was a certain sentiment among some of the younger population, particularly in the U.S. Many of them were protesting against the war in Vietnam and they were experiencing an overall disillusionment with some aspects of the society from which they came. They were looking for something different and something that would give them all of the answers to the questions they had" (VOICE 1996). The Krishnas' leader, Swami Prabhupāda, appeared to have provided them with such answers. As a consequence of following him, however, the early devotees "had begun to absolve themselves of any critical thinking that they might have engaged in with anyone else." Having placed their critical thinking aside, the early adult converts developed and operated schools in various places around the world (including the U.S. and Canada) in which a

27. Young former-members-turned-critics of the COG also have appeared on such television shows as NBC's "The Family–Children of God" (1993) and CBS's "The Children of the Children of God" (1998).

28. See, for example, British Columbia 1987; Gruson 1987; Harrison 1987; Hubner and Gruson 1988, 343–47, 399–400; Lieblich 1999; Rochford and Heinlein 1998; Das 1998; Raghunatha [1999?].

shocking level of child abuse took place. The website contains excerpts from accounts by young adults of beatings and punishments, sexual abuse, neglect, poor diet, privacy violations, and intimidation that they experienced and witnessed at the Krishna schools. Many of the first generation adult converts had become so subservient to Krishna leadership that the website designers felt compelled to remind them that "the perpetrator could be a friend of yours. Many of our abusers are in high and respected positions within [ISKCON]. Listen to your child, without defending the religion and the gurus." Clearly, the adult children felt that they had to educate their convert-parents about the atrocities and violence that had gone on within the Krishna organization. Soon after these disclosures, the Krishna governing body publicly acknowledged widespread abuse in its school system during the 1970s and 1980s (see Goodstein 1998; "Hare Krishnas Acknowledge" 1998; Raghunatha [1999?]).

To be sure, although such information about child abuse and related allegations is disturbing, it should not lead to blanket condemnation of the alternative religions that flourished during the early 1970s. In a large number of groups, presumably, no such crimes took place. Additionally, many adult converts to these and other alternative organizations left their new, high-demand faiths precisely *because* of concern for their children's well-being. Nevertheless, countless children in numerous groups suffered at the hands of adults who, ostensibly, were on paths of self-purification, aspiring to save the world from the abuses of the strong against the weak. Apparently, these same adults were unable to see (or, perhaps, chose to ignore) such abuses of power playing out in the very groups of which they themselves were members. While trying to save the world, the early converts to these religious groups lost much of themselves, and in the process forgot a basic lesson from the decade of the 1960s.

What they forgot from the previous decade was the importance of questioning authority—of holding people in positions of power accountable for their decisions and of ensuring that those decisions were not exploitative or based upon self-interest. As former political radicals and activists sat at the feet of gurus, swamis, and self-proclaimed enlightened masters, the new lessons that they learned about self-purity and about the importance of spiritual obedience obscured what the 1960s had taught about the importance of doubting what authority-figures told them. As disciples, converts who had railed against (what they perceived to be) political injustice sat passively as their new leaders initiated them into hierarchical social structures that were patriarchal, elitist, authoritarian, and often abusive.

Perhaps somewhere in these failed religious attempts at social transformation through personal purity lies a new lesson. In the social and political context of extraordinary frustration at a seemingly intransigent political system in the early 1970s, widespread conversion to apocalyptic religions and alternative faiths was understandable, especially because of the strong religious undercurrents in the 1960s counterculture. The religious path, however, is fraught with dangers that can harm if not destroy participants, their loved ones, and the communities in which they live. As my generation experienced, political frustration can make people desperate, and religions that feed upon people's desperation can blind their faithful followers.

Appendix

• • •

References

• • •

Index

Reexamining the Scholarship on Protesters' Religious Conversions

the wide-ranging approach to data collection that I took for this study may help to explain why my argument differs from ones offered by other researchers and scholars who have written on the late 1960s era. Several prominent sociologists and historians either downplay the politics-to-religion youth pattern or ignore the pattern entirely. Sociologists Jack Whalen and Richard Flacks, for example, scanning surveys of former activists from a variety of movements, concluded that the studies "contain no evidence that large numbers of New Left veterans have followed such paths" into " 'self-examining' religious and therapeutic communities." Whalen and Flacks (himself a former SDSer) collected life-history data from seventeen activists who were indicted for the Isla Vista, California, Bank of America bombing in 1970. After combining the data with biographical accounts by former civil rights activists such as SDSers Sharon Jeffrey and Tom Hayden (J. Miller 1987, 322–25), the sociologists concluded "that withdrawal into countercultural religious or therapeutic lifestyles in the days following the collapse of the mass movement was only a temporary resting place for many individuals who eventually resumed political commitments, albeit in less all-consuming forms" (Whalen and Flacks 1989, 291n. 5; see also 3–6; Adelson 1972, 208–9; Sale 1974, 733).

We must be careful to understand that Whalen and Flacks reached two separate but related conclusions. First, they claimed that not many activists and radicals turned to religious paths. Second, they seem to have decided that even those few activists who undertook spiritual or therapeutic quests in the early 1970s did not remain with them and most likely returned to "political commitments." This second point need not detain us, since I say very little about people's long-term life courses after their conversions to various spiritual paths. The first of these conclusions, moreover, must be taken cautiously, given that subsequent scholarship suggests that the conversion pattern of radical politics to mystical religion may have been more widespread than some initial data and surveys indicated and that Whalen and Flacks cited (1989, 3–4). Indeed, in cases like these the vagaries of data collection really matter. For example, Whalen and Flacks were unable to interview two of the activists involved in the Isla Vista bombing, one of whom they could not find and another of whom had left the country. Thus, they were unaware that one of these two activists probably was one who had joined the Children of God before his sentencing and for the next ten years remained on the run from the FBI while in the group.[1] Moreover, one of their activist informants, whom they call Kenneth Essian, was a follower of a guru called Kirpal Singh, whom they describe as "an Indian master of Sant Mat."[2] In short, at least two activists whom authorities implicated in the Isla Vista bank bombing subsequently became involved with alternative religions for lengthy periods of time.

As another example, we may consider more fully two activists whose accounts Whalen and Flacks specifically cited—Sharon Jeffrey and Tom Hayden. Jeffrey's account speaks clearly about how she "maintain[ed] an active interest in the psychological and spiritual traditions she discovered at Esalen" at the same time that she "remain[ed] an organizer" (J. Miller 1987, 322). Moreover, Hayden's more extensive autobiographical account listed activists who had been close to him and who became involved in spiritual quests (see Hayden 1988, 463–64). For example, Hayden recounted the feeling of illness that nearly overcame him as his good friend Rennie Davis shared his testimonial about converting to Guru Maharaj Ji. He then indicated that Davis "was not alone in developing an apocalyptic religious temperament," after which he outlined the spiritual journeys taken by former University of Michigan SDSer Al Haber (who "followed a strange and mystical path" leading to an immersion in biblical apocalypticism), Bob Moses of the Student Nonviolent Coordinating Committee (who under-

1. To be sure, Whalen and Flacks use pseudonyms for their activist sources, and so I cannot be absolutely certain that they missed this person. They do describe a person (whom they call Warren Newhouser) who "fled California after misdemeanor conviction in aftermath of Isla Vista riots" and who "lives under an assumed identity in rural New England" (Whalen and Flacks 1989, 19); however, the activist who converted to the COG apparently turned himself in to authorities (see Thompson 1988), which Whalen and Flacks's informant had not done.

2. The Sant Mat (Path of the Masters) is a guru tradition of spiritual transmission that adherents claim traces back hundreds of years in India. According to his followers, Kirpal Singh (1894–1974) was the first Sant (master) to personally visit the West.

took the study of Zen Buddhism), and Hayden's former wife, Casey Hayden (who helped to create the Integral Yoga Institute of San Francisco and more recently adopted "a Mayan view of 'harmonic convergence' ").[3] Although these anecdotes do not allow us to quantify the phenomenon of religious conversion, they at least alert us to the fact that some political activists were aware of the process among their friends.

Overstating the case would be as unfortunate as neglecting it. A noticeable number of radicals and activists converted to unusual religions in the 1970s, but by no means was the pattern universal. As Charles DeBenedetti has suggested (1990, 189), some people stayed with their politics despite changes in the national climate; a few even became more radical. Others entered jobs or professions that were humanistically oriented (such as teaching or social work), and yet others shifted their political energies to emerging movements concerned with feminism or with the environment (see, e.g., Sherkat and Blocker 1993). Some, of course, immersed themselves in the drug culture. Sociologist Richard Braungart (1984, 42) concluded that for the most part, in the 1970s the 1960s generation "mellowed considerably. The tightening of the international economy may have persuaded them to tone down their political activity." Thus, newly acquired mantras and prayers must be viewed as one in an array of options for those interested in toning down and mellowing out.

Widely varying patterns in people's life-directions showed up, for example, in a 1980 study conducted by Richard and Margaret Braungart, which attempted to determine "what happened to many of the radical young activists and leaders" of the 1960s. Directly pertinent to the central argument of this book, they specifically wondered whether 1960s activists and leaders had "retreat[ed] from politics into escapist pursuits such as religious cults and drugs" (Braungart and Braungart 1980, 237). After examining the lives of eighteen high-profile personalities from the 1960s, they concluded that "only a minority of former activists abandoned politics in the 1970s" (250).[4] The

3. The first Integral Yoga Institute in the U.S. was founded in 1966 by Swami Satchidananda (b. 1914); the San Francisco branch began a few years later. Satchidananda received temporary fame by his appearance at Woodstock, and among his devout followers was a popular songwriter from the 1970s, the late Carole King (Colker 1988, B5). The idea of "harmonic convergence" developed from José Argüelles's reading of the Mayan calendar, which supposedly foretold the first convergence of the planets on Aug. 16–17, 1987. This event (and subsequent ones) were supposed to facilitate the reception of "the realization of a larger, resonantly attractive force; a supersensible synthesis of mind and nature, hitherto undreamed of" (Argüelles 1987, 159).

4. The activists considered were Joan Baez, Rennie Davis, David Dellinger (considerably older than the others), John Froines, Tom Hayden, Abbie Hoffman, Staughton Lynd, Jerry

"minority" were Rennie Davis, Eldridge Cleaver, and Jerry Rubin, each having gotten involved with various religious groups or self-awareness programs that were popular in the 1970s.[5]

Worth noting about the Braungart and Braungart article is that most of the eighteen 1960s leftists whom they examined dated from early in the era. Their early political involvement in the decade may help to explain the low number of radicals-turned-religionists among their number. Similarly, James Fendrich studied fifty former activists who had taken direct political action in support of integration while attending Florida State University in 1960 and 1963. Much like the Braungarts, he concluded "that college activists of the early 1960s retain their distinctiveness as a generational unit," whose "political behavior reflects a radical commitment to political and economic changes in the United States" (Fendrich 1974, 115). Significantly, however, he added that

> it is uncertain whether later waves of student activists will demonstrate the same generational continuity. The political awakening of students in the later half of the sixties was different from the earlier idealistic reformist orientations. There are also presently available more avenues of escape from the frustration and disillusionment accompanying unsuccessful reforms, which might indicate that later activists would drop out rather than retain their radical political orientation. (115–16)

One avenue of escape that Fendrich did not mention is the focus of this study—mystical religion. A significant number of student activists went that route by the early 1970s.

Studying that route as it unfolded were sociologists Daniel Foss and Ralph Larkin. Their conceptual insights about various subcultural phases in the 1960s and early

---

Rubin, Mark Rudd, Mario Savio, Lee Weiner, Marion Barry, Stokely Carmichael, Eldridge Cleaver, Angela Davis, Jesse Jackson, Huey Newton, and Bobby Seale.

5. Braungart and Braungart (1980, 241) incorrectly say that Davis became involved with Transcendental Meditation, when in fact the group was the Divine Light Mission and its leader, Guru Maharaj Ji (whom they identify correctly). Interestingly, in another study on generational youth movements, Richard Braungart (1984, 30) indicates that the ending of the Vietnam War correlated with the appearance of "charismatic religious groups," but gives no reason for this apparent correlation. The likely reason is that former activists and radicals were converting to them in significant numbers.

1970s help clarify why researchers found small numbers of religious converts among *early* 1960s activists and radicals. In Foss and Larkin's terminology, the first subcultural phase of the era involved the *Old New Left*, whose actions predated the decade back to the 1950s (with concerns about racial integration) and extended until about 1965 (with the Free Speech Movement). The second phase saw the dominance of the *Hippies* and their lifestyle revolt from 1965 to 1967. The third phase involved the *New New Left* and dreams of social revolution from 1967 to 1969. That phase was succeeded by the *Woodstock Aquarian* phase for a brief time from 1969 to 1970 (Foss and Larkin 1976, 47–48). After this phase, however, the power redistribution Movement of the 1960s went into rapid decline: "By 1970–71 the two greatest cultural idols [John Lennon and Bob Dylan] officially declared the Movement at an end" (56). Out of this complex social and political decade emerged what Foss and Larkin called "post-Movement groups." The authors do not dwell (as I do) on the political events that contributed to their emergence, but these groups shared some characteristics with their subcultural predecessors even as they developed others that were unique: "Like their predecessors, they all believed in the inevitability of radical change; however, unlike dissident youth, they believed that social transformation could not be achieved by immediate action upon and conflict with objective social reality, but must be brought about by the attainment of spiritual perfection by the members and the diffusion of spiritual perfection to broad sectors of the population" (59). By 1974, this subcultural, post-Movement phase was itself in rapid decline (61), but in its brief heyday it experienced a major influx of "many former [1960s] Movement participants" (157). For these former participants, the post-Movement phase provided "alternatives to the meaningless participation in a dying Movement and to the meaninglessness of a middle class existence" (275).

The subcultural phases that Foss and Larkin identified help to explain the dilemma of researchers who examine the extent to which 1960s activists and radicals converted to mystical religious traditions. Persons involved with the relatively successful protests early in the era were not as likely to have experienced the frustration, anguish, and despair that their younger cohort members encountered a few years later. As writer Nicholas Lemann (b. 1954) revealed, "I am not someone to whom the idea that our country and its dominant institutions were deeply and fundamentally flawed was a dramatic revelation. It was what I grew up on" (1981, 210). In short, Fendrich's comments were correct about there being somewhat different social and cultural experiences and reactions among broadly defined generations. As Foss and Larkin themselves discovered about the religious and mystical groups that my study examines, "beginning in about 1973, post-Movement groups began to attract younger members who had not been participants in the youth movement" of 1960s social protest (Foss and Larkin 1979, 275). While a number of early activists made religious pilgrimages in the early-to-mid 1960s (and I managed to track down a few of them), the people most likely to have followed this conversion path were ones who had been intimately involved with the protests at the end of that frustrating decade.

By working through networks of current and former members of several religious groups that were prominent in the late 1960s and early 1970s, I located and interviewed persons who had been active in the civil rights movement, the Free Speech Movement, various antiwar activities, feminism, and the University of Michigan SDS chapter.[6] It is always difficult to extrapolate from a few examples, but almost all of the people whom I interviewed spoke of other former Movement people whom they knew who also had gone through similar spiritual pilgrimages. To be sure, some longitudinal surveys allow researchers to conclude (as did Whalen and Flacks) that not many of the converts *stayed* exclusively in the religious perspectives that they adopted in the early 1970s, but researchers must not overlook the fact that these conversions occurred in the first place.

Regrettably, even some sociologists of religion ignore the political backdrop to the religious conversions of the early 1970s. During this period, specialists in the study of religion were immensely interested in the groups into which youth were converting, but they knew little about most of them. Consequently, much early research involved scholars' attempts merely to identify doctrines, beliefs, and practices, and then to locate this body of material within existing sociological theory. This focus on the religious groups came at the expense of paying equal attention to the converts themselves, thus allowing some scholars to ignore or to deny the widespread conversions of activists and radicals to alternative religions. Sociologist of religion Thomas Robbins, for example, summarized the research of James Beckford (who wrote about the Moonies) and J. Stillson Judah (who wrote about the Hare Krishnas) by stating that members of these groups "were not politically radical or seriously alienated before recruitment" (Robbins 1988, 30). The evidence, however, is not quite so clear. Judah examined the results from sixty-three questionnaires (plus an undetermined number of interviews)

6. Apparently, few of the individuals with whom I made contact had been included in the surveys that Whalen and Flacks had examined, a research inadequacy that supported their conclusion that no evidence existed about large numbers of New Left participants joining alternative religions. Interestingly, Flacks himself knew Al Haber from SDS both at the University of Michigan and on a national level.

and from them concluded that "few [Krishna converts] were political activists" (Judah 1974, 117), but he also stated that "the Vietnam war was probably the most significant factor in driving the devotees [of Krishna] from the society of the establishment to the counterculture" (115). Judah did not state how many converts *had* been activists, nor did he specify when he conducted the survey. Indeed, in a subsequent article (that Robbins did not cite) in which Judah reported the findings of "a survey of members of the Hare Krishna movement living in temples along the Pacific Coast in 1969 and 1970," he stated unequivocally that significant numbers of Krishna members *had* participated in a variety of social protests prior to their conversions (Judah 1982, 13). Along the same lines, Judah reported that his survey of sixteen Unification Church centers in 1976 (which he realized was after the heyday of political dissent) indicated that "Unification Church members had still strongly protested against the establishment" (15). Once again, close examination of the sociological evidence *against* arguments that many activists converted to alternative religions is far less convincing than might first appear.

Even when we examine the presentations of scholars who believe that large-scale conversions of activists and radicals to religion *did* take place in the early 1970s, no definitive agreement exists about *why* this process occurred. Everyone who studies this era realizes how alienated many American youth were from the country's major social and political institutions, but researchers incorporate this realization into very different explanatory models. Among the most prominent interpretation of the process is the "crisis of meaning" or "moral crisis" perspective that sociologist of religion Robert Bellah outlined and which his student Steven Tipton elaborated and expanded in detail.

The "crisis of meaning" perspective explained the shift from politics to religion by viewing conversions as attempts to resolve individual moral crises that reflected widespread cultural trials and malaise. Bellah laid the intellectual background for this interpretation in his influential essay on American civil religion (originally published in *Daedalus* in 1967), in which he argued that in the late 1960s the United States was in the third great time of trial in its history. (The first two had involved the question of independence at the time of the American Revolution and the question of slavery during the Civil War era.) This "third great problem" that the American nation faced was one "of responsible action in a revolutionary world. . . . A successful negotiation of this third time of trial—the attainment of some kind of viable and coherent world order— would precipitate a major new set of symbolic forms" (Bellah 1974, 38). The new form of civil religion that would successfully reconcile the nation during this crisis "obviously would draw on religious traditions beyond the sphere of Biblical religion alone" (40). Bellah's articulate protégé, Steven Tipton, developed these ideas in what became the most prominent of the "1960s legacy" interpretations of the 1970s.

First, Tipton incorporated Bellah's assumption that the nation found itself in a time of crisis during the late 1960s. Second, he accepted Bellah's prediction that new attempts to "reconcile the nation" would involve some religious traditions that were nonbiblical, and likely non-Western. Through analyses of generational life-crises that youth experienced at the end of the 1960s, Tipton then examined the moral trauma of the period that Bellah had identified. His fundamental assertion was that "youth of the sixties have joined alternative religious movements of the seventies and eighties basically . . . to make moral sense of their lives" (Tipton 1982b, 185; see also Tipton 1982a, xiii). In an argument that resonated with the perspective of his mentor, Tipton claimed that American culture was in crisis by the early 1970s, and people gained a sense of moral purpose amidst this crisis by joining or participating in new religious movements (Tipton 1982b, 187). Conversion, therefore, was youth's attempt to solve individual moral crises that reflected larger crises in the culture. Appropriately, Bellah wrote the foreword to Tipton's seminal book *Getting Saved From the Sixties* (1982).

Despite the close sharing of ideas between these two colleagues and friends, they expressed different views on the extent of former activists' conversions in the early 1970s. In the late 1970s, Bellah deduced from his observations in the San Francisco Bay area:

> Far more of those involved in the cataclysmic events of 1968 to 1970 have turned to quiet politics or withdrawn from politics altogether than have become hypermilitant. Indeed, the burned-out activist was almost as common in the early 1970s as the burned-out drug user. For many of them "getting my head together" became the first priority. Every one of the new religious groups, from the Zen Center to the Christian World Liberation Front, has had its share of former activists for whom the group has helped to provide a new and more coherent personal identity. (Bellah 1976, 87; see also Wuthnow 1976, 276–78)

Bellah, therefore, had no doubt that the conversion pattern occurred. Tipton, in his work, would downplay the presence of former activists in the ranks of the new religions.

Once again, however, Tipton's actual evidence is in some tension with his own conclusions. For example, he did find some evidence that former activists and radicals had become involved in Zen Buddhism. Of ten Zen students that he had interviewed in 1976, "six had been active in political protest" (Tipton 1982a, 322n. 21) Indeed, one incident that Tipton recounted about the Zen students suggests that antiwar sentiment was widespread among them even after their conversions. In an interview, a Zen practitioner recounted how "a lot of people" studying under a particular roshi (Zen master) "kept asking him about the war and pacifism, pressing the point, 'What does he really think, is he against war or isn't he? What about this big peace demonstration next week? Should we go to it or not? What should we do?' " Presumably, the students would have gone to the demonstration had their roshi indicated the appropriateness of doing so, but instead he jumped up and beat a student with a stick as he roared, "Dreamer! Dreamer! What are you dreaming about?" The student recounting the story interpreted this outbreak to mean that "here we were against the Vietnam war but our minds were in the same state that produces war in the first place." He concluded by commenting that "that [outburst] was a big event for me because it shifted my awareness of where the real problem was from something outside to something not outside or inside; something that doesn't exclude myself or any other individual person" (168–169). In short, Tipton found evidence of the very shift in interpretation and action that my study explores. This evidence likely is strengthened by Tipton's citation of additional data about twenty-five students whom researcher David Wise had interviewed at the San Francisco Zen Center in 1970, of whom "one-fifth had participated actively in radical politics, and two-fifths peripherally" (323n. 21).

To be sure, Tipton was not quite able to replicate this same high level of political interest in his interviews with persons involved in another group, est (Erhard Seminars Training): of twenty est participants (called "graduates"), "nine had been in political demonstrations" (Tipton 1982a, 331n. 11).[7] Tipton specifically provided what he felt was the meaning that should be attached to these figures by clarifying that "many youths sympathized with political activists, some accepted radical diagnoses of what went wrong, why, and how it was to be changed. But virtually none committed themselves to enacting any such programs of change" (Tipton 1982a, 220). Tipton elaborated upon his findings in a lengthy footnote:

7. Erhard Seminars Training (est) began on Sept. 13, 1971, when Werner Erhard (formerly Jack Rosenberg) launched his program of personal development and transformation (Kornbluth 1976, 45). It ran until January 1985, when the founder began a new transformational program called the Forum. For a critical analysis of Erhard and his programs, see Pressman 1993. I cannot be certain of the dates of Tipton's interviews, but they appear to have been in 1978 (the year in which he calculated the average age of his est interviewees).

If we define the committed political activist by such indicators as leading or regularly participating in radical political activity, being arrested for so doing, belonging to a radical organization, mastering its formal ideology, resisting the draft or filing for CO [conscientious objector] status, then none of those formally interviewed could be classified as a committed activist. Of thirty additional [est] graduates informally interviewed, only one, an early sixties civil-rights worker and CORE member now turned massage teacher, would qualify, the case of est graduate Jerry Rubin notwithstanding. Seventeen of twenty interviewees reported sympathizing during the sixties with the view that American society seemed fundamentally wrong; only four of the seventeen accepted a full-blown radical political analysis of what was wrong, and none acted on it. (340n. 81)

Tipton's findings suggest that some of the psychotherapeutic groups that flourished in the 1970s drew members who may have been sympathetic to the political counterculture but remained outside its activist or radical traditions. Moreover, he specifically argued against viewing the groups that he studied as having diverted or siphoned off political activism within the 1960s generation: "To depict alternative religions as simply siphoning off would-be political activists or 'cooling out' the politically disaffected oversimplifies the peculiar relationship of political concern and disillusionment in these sixties youth, and, they would say, it oversimplifies the nature of social change itself" (244).

Without entering into the continuing debate about the "siphoning off" hypothesis, Tipton's conclusions about est and Zen must be regarded with caution. Here, as in many places in this scholarship, things are not as clear as they may seem. It is not enough to point out that Tipton appears to have carried out his interviews with est graduates rather late in the decade (probably in 1978) and so may have missed early participants whose backgrounds included political action. More important, est was not a religious organization but rather a psychotherapeutic one. Thus, its ideology did not appropriate political and cultural imagery into apocalyptic visions, as did some of the groups that I examine in this study. Admittedly, Zen Buddhism also was not apocalyptic, but Buddhism (broadly defined) had acquired an image in the 1960s as a religious tradition committed to peace and (following its Vietnamese example) opposed to the war.[8] It was a likely tradition to attract Western interest, and already had a countercul-

8. In Vietnam in 1963, Buddhist protest against the Catholic-favoring Diem regime led to the overthrow of the government; see Sheehan 1971, 158–233 (relevant sections are reprinted in

tural image within American society that dated back to the Beat generation. For these and other reasons, then, the previous scholarship on the relationships between religion and political activism in the early 1970s must be seen as posing more questions than it answers.

Gettleman 1985, 214–29). Throughout later periods of the war, Vietnamese Buddhist leaders called for a neutral "third solution" that deplored the violence on both sides and advocated a political coalition of Buddhists and noncommunist nationalists to rule the country. Some American peace groups supported this position. For a brief discussion, see DeBenedetti 1990, 189–190, 315.

References

Aagaard, Perille. 1978. The Children of God's Attitude Towards Politics. *Up-Date* 2, no. 1: 31–37.

Adelson, Alan. 1972. *SDS*. New York: Scribner's.

Adkins, Sharon. 1972. Prophets of Organized Medicine. *Los Angeles Free Press,* July 14, sec. 1.

Advanced Organization of the Church of Scientology. 1973a. The Meaning of the Way. *Advance!* no. 18: 5–11.

———. 1973b. The Vedic Hymns. *Advance!* no. 21: 6–8, 25–26.

———. 1974a. The Message of the Buddha. *Advance!* no. 23: 4–9, 20–22.

———. 1974b. Jataka (Birth Stories). *Advance!* no. 26: 3–5.

———. 1974c. A 2,500 Year Old Prophecy. *Advance!* no. 27: 4–5.

Albert, Judith Clavir, and Stewart Edward Albert, eds. 1984. *The Sixties Papers: Documents of a Rebellious Decade.* New York: Praeger.

Albert, Stewart Edward. 1973. Dear Rennie. *All You Can Eat* Sept.: 8, 38.

Ali, Tariq and Susan Watkins. 1998. *1968: Marching in the Streets.* New York: The Free Press.

Alsop, Stuart. 1970a. They Can't Go Home Again. *Newsweek,* July 20, 88.

———. 1970b. The Need to Hate. *Newsweek,* July 27, 80.

Amarendra/David Leiberman. 1988. Interview by author. Los Angeles/Culver City, Calif., Aug. 5. Tape and transcript in author's collection.

Ananda Marga: A Struggle Within and Without. 1974. *Northwest Passage,* Apr. 8–22, 18.

Ananda Marga Yoga Society: Banned in Bombay. 1975. *Take Over,* Aug. 1.

Anderson, Terry H. 1995. *The Movement and the Sixties.* New York: Oxford Univ. Press.

Another Hired Stranger. 1973. The Awful Truth About Scientology. *The Realist*, Oct., 1–8.

Argüelles, José. 1987. *The Mayan Factor: Path Beyond Technology*. Santa Fe, N.M.: Bear.

Atack, Jon. 1990. *A Piece of Blue Sky: Scientology, Dianetics and L. Ron Hubbard Exposed*. New York: Lyle Stuart.

Bailey, Raleigh Eugene. 1973. An Ethnographic Approach Toward the Study of a Spiritually Oriented Communal Group in the U.S.A.: The Healthy Happy Holy Organization. Ph.D. diss., Hartford Seminary Foundation.

Bainbridge, William Sims, and Daniel H. Jackson. 1981. The Rise and Decline of Transcendental Meditation. In *The Social Impact of the New Religious Movements*, ed. Bryan Wilson, 135–58. New York: Rose of Sharon.

Balavanta dāsa/William Ogle. 1987. Interview by author. Knoxville, Tenn., Dec. 15. Tape and transcript in author's collection.

Barker, Eileen. 1984. *The Making of a Moonie: Choice or Brainwashing?* London: Basil Blackwell.

Barker, Janet. 1985. Ex-Revolutionary Uses Bible as a Tool for Change. *The Daily Breeze* [Torrance, California], Dec. 14.

Barrett, David V. 1996. *Sects, "Cults" and Alternative Religions: A World Survey and Sourcebook*. London: Blandford.

Basham, A. L. 1959. Reprint. *The Wonder That Was India*. New York: Grove. Originally published in 1954.

Bauer, Bernard. 1982. Worldwide Cult Probed for Links to Terrorism. *Wisconsin State Journal*. Aug. 16, sec. 1.

Beidler, Philip D. 1994. *Scriptures for a Generation: What We Were Reading in the '60s*. Athens: Univ. of Georgia Press.

Bellah, Robert N. 1974. Reprint. Civil Religion in America. In *American Civil Religion*, ed. Russell E. Richey and Donald G. Jones, 21–44. New York: Harper and Row. Originally published in *Daedalus* in 1967.

———. 1976. The New Consciousness and the Berkeley New Left. In *The New Religious Consciousness*, ed. Charles Y. Glock and Robert N. Bellah, 77–92. Berkeley: Univ. of California Press.

Berg, David. 1976a. *The Mo Letters*. vols. 1 and 2. Geneva: Children of God.

———. 1976b. *The Basic Mo Letters*. Geneva: Children of God.

Best, Connie. 1973. Women Together or Out of the Frying Pan and Into the Fire. *And It Is Divine* 1, no. 9: 46–52.

Bianchi, Eugene C. 1972. *The Religious Experience of Revolutionaries*. Garden City, N.Y.: Doubleday.

Bibby, Reginald W. 1979. Religion and Modernity: The Canadian Case. *Journal for the Scientific Study of Religion* 18, no. 1: 1–17.

Billotte, Louise. 1978. Can The Left Find Room For Spirituality? *Alternative Media* 9, no. 6: 4–6.

Blaikie, Norman W. H., and G. Paul Kelsen. 1979. Locating Self and Giving Meaning to Existence: A Typology of Paths to Spiritual Well-Being Based on New Religious Movements in Australia. *Spiritual Well-Being: Sociological Perspectives*, ed. David O. Moberg, 133–51. Washington, D.C.: University Press of America.

Blau, Eleanor. 1973. Guru's Followers Cheer "Millennium" in Festivities at Astrodome. *New York Times,* Nov. 12.

Bloom, Alexander, and Wini Breines, eds. 1995. *Takin' It to the Streets*. Oxford: Oxford Univ. Press.

Boulanger, Betty. 1974. New England Peace Sale. *Divine Times* 3, no. 3.

Braungart, Richard G. 1984. Historical and Generational Patterns of Youth Movements: A Global Perspective. *Comparative Social Research,* 7:3–62.

Braungart, Richard G., and Margaret M. Braungart. 1980. Political Career Patterns of Radical Activists in the 1960s and 1970s: Some Historical Comparisons. *Sociological Focus* 13, no. 3: 237–54.

Bresler, Fenton. 1992. *Interpol*. New York: Viking.

British Columbia, Province of. 1987. Conviction Orders [for Stephen Phillip Kapitany in] the District of Burnaby. Filed Nov. 25. Copy in author's collection.

Bromley, David G., and Anson D. Shupe, Jr. 1979. *"Moonies" in America: Cult, Church and Crusade*. Beverly Hills, Calif.: Sage.

Brooks, Charles R. 1989. *The Hare Krishnas in India*. Princeton, N.J.: Princeton Univ. Press.

Brown, Peter, and Steven Gaines. 1983. *The Love You Make: An Insider's Story of the Beatles*. Toronto: McGraw-Hill.

Bugliosi, Vincent, with Curt Gentry. 1974. *Helter Skelter: The True Story of the Manson Murders*. New York: Norton.

Burroughs, William S. 1970. Burroughs on Scientology. *Los Angeles Free Press,* Mar. 6, sec. 2.

Burroughs, William S., and Daniel Odier. 1974. *The Job*. Rev. ed. New York: Grove. Originally published in 1969.

Butwin, Miriam, and Pat Pirmantgen. 1972. *Protest II*. Minneapolis, Minn.: Lerner.

Cameron, Charles, ed. 1973. *Who is Guru Maharaj Ji?* Toronto: Bantam.

[Campbell, John W., Jr.]. 1949. In Times to Come. *Astounding Science Fiction* December: 80.

Castaneda, Carlos. 1968. *The Teachings of Don Juan: A Yaqui Way of Knowledge.* Berkeley: Univ. of California Press.

Caute, David. 1988. *Sixty-Eight: The Year of the Barricades.* London: Paladin.

The Challenge of Scientology. *Astral Projection* 1, no. 3: 2.

Charity Frauds Bureau. 1974. Final Report on the Activities of the Children of God to Honorable Louis J. Lefkowitz, Attorney General of the State of New York. Albany, N.Y.: Office of the Attorney General.

Chatterton, Peter/Bahudak. 1989. Interview by author. Nanaimo, B.C., Aug. 2. Tape and transcript in author's collection.

Children of God Trust. 1973. *New Nation News* 5, no. 6.

The Children of the Children of God. 1998. Program televised on CBS's *Public Eye,* July 15.

Christian Activists: "The Problem is Not the System—But Man Himself." 1970. *Augur* 2, no. 2: 8.

Christian World Liberation Front (CWLF). ca. 1969. . . . And After This War? Self-published pamphlet.

———. 1969. Bulletin #1 (Oct. 3). Self-published pamphlet.

———. N.d. New Berkeley Liberation Program. Self-published pamphlet.

Church of Scientology Worldwide. 1970. In *The Background and Ceremonies of the Church of Scientology of California, World Wide.* Sussex, England: Church of Scientology World Wide.

Clark, Tom. 1980. *The Great Naropa Poetry Wars.* Santa Barbara, Calif.: Cadmus.

Clarke, Steve, comp. 1979. *The Who in Their Own Words.* New York: Quick Fox.

Cleaver, Eldridge. 1978. *Soul on Fire.* Waco, Tex.: Word.

Clecak, Peter. 1983a. *America's Quest for the Ideal Self: Dissent and Fulfillment in the 60s and 70s.* Oxford: Oxford Univ. Press.

———. 1983b. The Movement of the 1960s and its Cultural and Political Legacy. In *The Development of an American Culture,* ed. Stanley Coben and Lorman Ratner, 2d ed., 261–311. New York: St. Martin's.

Colker, David. 1988. Their Road's Less Traveled. *Los Angeles Herald Examiner,* Mar. 21.

Collier, Sophia. 1978. *Soul Rush: The Odyssey of a Young Woman of the '70s.* New York: William Morrow.

Connelly, Joel. 1972. "Praise the Lord, and Sabotage the Ammunition." *Northwest Passage,* Feb. 21-Mar. 5: 22–23.

Conze, Edward. 1967. *Buddhist Thought in India.* Ann Arbor: Univ. of Michigan Press.

———. 1975. Reprint. *Buddhism: Its Essence and Development.* New York: Harper Colophon. Originally published in 1951.

Cook, Bonnie L. 1974. Krishna Candidate is "God Conscious." *The Germantown Courier* [Philadelphia], Mar. 21.

Cooper, John Charles. 1972. *A New Kind of Man.* Philadelphia: Westminster.

Corydon, Bent. 1996. *L. Ron Hubbard, Messiah or Madman?* Fort Lee, N.J.: Barricade.

Cott, Nancy F. 1993. Domesticity. In *Family Patterns, Gender Relations,* ed. Bonnie J. Fox, 114–19. Toronto: Oxford Univ. Press.

Cowan, Edward. 1970. New Groups Help Exiles in Canada. *New York Times,* May 11.

Culpepper, Emily. 1978. The Spiritual Movement of Radical Feminist Consciousness. In *Understanding the New Religions,* ed. Jacob Needleman and George Baker, 220–34. New York: Seabury.

Cunningham, Alan. 1973. Young Guru is Denounced as Fraud by Rival Group. *Rocky Mountain News,* Oct. 23.

Daner, Francine. 1974. The Philosophy of the Hare Krishna Movement. *The Humanist* Sept.-Oct.: 11–12.

———. 1976. *The American Children of Kṛṣṇa: A Study of the Hare Kṛṣṇa Movement.* Toronto: Holt, Rinehart and Winston.

Darden, Anna. 1970. Is Political Activism a Noble Failure? *Los Angeles Free Press,* Feb. 27.

Das, Bharata Shrestha. 1998. ISKCON's Response to Child Abuse: 1990–1998. *ISKCON Communications Journal* 6, no. 1. Electronic journal at <http://www.iskcon.com/ICJ/6_2/62dhira.htm>.

Davidson, Sara. 1971. The Rush for Instant Salvation. *Harper's,* July, 40ff.

Davis, Deborah. 1988. Interview by author. Simi Valley, Calif., Aug. 6. Tape and transcript in author's collection.

Davis, Deborah, with Bill Davis. 1984. *The Children of God: The Inside Story.* Grand Rapids, Mich.: Zondervan.

Davis, James Kirkpatrick. 1997. *Assault on the Left: The FBI and the Sixties Antiwar Movement.* London: Praeger.

Day, Aidan. 1988. *Jokerman: Reading the Lyrics of Bob Dylan.* Oxford: Basil Blackwell.

DeBenedetti, Charles, with Charles Chatfield. 1990. *An American Ordeal: The Anti-war Movement of the Vietnam Era*. Syracuse, N.Y.: Syracuse Univ. Press.

de Herrera, Nancy Cooke. 1992. *Beyond Gurus: A Woman of Many Worlds*. Nevada City, Calif.: Blue Dolphin.

Delaney, Paul. 1972. 3,000 Youths Rally Peacefully at Miami Beach. *New York Times,* July 12.

de Mille, Richard. 1977. Carlos Castaneda—Fact or Fiction? *High Times* April: 44ff.

———, ed. 1980. *The Don Juan Papers: Further Castaneda Controversies*. Santa Barbara, Calif.: Ross-Erikson.

Derks, Frans, and Jan M. van der Lans. 1983. Subgroups in Divine Light Mission Membership: A Comment on Downton. In *Of Gods and Men: New Religious Movements in the West,* ed. Eileen Barker, 303–8. Macon, Ga.: Mercer Univ. Press.

Diamond, Sara. 1987. Shepherding. *Covert Action* no. 27: 18–31.

Dianetics Pair Pleads Innocent. 1953. *Detroit Free Press,* Apr. 10.

Divine Light Mission (DLM). N.d. Ashram Manual. Copy on file in the Graduate Theological Union, Berkeley, CA.

Douglas, Jim [pseud.]. 1988. Interview by author. Location confidential, Aug. 11. Tape and transcript in author's collection.

Downton, James V., Jr. 1979. *Sacred Journeys: The Conversion of Young Americans to Divine Light Mission*. New York: Columbia Univ. Press.

Dusenbery, Verne Andrew. 1975. Straight-Freak-Yogi-Sikh: A "Replace for Meaning" in Contemporary American Culture. M.A. thesis, Univ. of Chicago.

Ebon, Martin, ed. 1968. *Maharishi, the Guru*. New York: Signet.

Echols, Alice. 1989. *Daring to Be Bad: Radical Feminism in America, 1967–1975*. Minneapolis: Univ. of Minnesota Press.

———. 1994. Nothing Distant About It: Women's Liberation and Sixties Radicalism. In *The Sixties: From Memory to History,* ed. David R. Farber, 149–84. Chapel Hill: Univ. of North Carolina Press.

Editorial introduction to Lerner. 1971. *Ramparts,* July, 19–20.

Edwards, Joe. 1973. Pacified Hippies. *The Free Aquarian* [New Jersey]: 10, 28.

Elizabeth Daily Journal. 1951a. N. J. Starts Action Against Dianetics. Jan. 15, sec. 1.

———. 1951b. Dianetics Charges to Be Amplified. Mar. 28.

———. 1951c. Dianetics Group to "Quit City" Because "We're Not Wanted." Apr. 3.

Ellwood, Robert S. 1973. *One Way: The Jesus Movement and Its Meaning*. Englewood Cliffs, N.J.: Prentice-Hall.

———. 1994. *The Sixties Spiritual Awakening*. New Brunswick, N.J.: Rutgers Univ. Press.

Ellwood, Robert S., and Harry B. Partin. 1988. *Religious and Spiritual Groups in Modern America*. 2d ed. Englewood Cliffs, N.J.: Prentice Hall.

Elsberg, Constance Waeber. 1988. Graceful Women: An Ethnographic Account of Women's Experience in the Healthy-Happy-Holy Organization, and of the Interplay of Socio-Cultural Tensions, Organization-Building and Selfhood in One of the New Religions. Ph.D. diss., Univ. of Maryland.

Enriquez, Sam. 1986. Ex-Krishna Child Abuser Gets 50 Years. *Los Angeles Times*, June 6, sec. 2.

Enroth, Ronald M., Edward E. Ericson, Jr., and C. Brekinridge Peters. 1972. *The Story of the Jesus People: A Factual Survey*. Exeter: Paternoster.

Evans, Christopher. 1973. *Cults of Unreason*. New York: Farrar, Straus and Giroux.

Everett, Glenn, and Edward E. Plowman. 1973. "Psyching" Shiloh. *Christianity Today*, Jan. 19: 43 [423].

Everyman. 1969. "A Letter to Us—Brothers and Sisters in Madison" [letter to the editor]. *Madison Kaleidoscope* Oct.: 3.

The Family/Children of God. 1993. Program televised on NBC's *Now*, Sept. 9.

Farber, David R. 1988. *Chicago '68*. Chicago: Univ. of Chicago Press.

———. 1994. *The Age of Great Dreams: America in the 1960s*. New York: Hill and Wang.

Farrow, Mia. 1997. *What Falls Away*. New York: Doubleday.

Fendrich, James M. 1974. Activists Ten Years Later: A Test of Generational Unit Continuity. *Journal of Social Issues* 30, no. 3: 95–118.

Fichter, Joseph H. 1987. *Autobiographies of Conversion*. Queenston, Ontario: Edwin Mellen.

Fields, Rick. 1992. *How the Swans Came to the Lake*. 3d ed. Boston: Shambhala.

Ford, Joan. 1992. Interview by author. Location near Los Angeles, Calif., Dec. 14. Tape and transcript in author's collection.

Former Student [Fred Smith] Sent to Leavenworth Prison. 1968. *Daily Californian*, Aug. 2.

Foss, Daniel A., and Ralph W. Larkin. 1976. From "The Gates of Eden" to "Day of the Locust": An Analysis of the Dissident Youth Movement of the 1960s and its Heirs of the Early 1970s—the Post-Movement Groups. *Theory and Society* 3: 45–64.

———. 1978. Worshipping the Absurd: The Negation of Social Causality Among the Followers of Guru Maharaj Ji. *Sociological Analysis* 39, no. 2: 157–64.

———. 1979. The Roar of the Lemming: Youth, Postmovement Groups, and the Life Construction Crisis. In *Religious Change and Continuity*, ed. Harry M. Johnson, 264–85. Washington: Jossey-Bass.

Fowler, Robert Booth. 1982. *A New Engagement: Evangelical Political Thought, 1966–1976.* Grand Rapids, Mich.: William B. Eerdmans.

Franklin, Stephen. 1987. Murder, Abuse Charges Batter Serenity at Big Krishna Camp. *Chicago Tribune,* Sept. 2, sec. 1.

Franks, Lucinda. 1981. The Seeds of Terror. *New York Times Magazine,* Nov. 22.

Fraser, Ronald (et al.). 1988. *1968:A Student Generation in Revolt.* New York: Pantheon.

Freedman, Ralph. 1978. *Hermann Hesse: Pilgrim of Crisis.* New York: Pantheon.

Fritz, Leah. [1974?]. "The Faith of Our Fathers." *Catonsville Roadrunner* [U.K.], no. 54: 5–6.

"From Politics to Yoga." 1975. *Great Speckled Bird,* Aug. 7.

Gaines, Steven. 1986. *Heroes and Villains: The True Story of the Beach Boys.* Scarborough, Ont.: New American Library of Canada.

Gardner, Fred. 1970. *The Unlawful Concept: An Account of the Presidio Mutiny Case.* New York: Viking.

Garfinkle, Adam. 1995. *Telltale Hearts: The Origins and Impact of the Vietnam Antiwar Movement.* New York: St. Martin's.

Gelberg, Steven J. 1989. Exploring an Alternative Reality: Spiritual Life in ISKCON. In *Krishna Consciousness in the West,* ed. David G. Bromley and Larry D. Shinn, 135–62. Lewisburg, Penn.: Bucknell Univ. Press.

———. 1995. On Leaving the "Hare Krishnas." *Communities* 88 (fall): 39–42.

George, Carol V. R. 1993. *God's Salesman: Norman Vincent Peale and the Power of Positive Thinking.* Oxford: Oxford Univ. Press.

Gettleman, Marvin E., Jane Franklin, Marilyn Young, and H. Bruce Franklin, eds. 1985. *Vietnam and America: A Documented History.* New York: Grove.

GGM Second Anniversary Celebration. September 22, 1972. *Beads of Truth* (Dec.): 41.

G.I. Allowed to Clothe for Court. 1968. *Berkeley Barb,* May 10–16, 11.

Ginsberg, Allen. 1968. The Maharishi and Me. *San Francisco Express Times,* Apr. 11. Reprinted from *International Times.*

Gitlin, Todd. 1987. *The Sixties: Years of Hope, Days of Rage.* Toronto: Bantam.

Giuliano, Geoffrey. 1989. *Dark Horse: The Secret Life of George Harrison.* Toronto: Stoddart.

————. 1996. *Behind Blue Eyes: A Life of Peter Townshend.* London: Hodder and Stoughton.

Goines, David Lance. 1993. *The Free Speech Movement: Coming of Age in the 1960s.* Berkeley: Ten Speed.

Goldman, Albert. 1988. *The Lives of John Lennon.* New York: William Morrow.

Goldstein, Richard. 1989. *Reporting the Counterculture.* Boston: Unwin Hyman.

Gonzalez, Alberto, and John J. Makay. 1983. Rhetorical Ascription and the Gospel According to Dylan. *Quarterly Journal of Speech* 69, no. 1: 1–14.

Goodstein, Laurie. 1998. Hare Krishna Movement Details Past Abuse at Its Boarding Schools. *New York Times,* Oct. 9.

Gortner, Marjoe. 1974. Who Was Guru Maharaj Ji? *Oui* (May): 91ff.

Goswami, Jagadisha. 1987. Interview by author. Toronto, Oct. 10. Tape and transcript in author's collection.

Goswami, Satsvarupa dāsa. 1980–83. *Śrīla Prabhupāda-lilamrta: A Biography of His Divine Grace A. C. Bhaktivedanta Swami Prabhupāda.* 6 vols. Los Angeles: Bhaktivedanta Book Trust.

Gottlieb, Annie. 1987. *Do You Believe in Magic? The Second Coming of the Sixties Generation.* New York: Times Books.

Gray, Francine du Plessix. 1973. Blissing Out in Houston. *New York Review of Books,* Dec. 13, 36–43.

Greene, Bob. 1977. Meet the New Rennie Davis: He Sells Insurance to the People. *Philadelphia Inquirer,* May 1.

Gruson, Lindsey. 1987. 2 Hare Krishna Aides Accused of Child Molesting. *New York Times,* Feb. 18.

Guru Maha Ripoff. 1973. *Free For All,* Apr. 28: 18.

Haines, Steve. 1973–74. Pavlov's Divine Dog; Or I Saw The Light. *Ann Arbor Sun,* Dec. 14-Jan. 4: 8–9.

Halberstam, David. 1993. *The Fifties.* New York: Villard.

Hall, Mitchell K. 1990. *Because of Their Faith: CALCAV and Religious Opposition to the Vietnam War.* New York: Columbia Univ. Press.

Harder, Mary White. 1974. Sex Roles in the Jesus Movement. *Social Compass* 21, no. 3: 345–53.

Harder, Mary White, James T. Richardson, and Robert B. Simmonds. 1972. Jesus People. *Psychology Today,* Dec., 45ff.

Hare Krishna Devotee Plans Race for Mayor. 1973. *Dallas Times Herald,* Jan. 3.

Hare Krishnas Acknowledge Child Abuse at Schools in '70s, '80s. 1998. *Washington Post,* Oct. 10.

Harper, Tom. 1971. Jesus Freaks and Stars. *Great Speckled Bird,* Sept. 13.

Harris, James T. 1971. Just Call Me Allen. *Good Times* [San Francisco, Calif.], Sept. 17, 14–15.

Harrison, Eric. 1987. Troubled Paradise: Krishna Site Focus of Probes. *Philadelphia Inquirer,* Mar. 9.

Harvey, Peter. 1990. *An Introduction to Buddhism: Teachings, History, and Practices.* New Delhi: Munshiram Manoharlal.

Hayden, Tom. 1988. *Reunion: A Memoir.* Toronto: Random House.

Heath, G. Louis., ed. 1976. *Off The Pigs! The History and Literature of the Black Panther Party.* Metuchen, N.J.: Scarecrow.

Hedgepath, William. 1968. The Non-Drug Turn-On Hits Campus. *Look,* Feb. 6, 68ff.

Heenan, Edward F. 1973. The Jesus Generation. In *Mystery, Magic, and Miracle: Religion in a Post-Aquarian Age,* ed. Edward F. Heenan, 144–54. Englewood Cliffs, N.J.: Prentice-Hall.

Heineman, Kenneth J. 1993. *Campus Wars: The Peace Movement at American State Universities in the Vietnam Era.* New York: New York Univ. Press.

Heinz, Donald. 1976. The Christian World Liberation Front. In *The New Religious Consciousness,* ed. Charles Y. Glock and Robert N. Bellah, 143–61. Berkeley: Univ. of California Press.

Hesse, Hermann. 1970. *The Journey to the East.* Trans. Hilda Rosner. New York: Noonday.

Hiebert, Marylou. 1989. Interview by author. Richmond, B.C., July 28. Tape and transcript in author's collection.

A History of Hans Jayanti. 1973. *And It Is Divine.* Program for Millennium '73: 12.

Hoffman, Abbie. 1969. *Woodstock Nation: A Talk-Rock Album.* New York: Random House.

———. 1980. *Soon to Be a Major Motion Picture.* New York: Perigree.

Hofmann, Paul. 1968. 3,600 Hear Guru Urge Meditation. *New York Times,* Jan. 22.

Holloway, Bill. 1976. Mysticism, Fascism, and the Need for Transcendence. *Alternative to Alienation* no. 3 (Toronto): 12, 13, 20.

Hoshijo Calls Krishna Story Smear Attempt. 1977. *Honolulu Star Bulletin,* Aug. 22.

Hubbard Association of Scientologists, International. 1955. Project Celebrity. *Ability* (Phoenix: Hubbard Communications Office) Minor 2: 2.

Hubbard, L. Ron. 1950a. *Dianetics: The Modern Science of Mental Health.* New York: Hermitage House.

——. 1950b. Dianetics: The Evolution of a Science. *Astounding Science Fiction* (May): 43–87.

——. 1951. *Science of Survival: Simplified, Faster Dianetic Techniques.* Wichita, Kans.: Hubbard Dianetic Foundation.

——. 1958. Clearing: Some Facts. *Ability* no. 81: 1, 3, 5–6.

——. 1963. R-3M2: What You Are Trying to do in Clearing. *Hubbard Communications Office Bulletin,* Apr. 6.

——. 1964a. *Scientology: Plan for World Peace.* East Grinstead, England: Scientology Publications.

——. 1964b. International City. Transcript of tape number 6403C24. Saint Hill Special Briefing Course, March 24.

——. 1965. Five Years. *The Auditor* (East Grinstead, Sussex, England: HASI [Hubbard Association of Scientologists International]) World Wide edition 9: 3.

——. 1968. *The Phoenix Lectures.* Los Angeles: American Saint Hill Organization.

——. 1969. The Aims of Scientology. Flyer, Church of Scientology, San Francisco. Text written in Sept. 1965.

——. 1970. Celebrity Centre. *Hubbard Communications Office Policy Letter,* Feb. 22.

——. 1971. The Individual, Truth and Civilization. *Advance* no. 11: 3.

——. 1972. *Organization Executive Course.* 8 vols. Copenhagen: AOSH DK Publications.

——. 1974. *The Hymn of Asia.* Los Angeles: Church of Scientology of California.

——. 1975. *Dianetics and Scientology Technical Dictionary.* Los Angeles: Publications Organization.

——. 1976a. The Cessation of War. Pamphlet. N.p.: Founding Church of Scientology.

——. 1976b. *Modern Management Technology Defined.* Copenhagen: New Era.

——. 1976c. *The Technical Bulletins of Dianetics and Scientology.* 12 vols. Copenhagen and Los Angeles: Scientology Publications.

——. 1986. The Formation of the Sea Organization. *High Winds* 6. Church of Scientology International: 2–4. Edited from the taped lecture, "Ron's Journal, 1967," given on September 20, 1967.

——. 1988. The Sea Organization. *High Winds* 8. Church of Scientology International: 3–4. Originally issued as Flag Order 137.

Hubner, John, and Lindsey Gruson. 1988. *Monkey on a Stick: Murder, Madness, and the Hare Krishnas.* New York: Harcourt Brace Jovanovich.

Hunter, Glenn. 1992. Growing Role for the Sikhs. *Santa Fe Reporter,* Feb. 5–11, 15, 17.

Huxley, Aldous. 1963. *The Doors of Perception; and, Heaven and Hell.* New York: Harper and Row.

———. 1982. *Moksha.* Boston: Houghton Mifflin.

Instant Karma. 1972. *Lincoln [Nebraska] Gazette,* Nov. 6.

Investigative Party Group. 1977. *The Party: A Chronological Perspective on a Confrontation at a Buddhist Seminary.* Woodstock, N.Y.: Poetry, Crime, and Culture.

Isserman, Morris. 1972. I Like the Christian Life. *Portland Scribe,* May 2–8, 15.

———. 1973. Who Is Guru Maharaj Ji? *Portland Scribe,* Oct. 20–26, 6.

Jackson, Bruce [pseud.]. 1988. Interview by author. Location confidential, Aug. 14. Tape and transcript in author's collection.

Jacobs, Janet. 1984. The Economy of Love in Religious Commitment: The Deconversion of Women from Nontraditional Religious Movements. *Journal for the Scientific Study of Religion* 23, no. 2: 155–71.

———. 1989. *Divine Disenchantment: Deconverting from New Religions.* Indianapolis: Indiana Univ. Press.

Jacobs, Joshua [pseud.]. 1993. Interview by author. Location confidential, Mar. 5. Tape and transcript in author's collection.

Jamison, Andrew, and Ron Eyerman. 1994. *Seeds of the Sixties.* Berkeley: Univ. of California Press.

Jentzsch, Heber. 1974. Replace Warrant? Not for the IRS. *Los Angeles Free Press,* Mar. 22.

Jesus Communes—Sexism Revisited. 1973. *FPS,* Sept., 16.

Johnson, Gregory. 1976. The Hare Krishna in San Francisco. In *The New Religious Consciousness,* ed. Charles Y. Glock and Robert N. Bellah, 31–51. Berkeley: Univ. of California Press.

Jones, Edgar D., Jr. 1970. Scientology . . . Art is the Measure of Society. *Los Angeles Free Press,* Feb. 27.

Jorgensen, Bruce. 1973. Rennie Davis and God. *The Free Aquarian* [Passaic, N.J. and New York] 6, no. 51: 1, 6.

Joye, Barbara. 1971. Back to Godhead. *Great Speckled Bird,* Aug. 9.

Judah, J. Stillson. 1974. *Hare Krishna and the Counterculture.* Toronto: John Wiley.

———. 1982. From Political Activism to Religious Participation. *Update: A Quarterly Journal on New Religious Movements* 6, no. 1: 11–20.

Karie, Jack. 1955. Phoenix Man Jailed On Medicine Charge. *Phoenix Republic,* Sept. 4.

Karnow, Stanley. 1983. *Vietnam: A History.* New York: Viking.

Kaufman, Edward. 1970. Scientology Theatre. *Los Angeles Free Press,* Dec. 11.

Kaur, Hari Arti. 1973. Grace of God Movement for the Women of America. (On Service). *Beads of Truth* no. 20: 28.

Kelley, Ken. 1973a. Rennie Davis—Blissed Out . . . Hissed Out. *Vancouver Free Press/Georgia Straight,* May 3–10, 8–9.

———. 1973b. Blissed Out with the Perfect Master. *Ramparts,* July, 32ff.

———. 1973c. Guru Goons Loose. *Fifth Estate,* Dec. 8–21, 2–3.

———. 1974a. Over the Hill at 16. *Ramparts,* Feb., 40–44.

———. 1974b. I See The Light. *Penthouse,* July, 99ff.

Kellner, Douglas. N.d. American National Biography: Marcuse, Herbert. Webpage at http://www.uta.edu/huma/illuminations/kell12.htm.

Kempton, Sally. 1970. Cutting Loose. *Esquire,* July, 53–57.

———. 1976. Hanging Out With the Guru. *New York Magazine,* Apr. 12, 36–46.

Kendrick, Alexander. 1974. *The Wound Within: America in the Vietnam Years, 1945–1974.* Toronto: Little, Brown.

Kent, Stephen A. 1987. Puritan Radicalism and the New Religious Organizations: Seventeenth-Century England and Contemporary America. In *Comparative Social Research,* 10:3–46. Greenwich, Conn.: JAI.

———. 1988. Slogan Chanters to Mantra Chanters: A Mertonian Deviance Analysis of Conversion to the Religious Organizations in the Early 1970s. *Sociological Analysis* 49, no. 2: 104–118.

———. 1992. Slogan Chanters to Mantra Chanters: A Deviance Analysis of Youth Religious Conversion in the Early 1970s. In *Sights on the Sixties,* ed. Barbara L. Tischler, 121–33. New Brunswick, N.J.: Rutgers Univ. Press.

———. 1993. Radical Rhetoric and Mystical Religion in America's Late Vietnam War Era. *Religion* 23, no. 1: 45–60.

———. 1994a. Misattribution and Social Control in the Children of God. *Journal of Religion and Health* 33, no. 1: 29–43.

———. 1994b. Lustful Prophet: A Psychosexual Historical Study of the Children of God's Leader, David Berg. *Cultic Studies Journal* 11, no. 2: 135–88. Available online at <http://www.arts.ualberta.ca/~skent/Lustfulprophet.htm>.

———. 1996. Scientology's Relationship with Eastern Religious Traditions. *Journal of Contemporary Religion* 11, no. 1: 21–36. Available online at <http://wpxx02.toxi.uni-wuerzburg.de/~cowen/essays/eastern.html>.

———. 1999a. The Creation of "Religious" Scientology. *Religious Studies and Theology* 18, no. 2:97–126 (forthcoming).

———. 1999b. The Globalization of Scientology: Influence, Control, and Opposition in Transnational Markets. *Religion* 29, no. 2: 147–69.

———. 2000. Brainwashing in Scientology's Rehabilitation Project Force (RPF). Hamburg: Behörde für Inneres-Arbeitsgruppe Scientology und Landeszentrale für politische Bildung. October.

Kent, Stephen A., and James V. Spickard. 1994. The "Other" Civil Religion and the Tradition of Radical Quaker Politics. *Journal of Church and State* 36 no. 2: 301–15.

Kerby, David. 1972. Turn On, Tune In, Drop Out. *For Real* May: 4.

Kesey, Ken. 1962. *One Flew Over the Cuckoo's Nest.* New York: New American Library.

Kessler, Lauren. 1990. *After All These Years: Sixties Ideals in a Different World.* New York: Thunder's Mouth.

Khalsa, Gurubanda Singh. 1976. Editorial—Sikh Dharma and America's Future. *Sikh Dharma Brotherhood* 2, no. 2: [1].

Khalsa, Gurufatha Singh. 1983. "Sikh Religion." In *Spirit of Toronto,* ed. Margaret Lindsay Holton, 294–304. Toronto: Image House.

Khalsa, Gurutej Singh/Ted Steiner. 1987. Interview by author. Toronto, Feb. 20. Tape and transcript in author's collection.

Khalsa, Harinam Singh. 1987. Interview by author. Toronto, Sept. 16. Tape and transcript in author's collection.

Khalsa, Manjit Kaur. 1982. A Psychological Evaluation of Ladies' Camp. Ph.D. diss., Boston Univ. School of Education.

Khalsa, Shamsher Singh. 1986. Winning the Game of Life. *Beads of Truth* 11, no. 16: 8–9.

Kifner, John. 1970. Jury Convicts 4 in Bank Burning. *New York Times,* Nov. 8.

Klein, Darrel R. 1970. Revolution. *Los Angeles Free Press* [letter to the editor], May 22.

Kleinfelder, Rita Lang. 1993. *When We Were Young: A Baby-Boomer Yearbook.* Toronto: Prentice Hall.

Kopkind, Andrew. 1973. Mystic Politics: Refugees from the New Left. *Ramparts,* July, 26ff.

———. 1995. *The Thirty Years' Wars: Dispatches and Diversions of a Radical Journalist, 1965–1994.* Ed. JoAnn Wypijewski. New York: Verso.

Kornbluth, Jesse. 1976. The Fuhrer over est. *New Times,* Mar. 19.

Kostash, Myrna. 1980. *Long Way From Home: The Story of the Sixties Generation in Canada.* Toronto: James Lorimer.

Krassner, Paul. 1973. Rennie Finds Divine Light; CIA Glistens. *The Drummer* [Philadelphia], Apr. 10, 4–5.

———. 1993. *Confessions of a Raving, Unconfined Nut*. New York: Simon and Schuster.

Krishna Movement in for Politics. 1974. *Daily Breeze* [Torrance, Calif.], May 11.

Kunkin, Art. 1973. The Great Guru Hunt: Where Are the Consciousness Books Taking Us? *Los Angeles Free Press,* June 8.

Lambert, T. Allen. 1972. Generations and Change: Toward a Theory of Generations as a Force in Historical Process. *Youth and Society* 4, no. 1: 21–45.

Lapham, Lewis H. 1968. There Once Was a Guru From Rishikesh. *Saturday Evening Post.* May 4, sec. 1; May 18, sec. 2.

Late-Blooming Army Objector. 1968. *San Francisco Chronicle,* Apr. 20.

Layman, Emma McCloy. 1976. *Buddhism in America*. Chicago: Nelson-Hall.

Leary, Timothy. 1968. *High Priest.* New York: College Notes and Texts.

———. 1983. *Flashbacks: An Autobiography.* Los Angeles: Jeremy P. Tarcher.

Leary, Timothy, Ralph Metzner, and Richard Alpert. 1964. *The Psychedelic Experience: A Manual Based on the Tibetan Book of the Dead.* New Hyde Park, N.Y.: University Books.

Lee, Martin A., and Bruce Shlain. 1985. *Acid Dreams: The CIA, LSD, and the Sixties Rebellion.* New York: Grove.

Lelyveld, Joseph. 1985. The Enduring Legacy. *New York Times Magazine,* Mar. 31.

Lemann, Nicholas. 1981. The Post-Vietnam Generation. In *The Wounded Generation: America After Vietnam.* Ed. A. D. Horne, 209–13. Englewood Cliffs, N.J.: Prentice-Hall.

Lerner, Michael P. 1971. May Day: Anatomy of the Movement. *Ramparts,* July, 20ff.

Levine, Mark L., George C. McNamee, and Daniel Greenberg, ed. 1970. *The Tales of Hoffman.* New York: Bantam.

Levine, Richard. 1974. When the Lord of All the Universe Played Houston: Many Are Called but Few Show Up. *Rolling Stone,* Mar. 14, 36ff.

Levine, Saul. 1984. *Radical Departures: Desperate Detours to Growing Up.* New York: Harcourt Brace Jovanovich.

Levitt, Cyril. 1984. *Children of Privilege: Student Revolt in the Sixties.* Toronto: Univ. of Toronto Press.

Lewis, Gordon R., and Cal Thomas. 1973. The Millennium: A Bad Beginning. *Christianity Today,* Dec. 7, 51.

Lieblich, Julia. 1999. Child Molesting Charges Dog the Krishnas. *Detroit News,* June 20.

Link Acknowledged—Finally. 1977. *Sunday Star-Bulletin and Advertiser* [Honolulu], Aug. 21.

Lukas, J. Anthony. 1988. *Nightmare: The Underside of the Nixon Years.* Markham, Ont.: Penguin.

MacDonald, Robert. 1972. Kookie LIP Grants Make the Mind Boggle: MP. *Toronto Sun,* Mar. 2.

Mackenzie, Donald M., Sr. 1980. The Conversion of Bob Dylan. *Theology Today 37,* no. 3: 357–59.

Mailer, Norman. 1968. *The Armies of the Night.* New York: New American Library.

Makower, Joel. 1989. *Woodstock: The Oral History.* Toronto: Doubleday.

Mann, Jack. 1963. Scientology Claims Cures, Chases Reds, Vexes U.S. *Detroit Free Press,* Apr. 7.

Manning, Steve. 1980. Carp: New Moonies Rising. *Guardian,* Apr. 9, 10.

Manoff, Mark. 1973. Guru's Guru-dom Keeps Growing. *The Drummer* [Philadelphia], Nov. 6, 5.

Manuel, Frank E., and Fritzie P. Manuel. 1979. *Utopian Thought in the Western World.* Cambridge, Mass.: Harvard Univ. Press.

Marin, Peter. 1972. Children of Yearning: Meditations on the Jesus Movement. *Saturday Review,* May 6, 58–63.

———. 1975. The New Narcissism. *Harper's,* Oct., 45–56.

———. 1979. Spiritual Obedience: The Transcendental Game of Follow the Leader. *Harper's,* Feb., 43–58.

Marsh, Dave. 1983. *Before I Get Old: The Story of The Who.* New York: St. Martin's.

Marshall, Sue. 1970. Kent Massacre. *Los Angeles Free Press,* May 8.

Martin, William. 1991. *A Prophet With Honor: The Billy Graham Story.* New York: William Morrow.

Marx, Karl. 1964. Contribution to the Critique of Hegel's Philosophy of Right. Introduction. In *Marx and Engels: On Religion,* 41–58. New York: Schocken.

Massoglia (Sunshine), John. 1974. "Reality, a Guru, and Dead Flowers." *The Eugene Augur* Apr. 12: 7.

Mata Ji. 1974. Spiritual Marriage. *And It is Divine.* 2, no. 2: 22.

McAfee, Kathy. 1973. I Was a Teenage Guru. *Chicago Express,* Apr. 11–17, 1ff.

McCarthy, John D., and Mayer N. Zald. 1977. Resource Mobilization and Social Movements: A Partial Theory. *American Journal of Sociology* 82, no. 6: 1212–41.

McCray, Melvin R. 1983. The Two Lives of John Favors '72. *Princeton Alumni Weekly,* Feb. 9, 34–36.

McGuire, Meredith B. 1997. *Religion: The Social Context.* 4th ed. Belmont, Calif.: Wadsworth.

McLeod, W. H. 1989. *Who is a Sikh? The Problem of Sikh Identity*. Oxford: Clarendon.

McNamara, Tom. 1974. The Greedy Gurus and the False New Left. *The Match!* June, 6–7.

McRae, Earl. 1974. Blissing Out in Texas. *The Canadian Magazine,* Jan. 26, 2–4.

Melton, J. Gordon, ed. 1991. *The Encyclopedia of American Religions* 3 vols. Tarrytown, N.Y.: Triumph.

Messer, Jeanne. 1976. Guru Maharaj Ji and the Divine Light Mission. In *The New Religious Consciousness,* ed. Charles Y. Glock and Robert N. Bellah, 52–72. Berkeley: Univ. of California Press.

Michael Donner. 1976. *Divine Times* 5, no. 3: 1.

Mickler, Michael. 1980. A History of the Unification Church in the Bay Area: 1960–74. M.A. thesis, Graduate Theological Union, Berkeley, Calif.

Miles, Barry. 1989. *Ginsberg: A Biography*. Toronto: Simon and Schuster.

———. 1992. *William Burroughs: El Hombre Visible*. New York: Virgin.

———. 1998. *Jack Kerouac: King of the Beats*. London: Virgin.

Miller, James. 1987. *Democracy is in the Streets: From Port Huron to the Siege of Chicago*. New York: Simon and Schuster.

Miller, Russell. 1987. *Bare-Faced Messiah: The True Story of L. Ron Hubbard*. London: Michael Joseph.

Monk, Ed. 1972. Thots from Another Road. *Northwest Passage,* Apr. 3–16, 20.

Montgomery, Kathy [pseud.]. 1989. Interview by author. Location confidential, Aug. 13. Tape and transcript in author's collection.

Moon Comes Out for Nixon. 1974. *Great Speckled Bird,* Jan. 14.

Moon Goons. 1977. *Yipster Times,* Mar.-Apr., 14.

Moore, Kyle [pseud.]. 1987. Interview by author. Location confidential, Dec. 7. Tape and transcript in author's collection.

Morgan, Ted. 1973. Oz in the Astrodome. *New York Times Magazine,* Dec. 9, 38ff.

———. 1988. *Literary Outlaw: The Life and Times of William S. Burroughs*. New York: Henry Holt.

Morris, David. 1972. The Arrest of Guru Maharaj Ji. *Los Angeles Free Press,* Nov. 24.

———. 1974. Illusions: Illusions of the Spirit. *Green Revolution* 12, no. 3: 9, 10, 14.

Musgrove, Frank. 1974. *Ecstasy and Holiness*. London: Methuen.

Nadle, Marlene. 1967. The Power of Flower vs. The Power of Politics. *The Village Voice,* June 15, 1, 16.

Needleman, Jacob. 1984. Reprint (with new preface). *The New Religions*. New York: Crossroad. Originally published in 1970.

Nolan, James. 1971. Jesus Now: Hogwash and Holy Water. *Ramparts,* Aug., 20–26.

Nugent, Stephen, and Charlie Gillett, eds. 1978. *Rock Almanac.* Garden City, N.Y.: Anchor.

Oberschall, Anthony. 1978. The Decline of the 1960s Social Movements. In *Research in Social Movements, Conflicts and Change,* ed. Louis Kriesberg, 1:257–89. Greenwich, Conn.: JAI.

Olson, Helena. 1979. *Maharishi at "433": The Story of Maharishi Mahesh Yogi's First Visit to the United States.* 2d ed. Los Angeles: R. R. Donnelley.

On Being an Atheist in a Spiritual Age. 1975. *Communities,* Mar.-Apr., 27–29.

Organ, Troy Wilson. 1974. *Hinduism: Its Historical Development.* Woodbury, N.Y.: Barron's Educational Series.

Orwell, George. 1946. *Animal Farm.* New York: Harcourt, Brace.

Osborne, Jennifer [pseud.]. 1987. Interview by author. Location confidential, Dec. 6. Tape and transcript in author's collection.

Pahnke, Walter N. 1966. Drugs and Mysticism. *International Journal of Parapsychology* 8:295–314.

Pahnke, Walter N., and William A. Richards. 1972. Implications of LSD and Experimental Mysticism. In *Altered States of Consciousness,* ed. Charles T. Tart, 399–428. Garden City, N.Y.: Anchor. Reprinted from *Journal of Religion and Health* 5 (1966): 175–208.

Palmer, Susan Jean. 1994. *Moon Sisters, Krishna Mothers, Rajneesh Lovers: Women's Roles in New Religions.* Syracuse, N.Y.: Syracuse Univ. Press.

Peck, Abe. 1985. *Uncovering the Sixties: The Life and Times of the Underground Press.* New York: Pantheon.

People's Yoga. 1970. *The Fifth Estate* [Detroit, Mich.] 5, no. 16: 5.

People's Yoga: Daily Asanas. 1970–71. *The Fifth Estate* 5, no. 17: 17.

Perry, Charles. 1984. *The Haight-Ashbury: A History.* New York: Random House.

Perry, Paul, and Ken Babbs. 1990. *On the Bus: The Complete Guide to the Legendary Trip of Ken Kesey and the Merry Pranksters and the Birth of the Counterculture.* New York: Thunder's Mouth.

Plowman, Edward E. 1970. Battle for Berkeley. *Christianity Today,* May 8, 40 [752].

———. 1971. *The Underground Church: Accounts of Christian Revolutionaries in Action.* Elgin, Illinois: David C. Cook.

Plummer, Keith [pseud.]. 1987. Interview by author. Location confidential, Nov. 6. Tape and transcript in author's collection.

Poland, J. Fuck [*sic*]. 1970. Scientology Sucks!!! *Berkeley Barb,* May 1–7, 12.

Politics of Christianity. 1970. *Augur* 1, no. 17: 1, 3.

Polner, Murray, and Jim O'Grady. 1997. *Disarmed and Dangerous: The Radical Lives and Times of Daniel and Philip Berrigan*. Oxford: Westview.

Portuges, Paul. 1978. *The Visionary Poetics of Allen Ginsberg*. Santa Barbara, Calif.: Ross-Erikson.

Prabhupāda, Śrīla. 1987. *Letters From Śrīla Prabhupāda* . 5 vols. Culver City, Calif.: Bhaktivedanta Book Trust.

Pratt, John Clark, comp. 1984. *Vietnam Voices: Perspectives on the War Years, 1941–1982*. New York: Penguin.

Pressman, Steven. 1993. *Outrageous Betrayal: The Dark Journey of Werner Erhard from est to Exile*. New York: St. Martin's.

Quick Cuts. 1974. *Divine Times* 2, no. 3.

Raghunatha. [1999?]. Raghunatha's Response to the *New York Times* Publicity. Web-page at http://www.bhakti.com/vets/raghu.html.

Ram Dass, Baba. 1971. *Be Here Now*. Albuquerque, N.M.: Modern.

Reeder, Sharon [pseud.]. 1989. Interview by author. Location confidential, Aug. 28. Tape and transcript in author's collection.

Rennie Davis and the Underground Press. 1973. *Vancouver Free Press/Georgia Straight,* June 21–28, 11.

Rennie Davis On Tour. 1973. *Divine Times* (U.S. ed.) 11, no. 8: 2.

Reservist Guilty in Desertion Case. 1968. *New York Times,* June 18.

Revolutionary Yoga. 1970. *Berkeley Tribe,* Jan. 14–30, 17.

Richardson, Derek. 1986. Carry It On. *Mother Jones,* Jan., 42–43.

Richardson, James T. 1973. Causes and Consequences of the Jesus Movement in America. *Social Studies* [*Irish Journal of Sociology*] 2, no. 5: 457–73.

Richardson, James T., Mary W. Stewart, and Robert B. Simmonds. 1978. Researching a Fundamentalist Commune. In *Understanding the New Religions,* ed. Jacob Needleman and George Baker, 235–51. New York: Seabury.

———. 1979. *Organized Miracles: A Study of a Contemporary, Youth, Communal, Fundamentalist Organization*. New Brunswick, N.J.: Transaction.

Rintala, Marvin. 1974. Generations in Politics. In *The Youth Revolution: The Conflict of Generations in Modern History,* ed. Anthony Esler, 15–20. Lexington, Mass.: D. C. Heath. Reprinted from *International Encyclopedia of the Social Sciences,* 1968, 2d ed.

Robbins, Thomas. 1973. Contemporary "Post Drug" Cults: A Comparison of Two Movements. Ph.D. diss., Univ. of North Carolina at Chapel Hill.

———. 1988. *Cults, Converts and Charisma: The Sociology of New Religious Movements*. Beverley Hills, Calif.: Sage.

Robbins, Thomas, and Dick Anthony. 1981. Getting Straight with Meher Baba. In *In Gods We Trust: New Patterns of Religious Pluralism in America,* ed. Thomas Robbins and Dick Anthony, 191–213. New Brunswick, N.J.: Transaction. Reprinted from *Journal for the Scientific Study of Religion* 11, no. 2 (1972).

Roberts, Ron E., and Robert Marsh Kloss. 1974. *Social Movements: Between the Balcony and the Barricade.* St. Louis: Mosby.

Rochford, E. Burke, Jr. 1985. *Hare Krishna in America.* New Brunswick, N.J.: Rutgers Univ. Press.

Rochford, E. Burke, Jr., with Jennifer Heinlein. 1998. "Child Abuse in the Hare Krishna Movement: 1971–1986." *ISKCON Communications Journal* 6, no. 1. Downloaded from <http://www.iskcon.com/ICJ/6_1/6_1bharata.htm>, Feb.1, 2000.

Rodnitzky, Jerome L. 1976. *Minstrels of the Dawn.* Chicago: Nelson-Hall.

Rorabaugh, W. J. 1989. *Berkeley at War: The 1960s.* New York: Oxford Univ. Press.

Rose, Donna Sue. 1976. The Transcendental Meditation Movement: The Creation, Development and Institutionalization of a World View. Ph.D. diss., Southern Illinois Univ.

Rosenbaum, David E. 1970. 2nd Draft Lottery Selects Call-Up Order for 1971. *New York Times,* July 2.

Rossman, Michael. 1979. *New Age Blues: On the Politics of Consciousness.* New York: Dutton.

Rubin, Jerry. 1970. *Do It! Scenarios of the Revolution.* New York: Ballantine.

———. 1973. From the Streets to the Body. *Psychology Today,* Sept., 70–71.

———. 1976. *Growing (Up) at Thirty-Seven.* New York: M. Evans.

Russell, Leslye. 1973. New Mystics: The Great Guru Rip-Off. *Workers' Power,* Sept. 1–13, 14.

Sachs, Ron. 1979. Behind the Lines. *Miami Magazine,* Dec., 4.

Sale, Kirkpatrick. 1974. *SDS.* New York: Vintage.

Sanders, Ed. 1971. *The Family: The Story of Charles Manson's Dune Buggy Attack Battalion.* New York: E. P. Dutton.

Santelli, Robert. 1980. *Aquarius Rising: The Rock Festival Years.* New York: Dell.

Sarwer-Foner, Gerald J. 1972. Denial of Death and the Unconscious Longing for Indestructibility and Immortality in the Terminal Phase of Adolescence. *Canadian Psychiatric Association Journal* 17: SS51-SS57.

Schafer, Len. 1973. Divine Light or Divine Tricks. *The Drummer* [Philadelphia], Oct. 9, 8.

Schaffner, Nicholas. 1977. *The Beatles Forever.* Harrisburg, Penn.: Cameron House.

Scheflin, Alan W., and Edward M. Opton, Jr. 1978. *The Mind Manipulators: A Non-Fiction Account.* New York: Paddington.

Schultz, Gregg [pseud.]. 1988. Interview by author. Location confidential, Aug. 14. Tape and transcript in author's collection.

Schultz, John. 1993. *The Chicago Conspiracy Trial.* New York: Harper Collins.

Schumacher, Michael. 1992. *Dharma Lion: A Critical Biography of Allen Ginsberg.* New York: St. Martin's.

Schur, Edwin. 1975. *The Awareness Trap: Self Absorption Instead of Social Change.* Toronto: McGraw Hill.

Scientology Berkeley. [1969?]. No one bothered to ask us trees about People's Park! Self-published pamphlet.

Scientology: The Big Brainwash. 1971. *Guerilla* [Toronto] no. 18: 16–17.

Scientology Sues *The Realist* for Three-Quarters Of a Million Dollars for Libel and Conspiracy. 1971. *The Realist,* July-Aug.

Scranton, William W., chair. 1971. *The Report of the President's Commission on Campus Unrest.* Washington, D.C.: U.S. Government Printing Office.

The Serendipity of Peace: An Exclusive Interview with Rennie Davis. 1973. *Divine Times* 2, no. 6: 3–4.

Shachtman, Tom. 1983. *Decade of Shocks: Dallas to Watergate, 1963–1974.* New York: Poseidon.

Sharpe, David. 1987. *Rochdale: The Runaway College.* Toronto: Anansi.

Shaw, Miranda. 1994. *Passionate Enlightenment: Women in Tantric Buddhism.* Princeton, N.J.: Princeton Univ. Press.

Sheehan, Neil, et al. 1971. *The Pentagon Papers: As Published by the "New York Times."* Toronto and New York: Bantam.

Shelton, Robert. 1986. *No Direction Home: The Life and Music of Bob Dylan.* New York: Beech Tree.

Sherkat, Darren E., and T. Jean Blocker. 1993. Environmental Activism in the Protest Generation: Differentiating 1960s Activists. *Youth and Society* 25, no. 1: 140–61.

Shinn, Larry D. 1987. *The Dark Lord: Cult Images and the Hare Krishnas in America.* Philadelphia: Westminster.

Silverman, Jan. 1985. Spiritual Betrayal Turns Cult Member Into Counselor. *Oakland (Calif.) Tribune,* Apr. 28.

Singh, Baba. 1970. College Accreditation for Kundalini Yoga. *Beads of Truth* 1, no. 10: 8.

Smith, Fred [pseud.]. 1987. Interview by author. Location confidential, Dec. 1. Tape and transcript in author's collection.

Snell, David. 1974. Goom Rodgie's Razzle-Dazzle Soul Rush. *Saturday Review/World,* Feb. 9, 18–21ff.

Soll, Rick. 1975. Hare Krishna Followers Bow to a 64-Ounce Brain. *Chicago Tribune,* July 10.

Spinrad, Norman. 1970. Why the Present Ideological Revolution Will Fail. *Los Angeles Free Press,* Nov. 20.

———. 1971. How Far to the Rubicon? *Los Angeles Free Press,* May 14.

Spitz, Robert Stephen. 1979. *Barefoot in Babylon: The Creation of the Woodstock Music Festival, 1969.* New York: Viking.

Spofford, Tim. 1988. *Lynch Street: The May 1970 Slayings at Jackson State College.* Kent, Ohio: Kent State Univ. Press.

Stark, Rodney, and William Sims Bainbridge. 1980. Towards a Theory of Religious Commitment. *Journal for the Scientific Study of Religion* 19, no. 2: 114–28.

Starr, Jerold M. 1974. The Peace and Love Generation: Changing Attitudes Toward Sex and Violence among College Youth. *Journal of Social Issues* 30, no. 2: 73–106.

Stearns, Frederic. R. 1951. Dianetics. *Clinical Medicine* Mar.: 53.

Steckmesser, Kent. 1966. Robin Hood and the American Outlaw. *Journal of American Folklore* 79, no. 312: 348–55.

Steele, Lloyd. 1972. Amanda Ambrose Copes. *Los Angeles Free Press,* Nov. 17, sec. 2.

Steiner, Ted. 1969–72. Personal diary. Copy in possession of the author.

Stephenson, Gregory. 1990. *The Daybreak Boys: Essays on the Literature of the Beat Generation.* Carbondale: Southern Illinois Univ. Press.

Stevens, Jay. 1987. *Storming Heaven: LSD and the American Dream.* New York: Harper and Row.

Story of a Generation. 1973. *Divine Times* 2, no. 4: 8–10.

Strachan, Don. 1970. William Burroughs does The Job. *Los Angeles Free Press,* July 10.

Strozier, Charles B. 1994. *Apocalypse: On the Psychology of Fundamentalism in America.* Boston: Beacon.

Stuart, David. 1976. *Alan Watts.* Radnor, Penn.: Chilton.

Student Volunteers Scarce in Presidential Campaign. 1976. *New York Times,* Mar. 22.

Subhananda dāsa/Steven J. Gelberg. 1986. Interview by author. New York, N.Y., Aug. 29. Tape and transcript in author's collection.

Szatmary, David P. 1991. *Rockin' In Time: A Social History of Rock-and-Roll.* Englewood Cliffs, N.J.: Prentice Hall.

Tammeus, William D. 1977a. Exiles in Canada Vow to Seek Total Amnesty. *Kansas City (Kansas) Star,* Jan. 9.

———. 1977b. War Resisters Ready to Put Lives in Order. *Kansas City (Kansas) Star,* Jan. 9.

Tart, Charles T. 1975. *States of Consciousness.* New York: E. P. Dutton.

Teal, Donn. 1995. *The Gay Militants.* New York: St. Martin's.

Thompson, Gail [pseud.]. 1988. Interview by author. Location confidential, Aug. 7. Tape and transcript in author's collection.

Thompson, Tom. 1974a. The IRS is Watching You More Closely Than You Think. *Los Angeles Free Press,* Mar. 22.

———. 1974b. Coercion and Favoritism. *Los Angeles Free Press,* Apr. 12.

Tipton, Steven M. 1982a. *Getting Saved From the Sixties: Moral Meaning in Conversion and Cultural Change.* Berkeley: Univ. of California Press.

———. 1982b. The Moral Logic of Alternative Religions. *Daedalus* 111, no. 1: 185–213.

Tobey, Alan. 1976. The Summer Solstice of the Healthy-Happy-Holy Organization. In *The New Religious Consciousness,* ed. Charles Y. Glock and Robert N. Bellah, 5–30. Berkeley: Univ. of California Press.

Tonkinson, Carole, ed. 1995. *Big Sky Mind: Buddhism and the Beat Generation.* New York: Riverhead.

Townshend, Peter. *Who Came First?* MCA 2026. Originally released in 1972.

Transcendental Meditation Session Proving Popular at United Nations. 1976. *New York Times,* Oct. 20.

Trungpa, Chögyam. 1999. *Great Eastern Sun: The Wisdom of Shambhala.* Ed. Carolyn Rose Gimian. London: Shambhala.

Turner, Virginia. 1971. Children of God Leave Homes to Spread Gospel. *El Paso Herald-Post,* Nov. 11.

Turner, Wallace. 1968. Reservist Jailed for Not Reporting. *New York Times,* Apr. 28.

20,000 Protest Latin Policies, Hear Jackson. 1983. *San Diego Union,* Nov. 13.

2 Berkeley Banks Hit by Bombs; Damage is Slight, No One Hurt. 1970. *New York Times,* June 20.

University Microfilms International. 1985. *Underground Press Collection 1963–1985.* Ann Arbor. Mich.: University Microfilms International.

Van Ness, Chris. 1973. Guru Maharaj Ji: Spiritual Fascism. *Los Angeles Free Press,* Nov. 16, sec. 1; Nov. 23, sec. 2.

Van Zandt, David E. 1991. *Living in the Children of God*. Princeton, N.J.: Princeton Univ. Press.

Violations of ISKCON Children Exposed (VOICE). 1996. Website at <http://www.ccrgroup.com/voice>.

Wagner, Jon. 1982. Sex Roles in American Communal Utopias. In *Sex Roles in Contemporary American Communes*, ed. Jon Wagner, 1–44. Bloomington: Indiana Univ. Press.

Wallis, Roy. 1976. *The Road to Total Freedom*. New York: Columbia Univ. Press.

———. 1981. Yesterday's Children: Cultural and Structural Change in a New Religious Movement. In *The Social Impact of New Religious Movements*, ed. Bryan Wilson, 97–133. New York: Rose of Sharon.

Wangerin, Ruth. 1993. *The Children of God: A Make-Believe Revolution?* Westport, Conn.: Bergin and Garvey.

Ward, Justice Alan. 1995. W 42 1992 in the High Court of Justice. Family Division, London, England. Principal Registry in the Matter of ST (A Minor) and in the Matter of the Supreme Court Act 1991. Oct. 19.

Waskow, Arthur. 1969. The Religious Upwelling of the New Left. *Liberation*, July, 36–37.

Weiner, Bernard. 1970. The Jesus Freaks: "We're Building An Army." *Northwest Passage*, Sept. 29, 12.

Westhues, Kenneth. 1975. Inter-generational Conflict in the Sixties. In *Prophecy and Protest: Social Movements in Twentieth-Century Canada*, ed. Samuel D. Clark, J. Paul Grayson, and Linda M. Grayson, 387–408. Toronto: Gage.

Whalen, Jack, and Richard Flacks. 1989. *Beyond the Barricades: The Sixties Generation Grows Up*. Philadelphia: Temple Univ. Press.

What is Ananda? 1970. *Long Beach Free Press* 2, no. 2: 8.

Whitehead, Harriet. 1974. Reasonably Fantastic: Some Perspectives on Scientology, Science Fiction, and Occultism. In *Religious Movements in Contemporary America*, ed. Irving Zaretsky and Mark P. Leone, 547–87. Princeton, N.J.: Princeton Univ. Press.

Whitt, Lynn [pseud.]. 1989. Interview by author and Karyn Mytrash. Location confidential, Aug. 21. Tape and transcript in author's collection.

Who, The. *The Who: Thirty Years of Maximum R and B*. MCA MCAD4–11020.

Who Is Guru Maharaj Ji? A Brief Biography. 1973. *Divine Times* (U.S. ed.) 11, no. 8: 1–2.

Wilcock, John. 1967. Human Be-In. *International Times* [London, England], Feb. 13–26, 2.

Williams, Miriam. 1998. *Heaven's Harlots: My Fifteen Years as a Sacred Prostitute in the Children of God Cult.* New York: William Morrow.

Winter, J. A. 1987. *Dianetics: A Doctor's Report.* New York: Julian.

Wolfe, Tom. 1969. *The Electric Kool-Aid Acid Test.* Toronto: Bantam.

———. 1976. The "Me" Decade and the Third Great Awakening. *New York Magazine,* Aug. 23, 26ff.

Wolfe, Thomas Ross (Tom). 1994. Interview by author. Berwyn Heights, Md., Dec. 17. Tape and transcript in author's collection.

Wood, John. 1973. An Interview with Guru Maharaj Ji. *And It is Divine* 11, no. 2: 46–51.

Wood, Tony. 1973a. Whatever Happened to the Movement? *The Drummer* [Philadelphia], Jan. 30, 3, 5.

———. 1973b. A Candid Interview With Rennie Davis. *The Drummer* [Philadelphia], May 15, 6.

Woyce, Brian. 1973. And Is It Divine? *Georgia Straight,* Oct. 4-Oct. 10, 4, 6.

Wright, Walter. 1977a. IGG's 32 Big Donors: Giving and Chanting. *Honolulu Advertiser,* Aug. 21.

———. 1977b. Is Victory the Real Objective? Not to All Krishna Hopefuls. *Honolulu Advertiser,* Aug. 21.

———. 1977c. The Party Line: "Thou Shalt Not . . ." *Honolulu Advertiser,* Aug. 21.

———. 1977d. The Secret Spiritual Base of a New Political Force. *Honolulu Advertiser,* Aug. 21.

———. 1977e. Close Ties with IGG Found at 2 Papers. *Honolulu Advertiser,* Aug. 23.

Wuthnow, Robert. 1976. The New Religions in Social Context. In *The New Religious Consciousness,* ed. Charles Y. Glock and Robert N. Bellah, 267–93. Berkeley: Univ. of California Press.

Yogananda, Paramahansa. 1973. *Autobiography of a Yogi.* Los Angeles: Self Realization Fellowship.

Young, Karen. 1968. Military Protester [Smith] to Face Preliminary Court Battle Today. *Daily Californian,* May 7, 1, 12.

Zablocki, Benjamin. 1980. *Alienation and Charisma: A Study of Contemporary American Communes.* New York: Free Press.

Zald, Mayer N., and Roberta Ash. 1966. Social Movement Organizations: Growth, Decay and Change. *Social Forces* 44 (Mar.): 327–41.

Zaroulis, Nancy, and Gerald Sullivan. 1984. *Who Spoke Up? American Protest Against the War in Vietnam.* New York: Doubleday.

Zinn, Howard. 1995. *A People's History of the United States, 1492-Present.* Rev. ed. New York: Harper Perennial.

Zygmunt, Joseph F. 1972. When Prophecies Fail. *American Behavioral Scientist* 16, no. 2: 245–68.

Index